D0264990

GEOFF HAMILTON'S

YEAR IN YOUR GARDEN

GEOFF HAMILTON'S

YEAR IN YOUR GARDEN

A month-by-month celebration of a gardening genius introduced by Lynda Hamilton

Compiled by
ANDI CLEVELY
from articles written by
Geoff Hamilton
in the *Daily Express*
from 1991 to 1996

HEADLINE

Copyright © 1998 this compilation Lynda Hamilton
Copyright © 1998 original material Express Newspapers plc

The right of Lynda Hamilton to be identified as the Author of the Work has been asserted by Lynda Hamilton in accordance with the Copyright, Designs and Patents Act 1988.

First published in 1998
by HEADLINE BOOK PUBLISHING

10 9 8 7

All rights reserved. No part of this publication may be reproduced, stored in a retrieval system, or transmitted, in any form or by any means without the prior written consent of the publishers, nor be otherwise circulated in any form of binding or cover other than that in which it is published and without a similar condition being imposed on the subsequent purchaser.

Cataloguing in Publication Data is available from the British Library

Designed by Prue Bucknall
Picture research by Helen Flickling
Illustrations by Ann Winterbotham
Jacket design by Head Design

0 7472 2231 2

Printed and bound in Italy
by Lego Spa

HEADLINE BOOK PUBLISHING
A division of Hodder Headline PLC
338 Euston Road
London NW1 3BH

PREVIOUS PAGES A densely packed kitchen-garden bed promises a varied harvest of fresh home-grown produce.

THIS PAGE Swags of roses and clematis over a clipped green archway frame the view into an inviting garden beyond.

contents

6 *geoff in his garden*
Lynda Hamilton

Introductions to each month by Lynda Hamilton

12 *january*
26 *february*
38 *march*
56 *april*
72 *may*
88 *june*
106 *july*
120 *august*
134 *september*
150 *october*
164 *november*
176 *december*

186 Climate and the gardener
Glossary
188 Index
192 Acknowledgments

geoff in his garden

Lynda Hamilton

Geoff was passionate about gardening. He revelled in the physical work that it involved – being outside in all weathers, digging, sowing, hoeing, pruning and so on. But more than that, it was plants themselves that held him in thrall. Green shoots were the very basis of life, he said. They made his blood tingle.

In the years we shared together at Barnsdale, his enthusiasm for the garden never wavered. He was, at one and the same time, an idealist and a realist. He strove for the best – always. 'Spot on' he would say, or 'that's just right', but never 'that'll do'. But he would face setbacks with equanimity, openly admitting failure, but never defeat. Perhaps it was his willingness to share both his successes and his failures that made ordinary gardeners trust him. He certainly wanted to share the immeasurable joy that gardening gave him. Not only did it give him intense satisfaction and aesthetic pleasure, he also realised that it had a healing psychological role: gentle exercise and plenty of fresh air, fruit and vegetables are ingredients of any doctor's remedy for relieving stress. More importantly, the garden, Geoff felt, was the only place where most of our urbanised population can experience nature.

His absolute respect for nature was the bedrock of his deeply held belief in organic gardening. Long before organic gardening or 'green' issues became fashionable, Geoff had gardened in what he called 'the natural way'. As he saw it, organic gardening was 'very simply, a case of growing plants exactly as nature intended, only more so. Because we take much more out of our soil than nature does, we have to put more back.' Perhaps his chief concern – it was almost a mission – was to get people to stop using chemical pesticides and fertilisers. 'Just imagine,' he said, 'a garden filled with fabulous flowers, glorious greenery and perfect produce, and also buzzing with the activity of birds, bees, butterflies, hedgehogs, frogs, toads and all the rest of the gardener's friends.' Yes, of course

RIGHT Vegetables blend happily with flowers, as in this bed at Barnsdale where onions and beetroot mingle with fuchsias, petunias and marigolds.

LEFT Sweet peas and nasturtiums jostle for space on a fence at Barnsdale. Pots of summer bedding in the background echo the brilliant colours of the poppies and lupins in the borders.

it sounds almost too good to be true, yet Geoff proved that it was possible. Barnsdale has never been sprayed with a man-made chemical. And it thrives.

Although it is hard to believe now, Geoff was originally sceptical about the merits of organic gardening. He was trained as a commercial grower where rule number one was: 'If it moves – spray it.' So he started out with a trial aimed at proving that organic gardening didn't work. He set up four identical plots all growing the same vegetables and flowers. One was gardened organically, one with only chemicals, another with a mixture of the two, and finally there was a 'control' plot which had neither chemicals nor organic matter. In the first year the chemical plot produced very much better results. In the second there were signs that the organic plot was catching up. By the fifth year the organic plot was vastly outyielding the other three. And it was buzzing with insects while the chemical plot was sterile. So, although Geoff admitted that he couldn't honestly say whether the fruit tasted better or the flowers were brighter, he was absolutely convinced that they were healthier; the wildlife, he said, knew which plants were good for them.

But, again, he was a realist, and warned people what they might be in for if they tried this approach. 'If you decide to do away with chemicals entirely, you will be troubled with attacks from greenfly and caterpillars to begin with, and, in the first couple of years your crops might not be quite so good. But,' he said, 'nature's pest control methods are complicated. Every pest you consider your enemy has enemies of its own. Birds will eat caterpillars, slugs, snails, woodlice, greenfly and many other pests. Hoverfly larvae eat hundreds of greenfly, as do lacewings and ladybirds. Ground beetles go for slugs and caterpillars – if they get there before the frogs, the toads and the hedgehogs.'

To enlist the help of this green army, he suggested growing particular plants to attract specific insects and birds, but the first step, he said, was to grow a wide diversity of plants and pack them in together. 'Grow your flowers, fruit and vegetables, your roses, shrubs and herbaceous plants all in the same borders, just as the old cottage gardeners did. That provides cover for the shy species, and some food too. Provide trees for birds, and nesting boxes too if you

LEFT Geoff and Lynda in a corner of the courtyard garden at Barnsdale.

ABOVE Some of the loveliest violas have first appeared in private gardens. This is 'Barnsdale', an intriguing dark-coloured form which blooms profusely, especially in the cool shade that all violas prefer.

can, and think about making a pond somewhere for all the wildlife to drink.' Geoff also used physical barriers, netting fruit against birds, covering carrots with fine-spun polypropylene to protect against carrot fly and caterpillars, sticking bits of carpet underlay round the stems of cabbages to prevent cabbage root fly, and so on. 'Eventually you'll build up a balance of wildlife, but the process takes nerves of steel. You mustn't weaken once. If you do you'll be killing friends as well as enemies.'

Chemical fertilisers were also anathema to Geoff. 'They act fast and are like junk food to plants,' he said. 'They make them fat, soft, and attractive to diseases. Organic fertilisers, on the other hand, which feed the soil rather than the plant, are slow acting. They make for tough, strong plants which are much less prone to attack and better equipped to fight disease.' He explained that organic and chemical fertilisers work in different ways. 'Chemical growers don't rely on a fertile soil, often doing without manure or compost completely. Soil is used as an anchorage for the plants and as a store for water and plant food in solution. The growers add fertiliser that is immediately needed by the plant, which takes it up straight away and, it must be said, puts on a lot of growth. Organic growers rely on fertile soil that contains billions of micro-organisms. These slowly release plant food derived from organic matter, such as manure or compost, and any other organic fertiliser you may put on.' Geoff stopped using any of the suspect fertilisers from the time of the first BSE scare. Instead he used pelleted chicken manure and seaweed.

Geoff's concern with the environment went beyond the confines of his own garden: he was adamant that gardeners should stop using peat-based composts, or water-worn limestone for rockeries. He was horrified at the destruction of so much of our unique bogland and our limestone pavements, and spent a long time experimenting to find good substitutes. He found coir or coconut fibre worked well instead of peat, and also made his own soil-based mix using soil, garden compost, grit and chicken manure. And, after a spate of weekend trials, he found the perfect mix of hypertufa to give him artificial rock.

Serious as Geoff was about these issues, he had a huge sense of humour and could see the funny side of everything, including himself. Pinned up on a large notice-board in our downstairs loo – used by everyone who came to visit the garden, including the camera crews – were all the cartoons that poked fun at him, the photos that made him look ridiculous, and the rude letters that he'd received. He was always easy to tease and good-humoured about it – even when he was dunked in a water butt by three female production assistants who had been on the receiving end of one of his practical jokes. Geoff always had a fund of jokes and stories up his sleeve, which he would tell in the appropriate accent. And one of his favourite sayings, delivered at times of stress in the lilting Hertfordshire accent of an old and fondly remembered nursery colleague was, 'Thur's a whole noo day termorra, never bin star'ed.' He revelled in all aspects of the English language, especially puns, limericks and cryptic crossword clues.

He was a man without pretensions. Like the advice he gave, he was straightforward and honest. When he spoke or wrote, it was from the heart, about things that directly concerned him. That is why the articles on which this book is based, though compiled and edited, have been left largely untouched and in the present tense. It is Geoff's own voice that clearly comes through.

I'm not alone in still feeling his presence so strongly in the garden here at Barnsdale – several visitors have written to tell me that they feel it too. And just as his spirit lives on in his garden, I very much hope that it will live on in his words.

Lynda Hamilton

The cheerful, optimistic Geoff on screen was the real Geoff. Even on the shortest, coldest days he would enjoy doing something in the garden, and in January it was sowing. He thrilled, he said, to the very words 'seed pan' and 'seed tray' because 'they conjured up visions of the lovely round clay pans and wooden boxes that used to contain our dreams of a flowery summer'. He was bitten by the seedling bug when he was a young boy of seven, and never understood why gardening is generally regarded as an occupation for older people. His father gave each of his three sons a plot to cultivate, encouraging them by paying for the produce they grew. The strategy worked for the twins: Geoff eventually studied horticulture at Writtle, and Tony studied agriculture. Geoff's first job was with a commercial grower of chrysanthemums, but once fully trained he went on to do landscape gardening. At more or less the same time, his love of words pushed him into writing, and out of his columns and articles grew his broadcasting career – the cameras simply recorded him doing what he was writing about.

Hard frost at Barnsdale highlights the intricate patterns of shrub and tree growth that supply varied interest all winter in a mixed border.

January

key tasks for january

ANNUALS & BEDDING PLANTS

- ❍ Sow in modules to save time and space, page 14
- ❍ Buy new sowing compost, page 15
- ❍ Techniques for sowing in modules and seed trays, page 15
- ❍ Sow sweet peas, page 16

BORDER PERENNIALS

- ❍ Take root cuttings from dormant perennials, page 16

CONTAINER PLANTS

- ❍ Provide alpines with perfect winter conditions, page 18
- ❍ Sow alpines while the weather is still cold, page 18

SHRUBS, TREES & CLIMBERS

- ❍ Stake new trees and check supports of older ones, page 20
- ❍ Shape up young trees, page 20
- ❍ Prune those trees and shrubs grown for their leaf colour, page 21
- ❍ Winter-prune wisteria, page 21

LAWNS & HEDGES

- ❍ Improve the drainage by spiking the lawn, page 21

VEGETABLES & HERBS

- ❍ Plan now for an early start to the cropping year, page 21
- ❍ Set up early potatoes to sprout or 'chit', page 22

FRUIT

- ❍ Bring in strawberry plants in pots for forcing, page 22
- ❍ Prune hazelnut trees to keep them in check, page 22

MISCELLANEOUS

- ❍ Invest in a propagator for your first sowings, page 23
- ❍ Continue to pull out weeds, page 23

ANNUALS & BEDDING PLANTS

It's time to sow sweet peas, and it's also not too early to make a start on the annual bedding plants like salvias, petunias, busy lizzies and lobelia. Raising your own indoors is not too difficult, and it'll certainly save you quite a lot of money.

Sowing in modules

At one time, all bedding plants were raised in wooden trays. These were replaced by plastic trays, and then by expanded polystyrene strips. Now there is another option: to raise plants in modules, which are plastic trays divided into a number of cells. This is a welcome trend as it has several advantages.

First of all, there's no need to prick out the seedlings. Modules produce very even, uniform plants which can be potted up or planted out when they are large enough. When it's time to transplant, push each cell gently at the base and the rootball will pop up intact. The trays save a lot of space in the greenhouse or cold frame, or on the windowsill. They are even self-watering if you stand them on level staging that has been covered with polythene and then capillary matting.

Modules come in a wide range of sizes, usually the best being 4cm (1½in) across and, depending on the size of tray, you can easily raise several dozen plants of any one kind. You can use the modules now for tender annuals, and then use the same system in April for raising hardier plants. Modules are ideal for perennials such as pinks and delphiniums, and hardy annuals like marigolds and nasturtiums. They are also good for sowing ferns, and for starting garlic cloves if the ground's

SOWING IN MODULES

1 Using modules allows you to sow individual large seeds or a tiny pinch of small ones which can be left to grow unthinned, or you can remove all but the strongest seedling. Disturbance at planting time is reduced to a minimum.

2 Fill the cells, making a depression in the centre of each one to hold the seeds. Bury these under a thin layer of vermiculite or compost, and germinate in the same way as for a normal seed tray.

not suitable outside for planting; offsets and pips from flowering bulbs can be grown on in this way too. They are also valuable for early vegetables grown in clusters: sow onions or leeks with 6–8 seeds in each cell and then, instead of thinning them out, plant each clump 30cm (12in) square. You'll find they push each other apart to make their own space and mature into good-sized vegetables for the kitchen. Do the same with carrots (round varieties only, such as 'Rondo' or 'Parabel') and plant them out 15cm (6in) square.

Compost for sowing

Using last year's seed composts could be a bit dodgy – they eventually go off as the fertilisers in them break down and change into other chemicals that can harm seedlings. Use up your old compost as a soil conditioner in the garden.

For years most gardeners used peat-based composts, but now that we know that digging for peat composts has been responsible for the destruction of most of our unique bogland, it is vital to find substitutes. There are several available. The one that has performed well for me is coir or coconut fibre. It needs a different watering and feeding regime from peat: it tends to hold a lot of water but the top half-inch dries out fast.

Sowing in modules and seed trays

The techniques for sowing in modules or in seed trays are very similar. It's important not to firm any soil-less compost too much. It's usually enough to fill modules, pots or trays to the brim, tap them to settle the contents, and then water well and leave to drain. Do this before sowing, which avoids washing newly sown seeds into patches; alternatively soak the containers from below after sowing.

To cover seeds that don't need darkness to gerrminate, I like to use horticultural vermiculite: it lets some light through, so all's not lost if you

SOWING IN SEED TRAYS

1 Sow on top of the compost, very thinly to avoid too much competition. Tip a little seed into one hand, pick up a pinch with the finger and thumb of the other, and sprinkle evenly in the tray.

2 If the seeds need darkness to germinate, sieve a thin layer of compost over them; otherwise cover them with horticultural vermiculite which lets in some light.

3 Keep the seeds moist by covering the tray with a sheet of glass or clingfilm. Add a layer of newspaper if they need darkness, but remove this when the first seedlings emerge.

ABOVE Undeterred by frost, evergreen *Erica carnea* 'Springwood Pink' nestles against a prostrate juniper.

TYPES OF SEED

First read the seed packet: if the seeds are F_1 hybrids, you'll end up with plants that are uniform and all in flower at the same time. But they are expensive because the seedsmen have to re-hybridise every time they want a crop of seeds. It pays to grow F_2 hybrids instead – these cost less, and are often just as vigorous, but they usually only come in mixed colours.

Primed seeds are a great advance. They've been started into growth and then dried off again before packeting, so that they are raring to go just as soon as they hit moist compost and the right temperature, which can be as much as 5–6°C (10°F) lower than for normal seeds.

Some seeds need light for germination, so check the seed packet before sowing because most failures result from burying seeds too deep.

bury the seeds too deeply. Cover with clingfilm or sheets of glass to stop them drying out, and put them where they'll get a little gentle heat. Uncover as soon as seedlings show, move them into full light, and you're on your way to a glorious summer.

Sowing sweet peas

Sweet peas are best started in mid-autumn to make strong seedlings for planting out next month, but if you missed doing it then, now's the time to catch up. They grow best in deeper pots that let them develop a good root system, and you can buy coated paper tubes at the garden centre that are made specially for them. Stack these side by side in a deep seed tray, fill with peat-free seed compost, and water well. Read the seed packet instructions carefully. Most varieties can be sown straight away, but if the seeds are black and mottled it's often best to soak them overnight first. Those that haven't swollen next morning can be 'chipped' by removing a tiny bit of the seed-coat with a sharp knife, carefully avoiding the 'eye' where the root grows.

Plant 2–3 seeds in each tube, about 2.5cm (1in) deep, and keep them at about room temperature – they don't really need a propagator. Once they are through, give them a week on the windowsill or a sunny table, and then they can go outside into a cold frame. If frost threatens, cover the frame with old carpet or sacking. For instructions on planting outside, see page 58.

BORDER PERENNIALS

Taking root cuttings

Most gardeners find it hard to resist snipping off the odd shoot and turning it into a cutting to make a new plant. But at this time of year, instead of using your skill to grow roots on shoots, why not think of doing it the other way round by putting new shoots on to roots?

Plants with thick fleshy tap roots, such as Japanese anemones, are

RIGHT Don't be too tidy-minded with perennials. It's often a good idea to leave clearing the faded top-growth of plants such as *Sedum spectabile* until the spring, to create unexpected beauty in the depths of winter.

often quite difficult to propagate by division, but grow easily at this time of year from cuttings of their side roots, as shown on the right.

Plants with thin fibrous roots can be multiplied in a similar way, but their roots are laid horizontally on compost in trays. First trim the roots to about 8cm (3in) long and coat with fungicide; then lay them horizontally, covering them with another 1–2cm (½–1in) of compost. Water well, and stand in a frost-free cold frame or heated propagator.

PLANTS TO PROPAGATE BY ROOT CUTTINGS

Acanthus, anchusa, brunnera, catananche, ceanothus, crambe, dicentra, dictamnus, echinacea, eryngium, Japanese anemones, nepeta, oriental poppies, phlox, rhus, romneya and verbascum.

Remember that root cuttings taken from variegated plants lose their variegation and their leaves will turn out green.

TAKING ROOT CUTTINGS

1 Dig up the plant to be propagated or cut a portion from one side, and wash off as much soil as possible so that the roots can be separated from each other.

2 Cut off sound roots about the thickness of a pencil and divide into sections about 5cm (2in) long. Trim off small fibrous roots. Cut the bottom diagonally and the top straight so you know which way up to plant it.

3 Insert upright in pots of cuttings compost, with the tops just buried. Water well, and stand in a frost-free cold frame, or in a heated propagator for faster rooting.

CONTAINER PLANTS

Giving alpines perfect conditions

They say that adversity brings out the best in people, and that's true of alpine plants too. They revel in spartan conditions, with next to no food, and flower all the more spectacularly for this as soon as the sun comes out. In the wild, most alpines grow high in the cold dry mountains where the weather is pretty inhospitable. They're battered by cold winds and frozen by ice, followed by a summer of merciless sun, and some of them often get no more than one watering a year when their covering of snow melts in the spring. To grow them successfully in the garden, you'll need to reproduce those conditions as nearly as possible to make them feel at home. They need perfect drainage, which means making a raised bed or digging in plenty of coarse grit and pea shingle from the builders' merchant, and they may need protection from the damp winter mists and fogs that quickly rot some species.

The best way is to grow them in gritty compost in clay pots, which breathe and drain more efficiently and so avoid too much moisture at the roots. The pots can be plunged over winter in a sand or gravel bed in an unheated greenhouse, where the plants won't mind the cold but will be protected from excess dampness. In spring you can move them outdoors if you intend using the greenhouse for things like tomatoes during the summer. Alternatively you could make a permanent miniature rock garden on top of the staging, using a well-drained compost and lightweight tufa rock – having the small flowers at nose level is really the perfect way to appreciate them.

BELOW Alpines tend to be tough plants, adapted to a harsh environment, and will survive the worst winter weather provided they are grown in gritty soil in a well-drained raised bed.

Raising alpines from seed

Now is a good time to sow alpine pinks, saxifrages, houseleeks (*Sempervivum*), tiny primulas, stonecrops (*Sedum*) and hundreds of other fascinating species.

In the wild their seeds are mostly produced in late summer, and avoid the fatal icy grip of winter by delayed germination. But in order to trigger germination they need this cold spell, followed by rising temperatures, and you have to imitate this for success with bought seeds. You can do it artificially by putting the seeds in the fridge for 6–8 weeks before sowing, but I prefer to do mine the easy way by sowing them several weeks before the spring warmth arrives, leaving the seeds outdoors to freeze naturally.

Use a compost made with equal parts good soil, coir and coarse horticultural grit, or mix together equal amounts of John Innes seed compost and grit. Fill an 8cm (3in) clay pot to the top, and tap it firmly on the bench; firm gently and then water it well. Leave it to drain before scattering a small pinch of seeds on the surface and covering with a thin layer of grit. Stand the pots outside covered with a piece of glass or in a cold frame with the top positioned to keep off the rain but expose the seeds to the cold.

Most seedlings should be through in the spring, when they can be transplanted to individual pots and grown on. If germination occurs very early and this is followed by a cold snap, you'll have to close the frame or move the pots to a greenhouse or cold windowsill until the worst is over. In a warm season, seedlings may not appear until the second spring, so wait for at least a year before discarding any pots whose seeds haven't germinated. It's a bit of extra trouble, but the satisfaction of cracking nature's code for germinating these specialised plants makes it worth every second.

RIGHT At Barnsdale, deciduous winter-flowering viburnums such as *V. farreri* shrug off the frost that glistens on the large tough leaves of evergreen *Mahonia japonica* in the right foreground.

SHRUBS, TREES & CLIMBERS

Staking trees

There's a lot at stake when it comes to supporting newly planted trees for their first few years. Allowing the top to move around freely in the wind encourages a tree instinctively to strengthen its root system. A good buffeting actually triggers a mechanism that stimulates the roots to extend quite a distance to provide further anchorage. That's why it's now recommended that the stake should come no more than about a third of the way up the trunk of a tree, and in many cases even shorter stakes are preferred.

Leaving the base of the tree moving around in the ground, however, can spell disaster. Rocking in the wind at this time of year works a hole in the ground all round the stem and allows water to sit right on the crown of the roots, often causing rotting. So check that all your newly planted trees are solid at the base, especially after strong winds and also hard frost which can make the ground heave. Make sure the tree is tied securely to its stake, but if the ties have been on for more than a season, look to see that they're not so tight that they're strangling the tree.

Shaping up young trees

If you have planted 'feathered' trees, specimens with branches starting low down on the trunk, and you want to turn them into normal standards with long clean stems, now's the time to prune them.

Juvenile trees are full of youthful vigour, with a built-in urge to grow in all directions. Sideshoots often grow almost as fast as the vertical leading stem, so that a tree will end up shaped like a pyramid. If you stop or reduce the sideways growth, energy is redirected to the leader and your tree will gain more height.

Don't be tempted to produce a clean trunk straight away by shearing off all the sideshoots in one go. The extra leaves these carry help to thicken and strengthen the part of the trunk where they are growing. You can also shorten some of the sideshoots higher up to about 15cm (6in) long, removing them altogether next winter when you cut back the next two or three. In this way you can guide the tree's growth without giving it too much of a shock all at once.

SHAPING UP YOUNG TREES

A young fruit tree may have lots of sideshoots on the trunk that can be turned into fruiting spurs. Ornamental trees look best with a clean trunk, so you need to remove these 'feathers' gradually. Cut off the bottom ones completely, and shorten higher shoots in the first winter. Next year do this again, further up the trunk.

LEFT When supporting a tree after planting, avoid causing injury by driving in the stake at an angle so that it misses the rootball.

Pruning for good leaf colour

While you've got your secateurs handy, take a look at those shrubs and trees that produce their best leaf colour from young wood. Elders such as the lovely golden variety *Sambucus nigra* 'Aurea' and its dusky cousin 'Guincho Purple' (formerly 'Purpurea') will produce far better colour if their stems are cut back to 2–3 buds above ground level, as will the variegated maple *Acer negundo* 'Flamingo'. Others such as the purple-leafed smoke bush *Cotinus coggygria* 'Royal Purple' and the brilliant yellow *Catalpa bignonioides* 'Aurea' make much bigger leaves if pruned back hard now, although you will lose the flowers.

In small gardens pruning is a great way to keep trees and larger shrubs in check. The foxglove tree (*Paulownia tomentosa*) grows into a large tree if not cut back. But if it is pruned hard every year and the resulting suckers are reduced to just one, it will grow to about 2.4m (8ft) and produce absolutely huge velvety leaves up to 60cm (2ft) across, but you will lose the flowers.

Plants grown for their colourful winter bark can also be cut back hard, but don't be in too much of a rush. Wait another month or two, so as to enjoy the colour for as long as possible.

Winter-pruning wisteria

If you want to keep wisteria confined, and encourage flowering, this is the time to shorten the sideshoots back to 2–3 buds. Personally I prefer to take off as much growth as I feel necessary in August, but the advantage of doing it now is that you can see more of the plant's framework.

LAWNS & HEDGES

Improving lawn drainage

If you walk lightly over the lawn at this time of the year, and find areas that are actually squelching underfoot, it means that these bits need attention if the turf is not to suffer, and that means spiking.

I have to admit spiking the lawn is such a pain that I can sympathise with anyone who doesn't like the idea, and I doubt if many people do it on a regular basis. But it is a good way to remedy poor drainage. Note where the wet patches are and, as soon as the ground dries a bit, go over the area making holes at about 15cm (6in) intervals as shown below. If you don't act fast, they will simply close up again, so as soon as you have done a couple of square yards, brush in a good dressing of sharp sand (never builders' sand). Leave a shallow layer on top too, and the grass will tend to root into that in the spring.

IMPROVING LAWN DRAINAGE

A hollow-tine aerator will remove thin plugs of soil, but an ordinary garden fork, pushed in 15cm (6in) deep and wiggled about to open up holes, is equally effective.

VEGETABLES & HERBS

Planning for an early start

It's not too soon to be thinking about the vegetable plot to ensure plenty of fresh produce to harvest while shop prices are still high. But because of the weather and low temperatures, you'll need to make the first sowings indoors, and also prepare a small area of soil outdoors for planting later on.

Not only is it usually very cold at this time of year, but very often heavy rain will have turned the soil into a quagmire. Most of it will dry out over time, but the area set aside for the first sowings of the season needs special treatment. Cover it with cloches or, better still, with a sheet of thick polythene weighted down or tucked in at the edges. Not only will the cloches or sheet keep the bed dry and warmer than the air outside, but you will also be able to work the bed when you want to. (See the photo on pages 32–3.) Either prepare the seedbed first if the soil is in good condition and then cover it to keep it that way, or leave the polythene in place until the soil is dry enough to cultivate.

Meanwhile back indoors, in the greenhouse or on a windowsill, you can start sowing to produce plants that will be ready to go outside from mid-February onwards so long as they go under cloches or horticultural fleece to protect them from the worst of the weather. Sow small quantities of lettuce, early cabbage and cauliflowers in just the same way as shown for annuals on page 15. Varieties to choose include 'Hispi' and 'Kingspi' cabbages, 'Alpha Polaris' or 'Montano' cauliflowers, and fast-maturing lettuces such as 'Little Gem', 'Tom Thumb', or 'Novita' if you like the loose-leaf cut-and-come-again types. These vegetables do not need high temperatures, and will germinate easily at about 13°C (55°F). When they're big enough, prick them out to about 5cm (2in) apart if they are in trays and grow them on in plenty of light to prevent them becoming long and lanky.

Starting early potatoes

If you've never grown early potatoes before, let me urge you to try a few this year. Freshly dug, they're a different vegetable altogether from the bland, tasteless and expensive stuff you buy. (And I confess, I break all my own rules, and have my first serving obliterated with butter.) This is the time to order seed potatoes or 'sets', as they need a little preparation before planting out in March. All varieties need to be sprouted or 'chitted' to advance the date of the first harvest and also increase the size of the crop. Too many shoots on an early potato can be a disadvantage, leading to too much competition and resulting in reduced growth or smaller tubers. Overcrowded tubers tend to push themselves to the surface of the soil, where they're in danger of turning green in the light – green tubers contain poisonous alkaloids and should not be eaten. If possible choose smaller tubers for growing, as these will produce only a couple of sprouts; with the others, set them to chit, and rub off all but two sprouts as early as you can to prevent them from using up their reserves. If you are growing maincrop varieties, leave all the sprouts on as they can cope with the extra growth.

EARLY POTATO VARIETIES

Older varieties such as 'Arran Pilot', 'Home Guard' and 'Sharpes Express' are still available and worth growing. But there are more recent introductions for you to try, although you might have to buy them by mail order rather than from the garden centre. 'Accent' and 'Foremost' are two first earlies that produce heavy yields with little or no slug damage, while 'Concorde' has fine flavour. For extra-early crops, choose 'Rocket' or 'Swift' which, under favourable conditions, can be ready as soon as 8–10 weeks after planting. If you save a few tubers of these two varieties, you can plant them in August in pots under glass for Christmas.

CHITTING POTATOES

Lay the tubers out in a single layer in boxes or trays – egg boxes are ideal if you only have a few potatoes. Arrange the tubers with the ends that have the most eyes facing upwards, and stand them in maximum light in a cool but frost-free place. Very soon each eye will start to sprout a short bushy shoot, each of which is a potential plant.

FRUIT

Forcing strawberries

If you potted up strawberries last summer (see page 130), bring them into the greenhouse now, and they will soon be full of blossom, and give you fruit in May or even, if you are lucky, April. It's too late to start now if you don't have any plants potted up, but you can still push outdoor crops ahead by 2–3 weeks by covering a row with cloches or a double thickness of fleece. Tidy up the plants, taking off any leaves damaged over winter, loosen the soil with a handfork and remove any weeds. Scuffle in a dressing of general organic fertiliser, and then cover the plants with the cloches. You'll need to block the ends in order to keep out draughts, but remember to open up the flowering plants on sunny days so that bees can fertilise the blooms.

If you don't have strawberries in the garden, you can still plant maincrop varieties like 'Elsanta' even this late if you buy them pot-grown. They'll give you a crop this season, although a little later than usual. For really fast crops you can order deep-frozen runners from specialist fruit nurseries for delivery in the spring. Freezing holds them in check until they're planted, when the sudden change in temperature really boosts them into vigorous growth. In a good year they have been known to crop just 60 days after planting.

Pruning hazelnuts

Now's the time to prune mature hazelnuts. Shorten long branches by half of last year's growth. Save the trimmings to use as peasticks.

MISCELLANEOUS

Investing in a propagator

Raising your own plants still has to be the cheapest thrill of all. It's far from difficult, but you need to get geared up to the job and, at this time of year, that means providing a little heat.

Heating a whole greenhouse is much too expensive, and the few things that need starting this month can usually be raised in the house. Hardy annuals, most herbaceous plants and vegetables to be transplanted outside will germinate happily on a windowsill at ordinary room temperatures. But it will soon be time to sow the first tomatoes and half-hardy annuals, and these tender plants need extra heat.

Everyone has used the airing cupboard at some time for germinating seeds, and it is certainly a useful source of free heat. But there are pitfalls: never put seeds right on top of the hot water tank as they could cook. I find that two shelves up is about right. And remember that some seeds need light before they'll germinate, so the dark will hold these back. Finally you need to be extra vigilant, checking every day and removing the tray the instant the first seedling emerges.

All in all, a cheap propagator is definitely a better bet. The simplest are not heated at all and comprise a plastic top which fits over a seed tray, ideal for most windowsill propagation – put it near a radiator and you have the best of all worlds. But do check occasionally with a thermometer pushed into the compost to the level where the seeds are sitting, to make sure you're near the recommended temperature.

If you've no handy heat source, you'll need to buy a similar device with an electric element in the base. Generally these reach about 18°C (65°F), which is about right for most seeds, though not hot enough for some. If you want to germinate some of the more demanding subjects, spend a little more on a thermostatically controlled model, which will normally achieve 5–10 degrees more. Remember that the temperature inside varies according to that outside, so you'll have to set it by trial and error, and for that you need a thermometer.

And, of course, you're still stuck with one temperature. I've solved that problem by using a heated mat, just like an electric blanket complete with transformer and thermostat. The mats cover about 0.75 sq.m (8 sq.ft), so you get a lot of heated space for your money. Seeds that need about 18°C (65°F) go straight on the mat; I raise those needing less heat on an up-turned seed tray, and any needing more go under a plastic cloche. It's a bit Heath Robinson, but it works.

ABOVE At this time of year, cuttings and young plants appreciate the gentle warmth provided by a heated mat and trapped by a polythene cover.

Continuing to weed

Weeds such as chickweed and groundsel just never stop producing seeds, even in winter, so pull them out wherever you see them and you'll avoid a spring invasion of hundreds of offspring.

PLANTS FOR

january

1 Corkscrew hazel, *Corylus avellana* 'Contorta', has curiously twisted stems which spiral slowly to 3m (10ft) after 25 years and bear golden catkins in early spring.

2 Skimmias are robust slow-growing shrubs, up to 90cm (3ft) high, with evergreen leaves and fragrant blooms; the long-lasting berries appear only on female plants such as prolific large-fruited *S. japonica* 'Nymans'.

3 The spidery winter blooms of 3m (10ft) high *Hamamelis* x *intermedia* 'Pallida' are the softest coloured of all the witch hazels, but their pronounced fragrance is among the sweetest.

4 *Gaultheria* (*Pernettya*) *mucronata* is a shade-tolerant evergreen, about 60–90cm (2–3ft) high, that needs an acid soil. Heavy crops of showy berries depend on a male form growing nearby.

5 Common or English ivy, *Hedera helix*, is a hardy self-clinging evergreen ground-cover plant or climber, up to 5m (16ft) or more tall. The leaves on its climbing shoots are very variable, often deeply lobed with prominent veins, and can be very decorative.

1

2

3

4

5

February was the month in which the television cameras moved into the garden and into our lives. From now until October, Geoff's plans were geared to the day's filming each week. A team of six would arrive in the evening to discuss details and do a 'recce'. Filming began early the next morning and went on until everyone was satisfied. It was hard work, but judging from the shouts of laughter – and the occasional uninhibited expletive when something went awry – that rang round the garden, it was obviously also enormous fun. I was the 'gofer', making tea for the show's celebrity guests, and taking endless messages since no mobile telephones could interrupt shooting. I also had to keep track of what Geoff wore, just in case any re-shooting was needed the next day. On screen Geoff wore the same type of clothes he wore off it – comfortable ones. And though he was once pilloried as the worst-dressed television presenter he remained undeterred, and continued to wear jeans and sweatshirts because he strongly believed that he should be simply part of the background, allowing attention to focus on the stars of the show – the plants.

As the days begin to lengthen, hardy cyclamen, snowdrops, and hellebores carpet the leafy soil beneath the bare trees in Barnsdale's woodland garden.

february

key tasks for february

ANNUALS & BEDDING PLANTS
- ❍ Watch young seedlings under glass, page 28
- ❍ Revive stored dahlias for cuttings, page 29

BORDER PERENNIALS
- ❍ Take basal cuttings from strong young shoots, page 29

BULBS
- ❍ Start off tuberous begonias, gloxinias and achimenes, page 30
- ❍ Force spring bulbs for early colour, indoors and out, page 30

SHRUBS, TREES & CLIMBERS
- ❍ Prune late-flowering shrubs such as buddleias, page 30
- ❍ Prune late-flowering clematis, page 30
- ❍ Re-shape conifers after snow and frost damage, page 30

ROSES
- ❍ Start pruning in the middle of this month, page 32

VEGETABLES & HERBS
- ❍ Sow vegetables under cloches for early crops, page 32
- ❍ Plant shallot bulbs late this month, page 32
- ❍ Plan tomatoes and other tender greenhouse crops, page 33

FRUIT
- ❍ Force rhubarb for early pickings, page 34
- ❍ Choose and plant currants, gooseberries and raspberries, page 34

MISCELLANEOUS
- ❍ Choose or make cloches to protect early sowings, page 35
- ❍ Use cloches effectively by planning ahead, page 35

ANNUALS & BEDDING PLANTS

Looking after seedlings

Keep a close watch on your seedlings as they come up. They need all the light they can get, preferably on the windowsill if you don't have a greenhouse. But the problem with this is that the light only comes from one side, and doesn't encourage strong bushy upright growth. My solution is to transform an old cardboard box into a light box, as shown below. Push a table up to the sunniest window, and stand the light box there. Strong direct sunlight can scorch the tiniest seedlings so be prepared to protect them with a sheet of newspaper at midday, and remember to draw the curtains on cold nights – a little coddling now pays dividends later.

Remember that this is a dangerous time of year in the greenhouse for seedlings, so be extra vigilant. On cold nights, close the greenhouse

A LIGHT BOX FOR SEEDLINGS

The best way to deal with seedlings indoors is to cut the front out of a large cardboard box and paint the inside white to form a reflector. Line the base with aluminium foil.

early, and on sunny days be prepared to ventilate it. Standing the trays on capillary matting saves watering, but you can water and feed from above with a fine rose if necessary, but take care not to over-water.

Reviving stored dahlias

Planting time is still far away, but it's worth waking up dahlias and other stored tender perennials such as fuchsias to force some early growth for cuttings. The old tubers and stools have been kept in boxes of garden compost all winter, cool and almost bone dry. Now bring them out into full light, top up with compost so the stumps of last year's stems are just exposed, and give them a little water. Don't overdo it though: very soon the tubers and stools will start to put out new shoots, and then you can increase the watering gradually. Spraying them from the top from time to time helps stimulate the growth of those strong shoots that make the best cuttings.

BELOW *Helleborus foetidus* and *Anemone blanda* flourish in dappled shade.

BORDER PERENNIALS

Taking basal cuttings

Very soon many hardy perennials will be making short strong shoots near ground level, and these are ideal propagating material for making cuttings. This is the only way to propagate delphiniums and lupins, and is certainly the best way for many other plants.

Keep an eye on these shoots, because you need to take them before they grow too long: 5cm (2in) is ideal. There's no need to lift the plant before you take basal cuttings as shown on the right.

PLANTS TO PROPAGATE BY BASAL CUTTINGS

Achillea, border chrysanthemums, campanulas, gypsophila, lysimachia (loosestrife) and lythrum (purple loosestrife), macleaya (plume poppy), marjoram, platycodon (balloon flower), pyrethrum, sidalcea, and thalictrum (meadow rue).

TAKING BASAL CUTTINGS

1 Scrape away some of the soil to expose the base of the young shoots when they are about 5–8cm (2–3in) long, and cut them off with a sharp knife as near to the crown as possible.

2 Trim the cuttings, removing any ragged edges and older lower leaves. Dip the ends in hormone rooting powder or solution. Plant them in moist compost, 5–6 cuttings per 13cm (5in) pot, and water in.

3 Cover with a plastic bag to retain the humidity, and stand in a cold frame or gently heated propagator until new fresh growth shows the cuttings are rooted.

BULBS

Starting off tender bulbs

Tuberous begonias, gloxinias and achimenes can now be started off in the greenhouse or conservatory, or on a warm windowsill. Half bury the tubers in trays of compost, keep warm and evenly moist; then pot up individually once they sprout.

Forcing spring bulbs

If you potted up some spring bulbs at the same time as planting them outside (see page 140), you can now bring them indoors to force them into early flower. Move them to a sunny windowsill in a cool room until their flower buds begin to colour; then they can come into warmer surroundings. You could also think about planting some Dutch iris bulbs in the vegetable garden and covering them with cloches to produce superb early cut flowers for the house.

BELOW Snowdrops and the precocious *Crocus tommasinianus* are perfect companions for naturalising in a sunny spot.

SHRUBS, TREES & CLIMBERS

Pruning late-flowering shrubs

Most late-flowering shrubs, especially those which flower on stems they make this season, are best pruned at this time of year. Take your courage in both hands and have a really good go with the secateurs. You'll rarely do any damage, and generally a lot of good. Start now and continue whenever the weather is inviting, right up to the end of March.

Most buddleias, *Caryopteris clandonensis*, ceanothus such as *C. burckwoodii,* hardy fuchsias, *Hydrangea paniculata*, leycesteria, santolina and tamarix can all be cut back really hard to leave no more than two or three buds on last year's growth. You can leave some branches up to three-quarters their length if you want to build up the framework of a larger shrub – this works especially well with buddleias, where varying the amount of pruning will result in a strong bush covered with flowers in late summer. When you finish pruning, tidy up the soil around the plants and give them a good feed of general fertiliser to boost their new spring growth.

Mahonias with shoots that have gone woody and bare at the base can also be cut hard back as soon as the flowers fade to encourage them to produce new shoots.

Pruning late-flowering clematis

Clematis that flower after the middle of June can now be cut back to within a few inches of the ground. If you want them to flower high up though, cut back almost to the base of last year's growth.

Re-shaping conifers after snow and frost damage

Falls of heavy snow can play havoc with your conifers, especially varieties of cypress and other weak-stemmed species. Here and there the lingering weight of snow can force branches out from the main structure, spoiling their natural shape entirely. They can't be cut off as that would leave a gaping hole, but all is not lost. The answer is to tie them unobtrusively back in to the main trunk with a length of plastic-coated wire after wrapping a thick wodge of sacking round both stems to prevent the wire from cutting in. Once the branch settles back in place, the wire could be removed, although I've left it on for years with no harm to the plant.

This is also a good method of shortening conifers that have grown too tall, especially those like *Juniperus* 'Skyrocket', Irish yew, or Lawson's cypress (*Chamaecyparis lawsoniana*) 'Ellwoodii', bought optimistically as a 'dwarf' conifer and now about 6m (20ft) high – we've all done it. Prise the branches apart so that you can see the main central stem. This can then be cut down to well below where you want the finished height to be, leaving an outer ring of branches intact. You then wire these in individually to the trunk or loop a circle of wire round the outside to regain the original perfect shape – only now it will be three-quarters the size it was.

RIGHT All too often relegated to a minor role as background evergreens, ornamental conifers become important solid features in the winter garden, especially when encrusted with light snow and hoar frost.

ROSES

Starting to prune

For years now I have safely pruned my roses in mid-February rather than the recommended mid-March, when there's so much else to do.

The rose is Britain's most popular flower, and it's not hard to see why, but to get all that superb blossom and perfume plants need to be pruned every year. It's surprising how the prospect of this nearly gives so many gardeners a nervous breakdown, and yet rose pruning is not too difficult once you appreciate the ground rules. In fact there are many false assumptions about gardening that are often proved a bit of a myth. Trials by the Royal National Rose Society have shown, for example, that trimming roses with shears or a hedge trimmer can result in better flowers than plants pruned carefully with secateurs, although I still think this is the best tool for the job.

Remember that the harder you prune anything, the stronger will be the resulting growth. So when pruning roses, you cut out very spindly shoots completely, weak ones are cut back hard and vigorous ones not so hard. But what does 'not so hard' really mean? Well, that's up to you. Bear in mind that cutting back to about 2–3 buds will induce strong growth, but fewer flowers. Pruning to, say, four or five buds will produce weaker growth but more flowers, though of slightly lower quality.

The aim when pruning should be to open up a bush and so admit light and air for strong healthy growth. You can be a bit more particular with the different kinds of rose. For hybrid tea, floribunda, patio and English roses – in other words, most bush roses – reduce the thickest stems to leave about 10cm (4in) of last year's growth, and the thinnest to about 2cm (1in), with the rest anywhere in between. Larger shrub roses such as 'Nevada' only need thinning out where they're getting congested, and then you can trim them to shape with shears. Climbers can be pruned by cutting out overcrowded shoots near the base; reduce sideshoots to about 5–8cm (2–3in) long, and then tie in all the stems to their training wires or supports.

Once you've finished cutting off all that growth, clear up the prunings as they can attract pests and diseases, and then give the plants a dose of general organic fertiliser or special rose feed to encourage them to grow again.

PRUNING ROSES

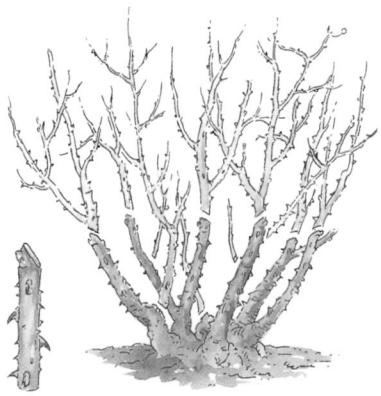

With all kinds of roses, pruning starts with the same routine. First remove dead and damaged wood, weak shoots and stems that cross the centre. Continue pruning bushy roses by shortening the strong stems by at least half. Always make a sloping cut just above a bud, as shown in the detail.

VEGETABLES & HERBS

Early sowings under cloches

If you got ahead and covered a patch of soil with polythene or fleece last month, and it has been in place for a fortnight, it should be warm and dry enough to sow lettuce, spinach, salad onions, cabbages, cauliflowers, radishes, turnips, broad beans and carrots.

Thinking ahead, you might also sow parsley and lettuce in small pots indoors, a pinch of seed in each; pot on the clusters of seedlings and grow on the windowsill for early cutting.

Planting shallots

It's almost possible to have a succession of onions all year round. The new crop is usually ready from August, and the onions will store

until late May or June. You can grow Japanese varieties and over-wintered onion sets to mature in July (see page 142), but that still leaves a gap, and that's where the earlier maturing shallots come in useful.

They are grown from small bulbs or sets, bought fresh or saved from last year's crop, and each one will split to form a cluster of new bulbs like small onions but with a distinctive flavour of their own. The ground needs to be well dug, with plenty of added compost and a sprinkling of general organic fertiliser. Plant the bulbs 15cm (6in) apart with 30cm (12in) between the rows, or 15cm (6in) square on deep beds. Never press the sets into the soil or the root plate may be damaged and subsequent root growth can push the bulbs out again. Instead make holes with a trowel or dibber, or take out a drill for planting in, just deep enough to cover the tip of the set – remove any old brown skin from the tops before planting, to prevent birds from pulling them out.

VARIETIES OF SHALLOTS
Old traditional varieties like 'Giant Yellow' and 'Giant Red' used to be planted on the shortest day for harvesting on the longest. More recent, improved kinds that make larger uniform bulbs might bolt if planted so early, and the second half of February is soon enough for 'Golden Gourmet', 'Topper', 'Pikant' and the handsome exhibition type 'Hative de Niort'. 'Santé' produces some cracking bulbs but should not be planted until April.

LEFT Warmed soil is vital when making early sowings, so cover seedbeds with polythene for a week or two.

Planning tender greenhouse crops

By summer most of us who own a greenhouse will want at least one side of it filled with tomato plants, even if we do then have enough ripe fruit to supply the whole road. Now's the time to be planning sowings, and perhaps using the valuable space more profitably by trying one or two plants of something else for a change.

Tomatoes

When they're grown well, a few tomato plants will produce enough to feed a family, so let me suggest that you grow fewer plants and concentrate on quality rather than quantity. Start by choosing a variety bred for flavour: 'Ailsa Craig' is still one of the best, or there's 'Tigerella' with red-and-gold striped fruits. If you like smaller tomatoes, try 'Sungold' which in my view puts all other varieties in the shade, while 'St Pierre' produces large tasty fruit perfect for slicing. Sow seeds now in gentle heat, transplant seedlings to 10cm (4in) pots when they have a full pair of seed leaves, and they'll be ready for planting in the greenhouse in April.

Other tender greenhouse crops

Sweet and chilli peppers are grown in the same way as tomatoes, but they are so prolific that you'll only need one or two plants. You can grow aubergines like tomatoes too, but finish them in 30cm (12in) pots for good root growth; they also need a longer growing season, so make sure you sow them now.

There's a misconception that you can't mix crops like tomatoes and cucumbers in the same greenhouse, mainly because older varieties of cucumber needed very high temperatures and humidity. All-female F_1 hybrids such as 'Athene', 'Petita', 'Tyria' and 'Pepinex' have changed all that, and give good crops under normal greenhouse conditions. Sow now, grow them on in 30cm (12in) pots or peat-free growing bags, and train them up strings. Unlike the old varieties, there shouldn't be any flowers to trim away, unless you let them go dry or forget to feed them regularly. Sideshoots can be trimmed after two leaves, as with older kinds, but don't remove fruits from the main stem because that's where most of them are borne.

FRUIT

Forcing rhubarb

The tartness of ordinary rhubarb is an acquired taste that many people never have the good fortune to achieve. Forced rhubarb, on the other hand, is entirely different. The sticks might look thin and anaemic but the flavour is superb – the acidity and slight stringiness of outdoor crops are replaced by sweetness and a tender texture.

Commercial growers dig up rhubarb crowns in late autumn and force them into growth inside darkened sheds to get those first juicy sticks. Outdoor forcing gives later pickings, which are just as good to eat and much easier to manage. First feed a strong crown with a dressing of general organic fertiliser or composted poultry manure; then cover it with a large bucket, a dustbin or, best of all, a clay rhubarb forcer with a separate lid so that you can check when sticks are ready to pull. In 6–8 weeks you'll be harvesting the best rhubarb you've ever tasted. But next year you must give the forced crown a rest, so if you've only got one plant buy another now – the best variety is 'Timperley early' – and then force them in alternate years.

BELOW Cover well-fed rhubarb crowns when the buds are just about to break, tucking them up with straw for extra warmth to force those first pale tender sticks.

Planting bush fruit

Most of our gardens these days are small, and that means we have to make choices. It would be nice to be self-sufficient in vegetables and have what the Victorians called a 'fruit room' that was fully planted, but when we come back down to earth, there'll probably be space for only a few fruit bushes, so we need to select carefully.

Perhaps the most important thing is to grow fruits you like. Choose them now and get them planted as soon as possible while they are still dormant. Soft fruit like blackcurrants, gooseberries, red currants and raspberries are all easy to grow, and should be fitted in if possible. There are space-saving ways of training them, which I show you on pages 99–100.

Blackcurrants are packed with flavour and vitamins, but can take up a lot of space unless you go for compact varieties like 'Ben Sarek' or 'Ben Connan'. These can be grown 90cm (3ft) apart, and should be cut back hard straight after planting, down to about two buds from the ground, to encourage plenty of vigorous new shoots that will bear fruit next year.

Older varieties of gooseberry can be badly attacked by mildew which often reduces the crop to next to nothing, so go for a disease-resistant one such as greenish-white 'Invicta' or red 'Pax' (which is also nearly spineless).

The red currant 'Redstart' and its pale cousin 'White Versailles' (now properly called 'Versailles Blanche') are popular varieties grown in the same way. These and the gooseberries should give you a small crop of fruit this year.

All bush fruit need sun and shelter from late frosts, with well-manured soil, to give of their best.

Planting raspberries

If you have no room for a row of raspberries, then grow them as a pillar (see page 100). 'Malling Admiral' is the best-flavoured summer variety, but it's not a heavy cropper, so try 'Glen Moy' which is very heavy and well-flavoured with spineless canes, or the disease-resistant 'Glen Prosen' which is also non-prickly. Plant now, and then cut each cane down to about 15cm (6in) high; the new strong stems that grow from the base are tied in and will fruit next summer. And while you're thinking raspberries, don't miss out on 'Autumn Bliss' which will guarantee you a superb crop from late August through to November. You should cut these down immediately after planting, and they'll fruit this autumn.

This is also the month to prune well-established, autumn-fruiting raspberries. Cut the old canes right down to the ground, and then tie in the new stems at waist level to support the next crop.

LEFT A planter bedded out with crocuses, primroses and dwarf narcissi, and kept under glass, supplies a splash of early spring colour.

MISCELLANEOUS

Choosing and making cloches

One of the most persuasive reasons for growing early vegetables, for me, is the joy of harvesting perfect crops when they're at their most expensive in the shops. And under cloches they really are perfect, safe from wind, rain and marauding insects. Not only that, but cloches lengthen the growing season by 2–3 weeks at each end, allowing you to get extra crops in spring and also autumn. Off-the-shelf cloches are not cheap, but even the best will pay for themselves within about two years if you use them well; it is also easy to make your own cloches for next to nowt.

If you arrange your crops in beds 1.2m (4ft) wide, with just one 45cm (18in) path each side to work from, there are three choices of cloche. The best type is the most expensive as it is built around strong tubular-steel field frames covered with polythene. It is far cheaper to bang in a few posts, staple bamboo canes to the top to make a kind of tent arrangement and cover this with clear polythene. You can also use 'floating' cloches, which are really based on horticultural fleece or a very fine mesh netting. You simply lay a single or double thickness on top of the bed, and the plants push it up as they grow. Although not as effective as a real cloche, the plants inside can be 2°C (4°F) warmer than in the open air, and coddling them by even this much can make a difference to harvesting time.

If you prefer growing in conventional rows, you can use tent or barn cloches. The good old-fashioned glass Chase cloches are dead easy to assemble, stay together and, because they're heavy, need no anchoring to the soil. There is a polycarbonate alternative if you feel glass is dangerous to have around. It is cheap, neat and simple to make your own polythene tunnel cloche, as shown on the right, and the polythene is easily replaceable.

Making the best use of cloches

Using cloches effectively depends on planning: set them in place a fortnight or so before you need them, to warm and dry the soil ready for sowing or planting. Once a crop is covered, start another next to it so that you can just move the cloche sideways when the first batch of plants is maturing. And make full use of the room inside – if you plant two rows of lettuce, for example, sow some radishes or spring onions down the middle to fill the space.

MAKING A POLYTHENE TUNNEL CLOCHE

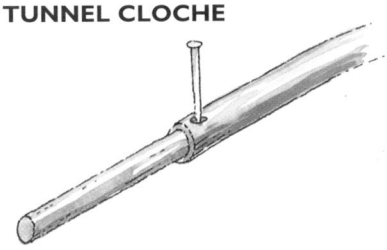

1 Cut the hoops from flexible alkathene tubing from the D-I-Y plumbing department, and plug the open ends with pieces of wooden dowel. Drill a hole at each end, then insert a nail right through the dowels and tubing.

2 Erect the hoops about 1.2m (4ft) apart and stretch the polythene over them. Loop a piece of string over the polythene and secure the ends to the nails.

3 Wedge the polythene securely into the soil at either end of the tunnel, pulling it taut and burying the ends.

PLANTS FOR
february

1 One of the brightest variegated evergreens, *Euonymus* x *fortunei* 'Silver Queen' makes a small compact shrub, but will climb to 1.8m (6ft) or more against a wall.

2 *Camellia* x *williamsii* hybrids withstand more cold and exposure than other camellias, and make handsome evergreen shrubs 4m (13ft) high. 'Debbie' bears large peony-like flowers.

1

2

3 Although individually small, the very fragrant blooms of *Viburnum* x *bodnantense* 'Dawn' are borne in large clusters from December to March, on the bare vigorous 3m (10ft) stems.

4 The 50cm (20in) tall flowers of the evergreen perennial Lenten rose, *Helleborus orientalis*, come in a range of colours from greenish-white through palest pink to deep maroon, some with upturned, saucer-shaped faces, others with nodding cups.

5 One of the winter-flowering heathers, *Erica* x *darleyensis* 'Arthur Johnson' ('Dunwood Splendour'), is a spreading 60cm (2ft) evergreen shrub, with very long flower sprays that are ideal for cutting and defy the coldest weather.

3

4

5

This is the time of year when Geoff started sowing vegetables in earnest. He loved his veg. Not only did he believe that he could save money by growing his own (and one year proved it conclusively by doing a detailed experiment, costing everything that he spent), but he was also convinced that the flavour of home-grown, fresh veg was infinitely superior to any in the supermarket. We never froze any vegetables. We stored onions and root crops over the winter, but everything else was picked or dug minutes before it came into the kitchen. Geoff liked his veg best either boiled or steamed until *al dente*, and served plain, unadulterated with any sauce. From sprouts stiff with frost, through the first new potatoes to sweetcorn, runner beans, artichokes and tomatoes warm from the vine, Geoff made sure there was a never-ending supply. He and his twin brother, Tony, competed with each other to see who could have the largest selection on the table at Christmas – never minding that I ran out of saucepans. The winning number was fourteen – though each later disputed which of them had achieved this.

Early spring is a season of excess, when thick clumps of narcissi jostle with blue scillas and the bright starry blooms of wild anemones to create a carpet of colour.

March

key tasks for march

ANNUALS & BEDDING PLANTS

- ❍ Start fuchsias into growth, take cuttings, and begin to train them as standards, page 40
- ❍ Take spring cuttings of tender bedding plants, page 41
- ❍ Plant sweet peas outdoors, page 41

BORDER PERENNIALS

- ❍ Grow perennials from seed, page 42
- ❍ Plant lily of the valley, page 42
- ❍ Split up polyanthus after flowering, page 43

BULBS

- ❍ Plant snowdrops in the green, page 43

CONTAINER PLANTS

- ❍ Pot up chrysanthemums for late colour, page 44
- ❍ Grow roses in containers, page 44

SHRUBS, TREES & CLIMBERS

- ❍ Prune shrubs with colourful stems and grow more from cuttings, page 45
- ❍ Revive heathers and hebes after the winter, page 45
- ❍ Prepare large shrubs for moving, page 46

LAWNS & HEDGES

- ❍ Give lawns early spring care by repairing damage, reviving growth and beginning to mow, page 47
- ❍ Start to plan dwarf hedges, page 48

VEGETABLES & HERBS

- ❍ Fit in vegetables, whatever the size of your garden, and plan a small-scale vegetable plot, page 49
- ❍ Plant asparagus crowns, page 50
- ❍ Plant early potatoes, page 50

MISCELLANEOUS

- ❍ Make or buy a cold frame, page 51
- ❍ Make the best use of a cold frame, page 51

Starting fuchsias into growth

Tender fuchsias are great favourites for bedding. They usually lose their leaves during their winter rest under the greenhouse staging, and end up looking like a mass of dead twiggy stems. But they'll soon be ready to spring back into life, and if you look carefully you might find tiny bright green or red buds about to break. Start them into fresh growth by treating them as shown on the right.

Keep the plants evenly moist and warm, and spray occasionally with water. New growth will soon appear, and you can then repot the plants, as shown on the right. Keep them fairly cool from now on, because you want the new shoots to be strong and short-jointed rather than long and leggy. When these shoots are about 8–10cm (3–4in) long, pinch them out to encourage bushy growth, nipping off about half their length.

The tips can be used as cuttings: leave the top pair of leaves and trim the stem just below the next pair, which should be cut off. Root as soft cuttings (see page 80).

Training fuchsias as standards

Training a cutting into a standard is not difficult, but it will take at least a season or two. When you first pot on the cutting, put a cane in the pot and tie the main stem to it at frequent intervals. Pinch out any sideshoots, but retain all leaves and keep the main stem growing unchecked until it reaches the required height, feeding every 7–10 days. It is important not to let the plant become pot-bound, so keep an eye on the rootball as it develops.

STARTING FUCHSIAS

1 Plunge the pots in water for a few minutes, then stand the plants in full light on the staging. At the same time you can prune them back quite hard, cutting out spindly lifeless shoots completely, and shortening all other shoots and sideshoots to about 2.5–5cm (1–2in) long.

2 Once new growth appears, knock the plants from their pots and tease out as much of the old compost as possible with your fingers. Then return them to their old containers with some fresh compost.

Taking cuttings of tender bedding plants

This is an excellent time to take cuttings of many greenhouse plants and tender bedding plants such as pelargoniums, marguerites and petunias. Rising temperatures and lengthening days are stimulating new growth on the plants, and the cuttings root quickly now – you might even be able to propagate the tips of cuttings rooted last autumn, so doubling your money. As a bonus, trimming off young shoot tips for cuttings encourages the parent plants to make bushier growth, so you win both ways. Treat the cuttings as shown on page 80, and root them in soil-less compost. Shade them from hot sunshine and keep them sprayed with water, and they'll get away in next to no time.

Planting out sweet peas

Seedlings started in the autumn or in January under glass will be ready to plant outside about now; those sown last month can wait until April. You'll need to train tall varieties against canes, like runner beans, so buy 2.4m (8ft) bamboo canes or some hazel sticks. In a sunny part of the garden, either arrange eight in a circle to make a wigwam, as shown on the right, or set them up 30cm (12in) apart in a straight double row. To save having to tie the stems to the canes in several places as they grow, attach a piece of pea and bean netting to the canes to form a continuous mesh; the plants' tendrils will naturally cling to this. But for the very best blooms, fit to win the village show, you will have to grow them up the canes as cordons, as exhibitors do.

Plant one sweet pea plant at the bottom of each cane. Never grow the main shoots up the canes as they quickly run out of steam and become 'blind'. Instead, tie in the strongest sideshoot from each plant to its cane and remove all the others – if there are no sideshoots, pinch out the growing tip to encourage them and then keep the best for training. As the stems grow, pinch out the sideshoots and tendrils to direct all the plant's energy into flowers. Once these form you'll want to cut them regularly, not just for their sweet scent but because leaving them to set seed will stop more forming.

PLANTING OUT SWEET PEAS

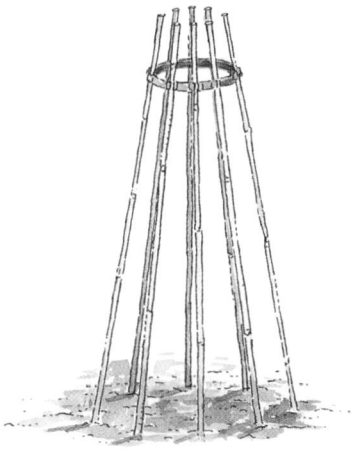

1 Space bamboo canes 30cm (12in) apart in straight rows or arranged in a circle, as above, and fasten the tops tightly to make a secure structure. Drape netting on the canes if you don't want to tie in each stem as it grows.

2 Plant a sweet pea at the bottom of each cane, and water in. If you are not using netting, hold the stem in place with a twist or wire ring to start it climbing, and continue to do this all the way up as the plants grow.

BORDER PERENNIALS

Growing perennials from seed

With a few packets of seeds, you can raise dozens of hardy perennials like lupins, delphiniums, pinks and many others, and you don't have to be an expert to do it. What's more, if you sow them now some could be in flower late this summer.

If you want to try and have plants that will flower this year, sow now in trays or modules (see page 15) of moist seed compost, very thinly and only just covered with a fine layer of compost. Put the trays in the greenhouse or on a not-too-sunny windowsill – they don't want a lot of heat, and 13°C (55°F) is usually ample. Cover with opaque polythene initially, but take a peek underneath every morning, and as soon as you see the first green shoots move them into full light.

Keep them watered but don't overdo it: it's much better for the shoots to be too dry than too wet. Don't force them along in high temperatures either. What you're after is short bushy seedlings, so as soon as they're about 1cm (½in) high transfer them to about 5cm (2in) apart in seed trays and, after a day or two, move them outside to the cold frame. When they're about 5cm (2in) high, they can be grown on in 9cm (3½in) pots until they're planted in their flowering positions, or they can be planted outside in rows in a nursery bed.

If you're not in a hurry for plants to flower, sow the seeds in shallow drills in a corner of the garden. Water down the drill before sowing in dry weather, cover the seeds with dry soil, and pack this in place gently with the back of the rake. Once the seedlings are big enough to handle, water well and then transplant them about 15cm (6in) apart. By autumn or early next spring, they'll be big enough to plant in the border where they'll give you a stunning display next year, all for next to nowt!

MY TOP DOZEN PERENNIALS

I wouldn't want be without any of the following: *Achillea*, with its large flat heads of yellow, pink or lavender shades; *Aquilegia* – more commonly known as columbines; one of the *Campanula* family with blue or white bell-shaped flowers; *Coreopsis*, which provides brilliant yellow flowers all summer – try 'Sunray'; blue, white and purple *Delphinium* spires; *Dicentra*, or bleeding heart, with its gracefully arching stems of pink and white lanterns; the thistle-like leaves and globe flowers of steely blue *Echinops*; *Geum*'s cup-shaped flowers in a range of bright colours; *Heuchera* for its excellent green or reddish foliage; *Lupinus* and *Nepeta* are old favourites; and finally *Rudbeckia* for late colour, with its masses of bright yellow or gold daisies.

Planting lily of the valley

These are supremely attractive spring perennials with their graceful sprays of scented white blooms, but don't be misled by their ladylike appearance. In some soils they are virtually thugs: plant a crown or two and, if they're happy, they'll romp far and wide. In fact some experts recommend digging up and dividing plants every three years. If you do so now, it will give you the

LEFT *Magnolia stellata*, which flowers while still young, is a good choice for small spaces; and crown imperials, *Fritillaria imperialis*, either in yellow or orange, are the aristocrats of the spring border.

RIGHT Blue *Scilla sibirica* spreads freely and makes a bright background to the checked inverted cups of native snakeshead fritillary, *Fritillaria meleagris*.

opportunity to pot some up to make early, highly perfumed houseplants.

They love shade, and grow contentedly under shrubs or fruit trees. They need well-dug soil with plenty of compost or rotten manure added, and make sure you take out any perennial weeds as these will be hard to get at once the lily of the valley plants are growing well. Plant the crowns about 5–8cm (2–3in) apart, with their growing points uppermost and just below the surface, and then mulch the surface with compost or leafmould.

You can plant them in September or now, but this month is certainly the best time to divide and replant if they're spreading where they're not wanted. Simply attack them with a spade, digging up the crowns in small lumps like miniature turves. Replant in freshly prepared soil, and keep a few clumps back for potting. Trim these to fit into 15cm (6in) pots of good potting compost, water well, and then stand them in the greenhouse or a cold frame until they start to bud up. Then you can bring them indoors to fill the house with their seductive perfume.

Splitting up polyanthus

The best moment to split up polyanthus is just after they have flowered. Each plant will make several more if you dig it up, divide the roots using two handforks, and then grow on the separate small plants 8cm (3in) apart in a spare corner until autumn.

BULBS

Planting snowdrops

There is something specially fascinating about bulbs: each of them is a prepacked plant with an embryo flower inside. These days there's a huge range available in garden centres in the autumn and most are excellent value, but there are some exceptions.

In my experience, for example, there is little point in buying dry snowdrop bulbs as they will often have dried out so much that many will have become completely useless and you'll be lucky to get a 50 per cent success rate – those that do grow often take a whole season to establish themselves. I think it's quite wrong that they should be sold in this way at all. Leave them alone, and instead buy pot-grown plants from a specialist or a garden centre that stocks them at the right time, which is now. They're a bit more expensive than dry bulbs, but they're almost guaranteed to grow.

PLANTING SNOWDROPS

Snowdrops, like winter aconites and hardy cyclamen, are best moved and planted during or just after flowering – in fact any time while they're making growth is fine as long as their roots aren't allowed to dry out. They'll appreciate some compost or leafmould worked in before planting if the ground is dry and sandy, or if you're growing them at the foot of hedges, shrubs and trees. Add a little bonemeal when forking over the soil, and then plant the whole clump or potful a little deeper than it grew before, and water in if dry.

CONTAINER PLANTS

Potting up chrysanthemums

Chrysanthemums can easily become a glorious obsession that just keeps on growing. I got hooked on them about thirty years ago.

Old hands like me will have overwintered their plants in a frost-free greenhouse, and will now be taking cuttings which usually root within days. If you're just starting though, you'll need to send away for some rooted cuttings. When they arrive, pot them up immediately in 9cm (3½in) pots of soil-less compost. They're tough customers and need no heat at this time of year so they'll be fine in a cold frame, but it's worth keeping an eye on the weather forecast – if a hard frost threatens, throw some sacking or a bit of old carpet over the frame to be on the safe side.

Mid-season and late-flowering varieties must be potted on into 23cm (9in) pots where they stay until flowering. They make big plants, so you'll need some kind of support – each plant needs a strong cane to tie the brittle stems to as they develop. If you've got several plants, rig up a couple of horizontal wires on the fence or between two posts to tie the support canes to. These varieties all need greenhouse protection from the beginning of October onwards, so they're ideal for following on from tomatoes.

If you don't want to go to so much trouble, grow early-flowering kinds which can be planted outside in late April or May about 38cm (15in) apart to bloom outdoors, but the plants will need digging up and bringing indoors for the winter. There are some really good ones that are bone-hardy for growing in the border, particularly the Pennine varieties. They are potted up in the same way as rooted cuttings when they arrive, but they can go straight out in the border as soon as they're big enough, and there they stay. For all these outdoor kinds, prepare the soil now with plenty of manure, compost or spent mushroom compost, and if your soil is heavy, dig in a barrowload of coarse grit because the one thing chrysanths object to is bad drainage.

Growing roses in containers

If you love roses and can't wait to have them in flower, get a head start now. Ground-cover roses, patio roses and the miniatures are all perfect for pots and containers.

Ideally they should be bought in threes to make a knock-out show in a big tub, but single plants look fine in 30cm (12in) pots. It's the depth that is important, to give plants a good root run, so allow 25cm (10in) for the smallest varieties, and up to 40cm (16in) deep for ground-cover roses. Use a soil-based compost such as John Innes No. 2 – although soil-less compost is fine if moving heavy pots might be a problem – and set the plants a little deeper than they grew before.

Prune them hard, cutting thicker shoots back to about four buds and thinner ones to two, always cutting to just above a bud that faces outwards. You can then stand the plants in a sunny cold frame until next month, or put them straight in a cool greenhouse or conservatory where they'll grow a little taller than normal and flower several weeks earlier. Water them regularly but don't let them get waterlogged, and give them a good feed after 6–8 weeks and then every fortnight.

There's a huge choice of varieties: 'Anna Ford', 'Festival' and 'Pretty Polly' are prize-winning patio roses; 'Baby Masquerade', 'Fire Princess' and 'Starina' are some of the best miniatures, while the County series of ground-cover roses, such as 'Avon' and 'Kent', are hard to beat.

LEFT Roses and small shrubs such as *Skimmia japonica* and *Euonymus fortunei* form centrepieces in outdoor containers, here edged with ivies and ornamental cabbages.

SHRUBS, TREES & CLIMBERS

Pruning shrubs with colourful stems

A number of shrubs, including willows, dogwoods and even one or two of the bramble family, are often grown for the attractive colours of their winter bark. Of the willows, *Salix alba* subsp. *vitellina* has brilliant orange-yellow bark; that of *S.* × *ruhens* 'Basfordiana' is a red-orange which really glows in the spring sunshine, while that of *S. acutifolia*, especially 'Blue Streak', is damson-coloured with a white 'bloom'. Of the dogwoods, *Cornus alba* 'Elegantissima', which has the bonus of leaves that are edged and splashed with white, has ruby-red stems though these are not as bright as those of the green-leafed variety, *C. a.* 'Westonbirt'. And the purplish stems of the brambles *Rubus cockburnianus* and *R. thibetanus* become covered in an eye-catching white bloom in winter. They're all looking so good now, it seems a pity to prune them. It's the youngest growth which gives the most vivid display, however, and cutting the stems back to within 2.5cm (1in) of their base about now keeps the plants in check and helps produce new stems with the best bark colour for next winter.

Don't throw the cut stems away – if they are trimmed into 15cm (6in) lengths and stuck in the ground they will root easily. If you push quite large branches into the soil they'll still root, and a row can make an attractive hedge. I've even seen them woven together to make a very attractive living screen which looks almost as good in winter as it does in summer.

ABOVE Firm annual pruning is the key to a regular display of vivid red dogwood stems

PRUNING SHRUBS WITH COLOURFUL STEMS

To ensure brightly coloured new shoots, cut back the old stems to within 2.5cm (1in) or so of their base, then feed the plant well. If you want flowers as well, cut out between one and two thirds of the stems each year to leave some older ones which will bloom later this year.

Reviving heathers and hebes

As soon as winter-flowering heathers are past their best, clip them lightly over the top with shears as this ensures that they remain compact and sturdy.

At the same time, have a look at any hebes. Many of the best hebes are slightly tender, and are only really reliable grown outdoors in sheltered or coastal areas or kept in containers for bringing inside in winter. Elsewhere they can often look tattered and damaged after hard weather, and sometimes there's no saying if they're alive or not. They will grow out from the base, however, if the roots are still alive, so cut them back almost to the ground and keep your fingers crossed. If the weather looks like

LEFT This month is truly blossom time, with magnolias and flowering cherries competing for attention.

being as bad next winter, you can always cut them back before the worst sets in, and protect them with a thick layer of bark mulch.

Preparing to move a large shrub
Although the job might look daunting at first sight, a large shrub in the wrong place can be transplanted to another position quite successfully if you get it ready well in advance to reduce the inevitable shock to the plant. The best time to move it is the autumn (see page 156), but start preparing it now by severing the long side roots. This gives the plant the rest of this season to recover and make a compact fibrous rootball.

PREPARING TO MOVE A LARGE SHRUB

Reduce the shock to a shrub by trimming its roots now. Simply slice down with a spade all round the plant, or dig out a trench the width of the spade, cutting roots as you go, and refill it with a blend of soil, compost and general fertiliser to encourage new fibrous roots by the autumn.

LAWNS & HEDGES

Britain's climate allows us to grow the very best grass in the world. Compared with warmer drier countries it's really hard to go wrong, but to keep your lawn in top condition it needs a bit of regular care, starting now. So if it isn't quite up to scratch, here's my three-point plan for success: repair, revive and mow.

Repairing damage to lawns
This is an ideal time for covering up bare patches. On hard compressed soil, scratch the surface of the patch with an old kitchen knife to form a fine but shallow tilth. Mix a little seed with some soil, and spread it over, and then cover the patch with clear polythene held down with wire pegs. Cut a few slits in the plastic to let in air and water, and the seed should germinate in a matter of days.

Cut and repair the edges. This is best dealt with by cutting out a section of turf: turn it around with the ragged edge towards the centre and then you can repair this with a handful of seed and fine soil. No amount of rolling will remove bumps, because the flattened areas simply rise up again after rain. Instead make up a top dressing of sieved soil, garden compost and sharp sand in a 3:2:3 ratio. Spread this over the area, levelling it into the depression and leaving the high areas uncovered.

Reviving lawn growth
Old dead grass or 'thatch' builds up at the base of the grass, choking it out where amounts get bad. It should be raked out at the beginning of the season with a spring-tine rake or a hired electric machine. If you've got moss in the lawn, spread a special moss killer first and then, after it has gone black, rake out the dead stuff with the thatch. Organic gardeners don't use chemical moss killers, and just rake the worst out or learn to live with it. It's too early to do any weeding just yet – wait until the grass is growing vigorously, and then either water on a lawn weedkiller or combined weed and feed product, or dig the weeds out individually. You can give the grass a feed of nitrogenous lawn fertiliser as a spring boost at the end of this month, in which case you will need to give it another in June. Alternatively, you can apply a slow-release fertiliser just the once in May (see page 81).

Mowing
Sometime this month or next, when the grass starts to look ragged, you can begin the mowing regime. Avoid slashing grass close to the ground for the first cut, as this can set growth back if the weather turns cold again. It's much better to set the mower at its highest and just trim the top. Then you can lower the cutters a little each time each time you mow over the next few weeks until you leave the grass at its summer level. During the season, aim to mow a minimum of once a week, and 2–3 times each week for the finest lawns. If you can, mow diagonally in the opposite direction each time as this ensures that you pick up long grass flattened by the roller last time, and makes for a finer finish. And never kill worms: just brush their casts into the grass with a broom before mowing.

ABOVE A framework of neatly clipped dwarf box provides a disciplined surround for small beds of spring bulbs.

Starting dwarf hedges

Plant breeders are forever recommending pygmy versions of taller plants as 'ideal for small gardens'. But even if your plot is small, this doesn't exclude you from growing tall plants here and there, with a few larger drifts for more impact. And one of the ways to make ambitious ideas work in a small space is to tie the scheme together with dwarf hedging. If you edge borders or paths with a continuous run of the same plant the effect is to bind all the various plants together into a coherent scheme, and the last thing it looks then is bitty or boring. One of the traditional features of cottage gardens was a hedge of catmint or lavender running down both sides of the path that led to the front door. Although both sides of the path were largely planted with vegetables, this didn't look out of place or ugly. Dwarf box is a more formal, evergreen alternative.

The trouble is that a long run of hedging needs a lot of plants, and that could just break the bank. But if you have a bit of patience you can do it for next to nothing, because many of the best hedging plants can be raised from seed or from cuttings. Take catmint, for example: sown early in warmth, it will actually flower in its first year; otherwise sow it this month or next in a cold frame. Go for *Nepeta mussinii* (now called *N. racemosa*), or *N. nervosa*. Lavender can be raised in the same way. It's a superb traditional hedging plant, with greyish foliage all year round and scented blue flowers. Most of the popular varieties like *Lavandula* 'Hidcote' or 'Munstead' are available as seed. Cotton lavender (*Santolina chamaecyparissus*, also called *S. incana*) is another excellent hedger with silver filigree foliage. It also produces yellow flowers but is best cut back before these appear, to keep the hedge neat and compact.

Pot up the seedlings individually when they are large enough or line them out in a spare bit of the garden, and then plant them finally 15–20cm (6–8in) apart in the autumn. The one thing to bear in mind is that seed-raised plants are not as uniform as those grown from cuttings, but for hedging I don't think that matters at all. Since it's going to be clipped regularly, any difference in height won't show and slight variation in leaf or flower colour is to be welcomed.

Dwarf box needs the most patience but, once established, is disease-free and will last a lifetime. One decent-sized plant bought now could give you dozens of semi-ripe cuttings later in the year. These root easily, (see page 125), and in a year or two will provide yards of hedge.

VEGETABLES & HERBS

Fitting in vegetables

Some gardens are just too small to accommodate a kitchen plot. If you are in this position and haven't the time to rent an allotment locally, don't despair. You can always grow a few vegetables in your flower borders. Many vegetables are very attractive and, far from spoiling a flower bed, will enhance it. And by camouflaging vegetables among other plants you'll confuse many insect pests, so there's no need to cover your food with chemicals.

Leave a few spaces, ideally near the front of the border so that you can reach them from the path. Dig 15–20cm (6–8in) deep with a border fork, preferably working in garden compost, well-rotted manure or spent mushroom compost at the same time. Add a handful of organic fertiliser, and then rake the surface with the back of the fork to bring up a fine tilth. Scratch shallow rows about 15cm (6in) apart using a bit of garden cane, and then this month you can sow radish, lettuce, carrots, spinach, turnips or summer cabbage. Later on you can add courgettes, bush cucumbers, tomatoes and sweetcorn.

Herbs, of course, are even easier to fit into a border scheme because most have very decorative leaves or flowers. Try chives or parsley as an edging, or plant thyme, marjoram and pennyroyal to tumble over the sides of a path, while giants like angelica, lovage and bronze fennel look great at the back of a border.

Planning the small-scale plot

If you do have a small plot, you'll have some hard decisions to make about what to grow and how to get maximum yields from every square inch. If your plot is small and your freezer's big, it's worthwhile growing things like spinach, Swiss chard and beans to stock up for the winter – frozen peas are the one exception though, because commercial growers do them so much better than we can. Try some roots like carrots and beetroot: you can store all you can grow by putting them in boxes of garden compost in the garage. Then there are the vegetables that are expensive or hard to come by. I certainly wouldn't be without things like asparagus, globe artichokes, sweetcorn and courgettes, which are all very much cheaper to grow and taste a million times better when harvested minutes before cooking.

Above all, make the most of your space. Grow plants close together, perhaps in a deep bed (see page 117), and sow just the right amount and no more. That means crops grown in succession – lettuces, summer cabbages, radishes, carrots, beetroot – must be sown in short rows at frequent intervals. It all depends on how fast you eat them, but I'd suggest sowing a short row

BELOW Hardening off early vegetable sowings or tender plants is easy with a simple cold frame, equipped with a clear lid that can be opened a little more each day (see page 51).

MARCH SOWING LIST

In a small bed try: lettuce 'Tom Thumb'; carrot 'Early Nantes'; turnip 'Purple Top Milan'; salad onion 'White Lisbon'; radish 'Sparkler'; beetroot 'Boltardy'; spinach 'Medania'; cabbage 'Kingspi'; pea 'Douce Provence'; broad bean 'The Sutton'; parsnip 'White Gem'. The only tools you'll need are a border fork, a stick and a bucket for as much compost or manure as you can spare. Sow rows at close spacings, thin seedlings early and pick while crops are young.

of radishes once a week and a longer one of lettuces every fortnight: thin the lettuces when they're large enough, and use the thinnings for another, slightly later, row.

Turnips, carrots and beetroot are tastiest when they're pulled small, so I get them in once a fortnight too, but the winter storage varieties are sown just once, of course. If you like a succession of summer cabbages and cauliflowers, sow those once every three weeks – bear in mind, though, that when beans, sweetcorn and tomatoes come in, you might lose interest in cabbages.

If space is really scarce, you can always try growing 'mini-veg', specially bred compact varieties (see page 182).

Planting asparagus

Now is a good moment to make an asparagus bed, which I suggest should be about 1.2m (4ft) wide and as long – or short – as you like. Dig it deeply and add plenty of compost. On heavy soil also add some coarse pea shingle for better drainage. Mound the bed 15cm (6in) higher than its surroundings to improve drainage. For heaviest yields order crowns of an all-male variety such as 'Franklim', 'Lucullus' or 'Dariana', and when they arrive soak them for a couple of hours. Dig out shallow trenches about 15cm (6in) deep and 45cm (18in) apart, and mound up the centre of each trench to make a gentle ridge. Rest the crowns on the top, 45cm (18in) apart with the fleshy roots spreading down each side of the ridge, and replace the soil over them. You won't be able to cut any spears this year, and will have just a taste next season. But after that, gastronomic bliss!

Planting early potatoes

Potatoes can be put in now, although if the sprouts are still small there's plenty of time. Provided the sprouts are healthy, the potatoes can last unplanted until early April, but yields begin to decline after that.

If the ground is well prepared in advance, you can plant potatoes with a trowel. Otherwise dig out planting trenches about a spade deep and 60cm (2ft) apart, and put manure or compost in the bottom. Don't use spent mushroom compost as this contains lime which could encourage unsightly potato scab.

Plant the tubers on top, 30cm (12in) apart. Since they're gross feeders, add about 136g/sq.m (4oz/sq.yd) of pelleted chicken manure or Growmore to the soil you dug out, so that it's worked in when you refill (alternatively scatter the dressing down the rows after planting). You'll find the soil naturally mounds up slightly over the top of the rows, and they'll need a further mounding later when the shoots have grown about 15cm (6in) high. Once these appear, watch out for frost and if this is threatened cover the plants with horticultural fleece.

For extra-early crops, prepare the ground in the usual way and then ridge the soil into mounds 30cm (12in) high and 60cm (2ft) apart. Plant an early tuber in each mound, as deep as possible. Cover the area with clear polythene held down with bricks or pieces of timber, and when the foliage appears cut slits to let it through. It is even easier, because the potatoes are grown on the surface, to use black polythene, as shown above. If you protect the plants with fleece in the event of frost, you should be harvesting new potatoes in mid- to late May.

Maincrop varieties can also go in now, planted in the same way, except that they're spaced 38cm (15in) apart with 75cm (30in) between the rows. Frankly though, there's not such a huge difference in taste over shop-bought supplies so, unless you have plenty of space or want to clear new ground, perhaps maincrops are not so worthwhile.

PLANTING POTATOES

1 Prepare and level the bed, and cover with a sheet of black polythene tucked in all round. Cut a small cross for each potato, large enough to push the tuber into place just below the surface.

2 The foliage will grow through the slits and then, at the end of the season, it's simply a matter of peeling back the polythene to expose the crop, right at the surface and ready to harvest.

MISCELLANEOUS

Make or buy a cold frame

You'll soon find the greenhouse overflowing, or your windowsills so full of young plants that you can't see out. What you need is a cold frame, a fairly modest but worthwhile investment that's sure to reap dividends.

Frames come in all shapes and sizes, in wood or aluminium, with a glass or plastic lid, and either with solid sides or fully glazed right down to the ground. Naturally, all-glass frames let in more light but can be colder – in early spring it's a good idea to line one of these with bubble plastic or even insulate the sides with sheets of polystyrene. Some frames are glazed with twin-wall polycarbonate, which lets in almost as much light as glass does, and is warm and completely shatterproof. Wooden frames look attractive and they tend to retain more heat than aluminium ones.

Alternatively, it's very easy to make your own. In fact, a wooden apple box with a piece of rigid plastic on top, held down with a bit of string and an elastic band, served me well for years. You can make a more elaborate version from old timber, as shown above. A cast-off window frame or even a surplus car windscreen would do for the lid.

You could paint the inside of the frame white for maximum light, and treat the outside with a couple of coats of timber preservative.

There's no need to make a solid floor, indeed, a frame is better without one at all. It will be more use if you can stand it on the soil, partly because bare soil provides better drainage for trays and pots, especially if you cover the ground with a layer of capillary matting; but also because you can actually sow and grow plants directly into the soil inside the frame.

To make maximum use of the frame, cultivate the the ground it stands on as a seedbed, forking in plenty of compost and then levelling the surface. Cover this with the matting while you are hardening off your pots of plants – once they're safely out, remove the matting and the seedbed will be ready.

Using a frame

Site your new frame in a sunny spot and it will deliver enough light to allow you to grow good short bushy plants in complete safety from frost and wind. Right now its main use is to 'harden off' tender plants. Any you've raised on the windowsill will be desperate for full light to keep them sturdy. Put them inside the frame, close the lid and cover it with a bit of old carpet or a blanket if frost threatens at night. In April you can open the lid a fraction during warm days, gradually giving the plants a bit more air each day. Then start opening it at night, depending upon the temperature. By late May you should be able to leave the plants exposed day and night – they should be hardy enough by then to take anything the weather can throw at them.

During June you can use the frame for soft-wood cuttings, or for a batch of self-blanching celery. In the autumn it can be used to help to root semi-ripe cuttings, and then in winter it could house November-sown sweet peas, or you could plant crops of winter lettuce, endive and chicory in the ground. In a well-run garden a cold frame should never be empty, and will earn its keep over and over again.

MAKING A COLD FRAME

A sturdy and durable frame can be made from strong recycled timber that has been treated with preservative. Make sure the lid slopes to shed rain and collect maximum light. If you make the frame to fit one of your vegetable beds and add a handle at each end, it can be placed over growing plants to protect them out of season.

PLANTS FOR
march

1 The hardy evergreen lesser periwinkle, *Vinca minor*, is more restrained than its large cousin *V. major*; the 20cm (8in) gold-splashed stems of 'Aureovariegata' spread 60cm (2ft) after three years.

2 'Rose Queen' is one of the finest varieties of hardy perennial *Epimedium grandiflorum* (*E. macranthum*). Its 30cm (12in) high clumps of richly tinted leaves last all winter. Trim them off in spring to reveal its crimson-pink blooms and the newly emerging shoots.

1

2

3 The flowering quince, *Chacnomeles × superba* 'Knap Hill Scarlet', is a dense spreading deciduous bush, eventually 90cm (3ft) high and 1.5m (5ft) wide, with a long season of brilliant blooms.

4 As its name implies, *Daphne odora* has intensely fragrant flowers which stud the 1.5m (5ft) evergreen shrubs from late winter onwards. *D. o.* 'Aureomarginata' has creamy-yellow edged leaves and is slightly hardier.

5 Perennial double primroses are often sold unnamed in collections of mixed colours. At 15cm (6in), they are ideal highlights for small beds and containers in March and April.

OVERLEAF Parrot tulips have large heads of fringed petals, and provide an extravagant display both in the garden and as cut flowers.

3

4

5

Geoff would complain loudly at this time of year about lack of sleep, having frequently been woken at first light by what he called the 'twittering cacophony of lustful birds'. In truth, of course, he loved the dawn chorus, and it was one of the reasons why planting a variety of mature trees was among his first priorities at Barnsdale. Now there are finches, wrens, robins and owls in the woodland; we have bird boxes for blue tits, house martins have nested in the eaves, and we have to leave the barn doors open all summer for the swallows. Geoff loved their songs – even the bullfinch's, which he said sounded like a squeaky wheelbarrow. But he also loved them for being allies in the fight against greenfly, slugs and caterpillars.

Geoff felt passionately about encouraging these garden pests' natural predators, and never, ever used pesticides or slug pellets. He was even known to have 'hardened off' the ladybirds which hatched in his office by gently scooping them up and taking them into the garden where he installed them under a cloche to get them used to the lower temperatures outside.

The popular weeping willow-leafed pear, *Pyrus salicifolia* 'Pendula', takes centre-stage as its young foliage opens above a border packed with tulips and hardy perennials.

april

key tasks for april

ANNUALS & BEDDING PLANTS

- Sow hardy annuals outdoors where they are to grow, page 58
- Sow annual climbers early in the month, page 58
- Buy summer bedding as plugs for growing on, page 59

BORDER PERENNIALS

- Clean up borders now growth is well under way, page 60
- Start to plant borders, page 60
- Make a scree garden for alpines and drought-tolerant plants, page 60

BULBS

- Pinch off spent bulb heads, page 63
- Plant gladioli corms, page 63

SHRUBS, TREES & CLIMBERS

- Plan climbers to add height to the garden, page 64
- Support and tie in climbers, page 64
- Prune quinces after they have flowered, page 65

ROSES

- Feed and mulch roses, page 65

LAWNS & HEDGES

- Assess your mower at the start of the season, page 65

VEGETABLES & HERBS

- Sow French beans in pots under glass, page 66
- Sow maincrop leeks outdoors, page 66
- Sow peas, and keep on sowing at regular intervals, page 66
- Make plans for late crops and winter supplies, page 67

FRUIT

- Choose fruit trees for training into compact shapes for small gardens, page 68

MISCELLANEOUS

- Feed outdoor plants to stimulate growth, page 69
- The benefits of organic fertilisers, page 69
- Grow your own manure, page 69

ANNUALS & BEDDING PLANTS

Sowing annuals outdoors

Hardy annuals can produce probably the cheapest and most cheerful flower borders possible, and they're also useful for providing flowers in new beds while slower plants are still settling in. A sprinkle here and there will help to fill gaps in established borders, and many annuals will also attract a lot of bees and butterflies to the garden.

At this time of year annuals can be sown direct into the soil, but don't start before the ground is warm enough as the seeds won't germinate until the temperature has reached about 7°C (45°F). Wait until the soil is dry enough to rake down to a fine crumbly tilth – there's no need to add any fertiliser, because most annuals flower much more prolifically in poor soil.

Although they are great for filling in gaps in borders, annuals always look most impressive in big bold blocks of colour. The easiest way to mark these out on the ground is to fill a wine bottle with fine dry sand and then use this to outline planting areas for each variety. Then sow as shown on the right.

For early flowers, or if your soil lies wet and cold until late in spring, sow early this month in the greenhouse. Fill seed trays with moist soil-less compost, sow the seeds very thinly and allow them to grow on without thinning. Harden them off when they're about 5cm (2in) high, and plant them out in small clumps – just lift the whole block of seedlings out of the tray and cut it into 4cm (1½in) squares with a knife.

SOWING ANNUALS OUTSIDE

1 Mark the outlines of planting areas with dry sand trickled from a wine bottle; then make parallel drills for sowing within each patch with a cane.

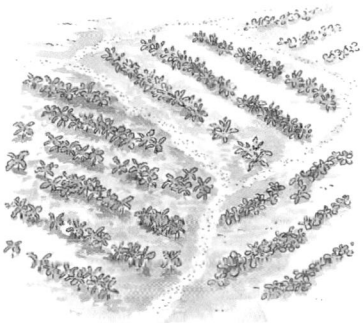

2 Sow a different variety in each patch, arranging heights and colours to produce a balanced design. Water and weed the area until the seedlings are through.

3 When the seedlings are 5cm (2in) high, thin them to about 15–20cm (6–8in) apart, depending on the variety. Water them with a diluted feed after you've finished.

Growing annual climbers

A little social climbing will do you and your garden no harm at all, and it needn't cost a fortune. There's a small range of annual climbers that are easily raised from seed.

Sweet peas (*Lathyrus odoratus*) should have been planted earlier (see page 16), but there are three other annuals that will flower from late summer onwards if you get the seeds in early this month. Morning glory (*Ipomaea*) has large blue or pink trumpets with white centres; cathedral bells (*Cobaea scandens*) has large bell-shaped flowers that are violet and purple on the outside and green inside; and climbing nasturtium (*Tropaeolum speciosum*) is a knock-out in brilliant reds, oranges and yellows. All three need to be planted in a sunny spot with some support, such as a pergola or fence. They are also ideal for growing through evergreen shrubs.

Buying bedding as plugs

These days most seedsmen offer more than just seeds in their catalogues. There are all kinds of accessories, plus an increasing range of half-hardy bedding as plants, which could save you a lot of worry if you haven't the time or space to raise your own. The trouble with the more tender kinds of bedding like petunias, busy lizzies and begonias is that they usually need heat early in the year to get them to germinate. New F_1 hybrids are getting quite expensive and if the seeds don't grow, or only a few do, that can prove far too costly. Buying plants at bedding out time can work out expensive too, but there is a way to grow the best bedding ever, while leaving all the early risks to someone else.

Growers now tend to raise all their bedding by precision-sowing large trays divided into dozens of tiny tapering cells, and these produce 'plug' seedlings. At this stage they have got past all the hazards of germination, and don't need such high temperatures. When you buy plugs from a seed catalogue or garden centre they'll be ready for transplanting, each with its own perfect root system.

With no disturbance to the roots, they're off and away before you can say 'petunia', and they are comparatively easy to grow on until you plant them out when the danger of frost has passed in late May or early June. They should be in flower when you plant them, and considerably bigger and bushier, so you might need fewer of them than

BELOW Violas and winter-flowering pansies are favourite choices for spring bedding and for combining with low-growing bulbs.

if you'd raised your own. They could work out cheaper too.

When they arrive, pot the plugs up in 9cm (3½in) pots of soil-less compost and put them in a cool greenhouse or a cold frame. Although no extra heat is necessary from now on, they must be kept frost-free, so keep an eye on the weather forecast and, in the unlikely event of very hard frost, cover the frame with a blanket or a bit of sacking. Start to feed the plants with a general liquid fertiliser a fortnight after potting.

They should be pinched back two or three times by nipping out the tips of leading shoots with your thumbnail. This encourages them to bush out and produce big fat flowering plants to brighten up your summer borders. Make sure that you harden them off thoroughly for a fortnight or so before planting, by gradually opening the top of the frame a little more every few days until they're used to outside conditions.

BORDER PERENNIALS

Cleaning up the borders

Some time this month you'll find just about everyone outside in the fresh air, both fair-weather gardeners and those of us who are at it all year round. If your garden hasn't been worked on since the winter, the first job is a general clean-up of the borders.

Cut away any old dead growth from last year's herbaceous plants, pull out the weeds and then give the soil between the plants a light forking over, just the top couple of inches or so. I like to spread a layer of compost on the surface first, and tickle this in as I fork. If you have no compost or manure, spent mushroom compost is the next best thing, except around acid-loving plants. Never, of course, use peat.

Add a sprinkle of rose fertiliser or a general organic one if you are moving plants or planting new ones. Check for any herbaceous plants that are overcrowded or have become old and tired. It's getting a bit late to lift and divide them, and I prefer to do this in the autumn anyway (see page 138), but I'd still do it now if it's really necessary. (Though this is the best time to divide sweet violets, which will have flowered by now, and move them to a shady spot for the summer.) Make sure you water in any newly divided plants well.

LEFT A raised scree bed, like this one constructed for alpines at Barnsdale, is an attractive and practical alternative to a rock garden for displaying arabis, alyssum and other compact alpines that need perfect drainage to do well.

Starting to plant

This is the perfect time to put in new herbaceous plants, and it's worth paying a visit to the garden centre or nursery if you have any bare spaces in the border. But please don't buy everything that's in flower now or you'll have a garden that only flowers in the spring. Look for summer-flowering plants, such as achilleas, delphiniums and lupins. They'll produce masses of colour year after year, are generally soil-tolerant and easy to grow.

Before you buy, check on heights, spread, required position, colour and flowering time: this is where a good book becomes essential. But many books encourage you to plant three, five or even seven plants in a group; that can be mighty expensive and, if you have patience, could be completely unnecessary. If you wait until next year, you'll be able to lift most of your new plants about this time and split them up to produce the extra plants you need, all for the cost of just one plant.

Although we expect spring to start with buckets of rain, don't be lulled into a false sense of security. The plants will need watering in and, if the weather remains dry, watering again in a week or so.

Making a garden for alpines and drought-tolerant plants

As I said in January, alpines can withstand most extremes of weather, but the one condition they can't abide is excess wet, a condition they share with drought-tolerant or Mediterranean plants. Efficient drainage is a must.

While a full-scale rock garden will provide the right drainage conditions, it will also take up a lot of space. Instead, you could always

ABOVE As well as being a wonderful aid to drainage in alpine beds, gravel can be added to the soil and spread as a mulch, as here at Barnsdale, to provide the conditions that drought-loving Mediterranean shrubs and perennials most enjoy.

make yourself a small scree garden which will re-create the gravelly conditions found at the bottom of mountains, where some of the best alpines grow, or the dried-up river bed typically colonised by heat-loving plants.

You can make a scree garden as large as you like and with a natural appearance, or do what I did and make it small and formal. Mine is a circle edged with bricks and looks good all year round. Simply mark out the area you want to plant, and dig a lot of grit into the soil: a barrow-load per square yard is certainly not too much. Make sure the grit is at least 0.25cm (⅛in) in diameter; never use sand, which is too fine. Pea shingle from builders' merchants is ideal, and you can also incorporate about half as much well-rotted garden compost. Mix all this in thoroughly.

If you want to make a rock garden, position a few groups of rocks here and there, burying them about one-third of their depth to make them look natural. And always put them in random clumps, rather than spreading them around evenly like currants in a bun. But please be careful that you don't buy water-worn limestone for the rocks – it is robbed from rare and irreplaceable limestone pavements in the countryside.

After planting mulch with more pea shingle or coarse grit, tucking it under the plants where you can to keep their leaves off the damp soil. I like to mix the sizes of the gravel to make an interesting texture, and find that larger pebbles deter cats from scratching it about. The mulch will greatly reduce water loss and

suppress most of the weeds – any that do blow in and germinate will be a lot easier to control. Water and feed your plants only if they look as though they are not growing well.

CHOOSING ALPINES

Start with one or two taller plants like dwarf conifers, but make sure they are truly dwarf: slow growers like the little Noah's Ark juniper, *J. communis* 'Compressa', are ideal. When you buy the smaller plants check that they're not too rampant – too much arabis or aubrietia will soon swamp the garden. There are hundreds to choose from, so go for the tougher customers like saxifrage, thrift, rock pinks, houseleeks, sedums, miniature aquilegias, thymes, raoulias and dwarf hypericum.

CHOOSING DROUGHT-TOLERANT PLANTS

I would start with lavender and rosemary, the many varieties of *Cistus* or rock rose that thrive on sun-baked hillsides, and smaller hebes like *H. pinguifolia* 'Pagei' and *H.* 'Red Edge'. You can grow yuccas, cordylines and sea-hollies, and some kinds of osteospermum and penstemon; in summer interplant with tender perennials such as marguerites and cannas, as well as annuals like Livingstone daisies.

LEFT This bold grouping of yellow and orange crown imperials (*Fritillaria imperialis*), with blue pulmonaria and muscari at their feet, is one way to illuminate a border of summer-flowering perennials still in their early stages of growth.

BULBS

Treating flowered bulbs

April is the prime month for bulbs. Daffodils are at their peak, with tulips coming on fast and many smaller bulbs such as fritillaries also making a show. In order to channel the plants' energy into building up flowering bulbs for next year, prevent them from forming seedheads by pinching off the flower heads as soon as they fade.

Planting gladioli

Although there's no doubt that the large-flowered hybrid gladiolus deserves its reputation as a 'mega-star' of the border, there are few better flowers for cutting, so a row or two in the vegetable plot is a must. If you cut them when the first floret is just opening, the flowers will continue to develop in water and last for ages.

A good mixture is perhaps the best choice for cutting. That way you should get a superb range of colours, from delicate pastels to flaming scarlet, often with exotically frilled petals and contrasting markings. If you decide to go for individual varieties to fit in with your border scheme, choose them from a good catalogue that lists them according to season because there are early, mid-season and late kinds. Not only that, but if you plant a few every fortnight between early April and late May, they'll flower in succession through the summer and autumn months. If there's a choice of sizes, I'd recommend the '14cm (5½in) upwards' grade, as these are the largest corms and produce the best flowers – for the biggest spikes, peel the corms before planting and nick out any shoots coming from the sides with a knife, to concentrate all the energy in the spike at the top.

Gladioli can look a bit ungainly in borders if you grow them singly or in rows, so group about five or six in a circle to make a stunning column of colour. That way you can also stake the lot with one unobtrusive cane in the middle. Straight rows often fit in better among vegetables – set up a couple of strong stakes and a horizontal wire or two for tying them to, or simply tie each stem to a cane.

Prepare the soil well with plenty of manure or compost, and a handful or two of pelleted chicken manure. If you are on heavy soil, plant the corms on a layer of coarse grit, just to keep the base-plate dry and free from rot. Space large-flowered kinds 15cm (6in) apart each way, or with 30cm (12in) between rows if you're growing them in this way. The corms need to be 10–15cm (4–6in) below the surface, a little deeper on very light soil because the tall stems are more likely to topple over if they're not well supported at the base.

For me, the smaller Butterfly hybrids have a special charm and come in a range of superb colours with bright patches on the lower petals – try white and scarlet 'Bizar', pink and yellow 'Jackpot' or violet 'Pop Art' with its brilliant white markings. My own favourites are the *Primulinus* hybrids with flowers more loosely arranged and in slightly more restrained colours. Try potting some of these smaller types, about 8cm (3in) apart and 10cm (4in) deep in 20cm (8in) pots of John Innes No. 2 compost with about 25 per cent added grit.

SHRUBS, TREES & CLIMBERS

Planning for climbers

Cover the boundaries of a tiny new garden with climbing plants and you'll transform a confined space into a secret haven. Even in large gardens, climbers will give height and increase your growing space three- or four-fold. They can be used to clothe the walls of the house and hide ugly features such as a central heating oil tank. And don't forget, many climbers will also provide a home for all kinds of wildlife.

Everyone would like a climber that is evergreen, fast growing, loaded with flowers all year long and thrives on a freezing north-facing wall. Well, I have to tell you that such a plant doesn't exist. For a start, you'll miss a lot if you insist on evergreens. There are certainly some very good ones (pyracantha and garrya, for example) but to be without clematis, most of which are deciduous, would be a sin. Don't get hung up on their speed of growth either, for the faster a climber grows, the bigger the problems can be later on – choose a Russian vine, *Fallopia* (*Polygonum*) *baldschuanica*, and although it will clothe your garden shed in two years, it will bury it in five. And although there are climbers for every wall, it's the east- and north-facing ones that really sort the men from the boys, because lack of light and the possibility of biting winds make these positions suitable for only the hardiest climbers. It's no good putting wisteria, for example, on an east- or north-facing wall: it will certainly grow perfectly well, but the flowers will be as rare as hen's teeth.

BELOW Early-flowering *Clematis armandii* scrambles through a white camellia, making a perfect partnership.

There is no need, however, to be satisfied with just one climber. Walls can actually be gardened just like borders, allowing one less vigorous plant to scramble through another. A favourite combination of mine, for example, is a climbing or rambling rose with a clematis growing through it, but be careful which kind of clematis you choose. A vigorous species such as *C. montana* will swamp anything smaller than a large tree. The best bet is to use a less rampant variety and, if you go for one that flowers late, you'll be able to cut it to the ground after flowering and pull out all the shoots to give the rose a chance. The following year the rose will flower well, and the clematis will grow back again to flower afterwards. The best kinds would be any of the *C. viticella* or *C. texensis* varieties.

Supporting climbers

There are a few climbers that will cling to a fence or wall without any support at all. If you grow Virginia creeper, one of the ivies or a climbing hydrangea, all you need do is plant it and then point the growing tip towards the fence. But there are many more that need some support. The best method is to staple wires to fence posts. If you want to grow plants on an old wall, you should be able to drive 'vine eyes' into the mortar – these are small hardened steel wedges with a hole in one end for the wire. On modern walls with strong mortar, you'll have to drill and plug holes for screw-in eyes. Horizontal wires set 30cm (12in) apart will be enough for tying in most perennial climbers with woody branches, but for twiners such as honeysuckle or clematis, you should add thinner vertical wires at 15cm (6in) intervals to make a wide mesh.

Don't be afraid to plant restrained climbers in the middle of a border. You can support climbing roses by tying the stems in to an upright pole; for self-clinging climbers, wrap a couple of thicknesses of chicken wire or dark-coloured plastic netting round the pole to help give them a grip. Alternatively, you could build a wigwam like the structure you'd make for sweet peas or runner beans (see page 41). You can use garden canes for lighter climbers such as a late-flowering clematis that is pruned to ground each spring, or stronger poles for heavier climbers like roses or early-flowering clematis that keep a permanent framework of branches.

Finally, don't forget that walls, especially house walls which are protected by the eaves, are some of the driest places in the garden. Dig in lots of manure or compost before planting, position the climber at least 30cm (12in) away from the wall, and give it a good soak from time to time in its first year or two, at least until it has been able to root out into moister soil.

Pruning flowering quinces

Flowering quinces can be wall-trained as well as grown as free-standing specimens. If they are wall-trained they must be cut back annually to keep their shape and hug the wall, but even free-standing quinces will become choked with growth if they are left to their own devices. They are best pruned as soon as the flowers fade: cut back the flowered shoots to 1–2 buds.

CLIMBERS FOR SHADY WALLS

Akebia quinata; camellias – though not on an east-facing wall; some clematis such as *C.* × *jackmanii*; flowering quince (*Chaenomeles*); silk tassle bush (*Garrya elliptica*); most ivies (*Hedera*); climbing hydrangea (*H. petiolaris*); winter jasmine (*Jasminum nudiflorum*); honeysuckles such as *Lonicera americana* and *L. tellmaniana*; Virginia creeper (*Parthenocissus quinquefolia*); firethorn (*Pyracantha*); flowering currant (*Ribes speciosum*); some roses such as 'Golden Showers', 'Mme Alfred Carrière' and 'Zéphirine Drouhin'; and *Schizophragma*.

ROSES

Feeding and mulching

A large part of the enjoyment of gardening is the actual doing, but reducing work in certain areas will allow more time for the most agreeable jobs. Growing plants well will greatly reduce labour, and one of the most important ways is to get the soil fertile in the first place and then keep it that way afterwards so that plants almost look after themselves. Nowhere is this more critical than for roses, which really enjoy good living.

After pruning and cutting back roses earlier in the year, it's a good idea now to show you care by giving them a liberal feed and a heavy mulch to sustain all that new growth and flowering. Some gardeners mulch straight after pruning, but the soil is still cold and will take longer to warm up under a blanket of manure so wait until this month when temperatures are rising. And before you mulch, give the plants a feed so the fertiliser is in direct contact with the soil.

You can use a standard rose fertiliser at the rate suggested on the packet, or spread an organic feed such as blood, fish and bone or pelleted poultry manure at about 136g/sq.m (4oz/sq.yd). Then dress the plants with a good mulch of garden compost or well-rotted manure all round, 5–8cm (2–3in) deep and covering the same area as the spread of the branches. This will help keep the soil moist in summer and stop annual weeds in their tracks. About mid-summer, after the first main flush of bloom, you can give the plants another feed to encourage later colour.

LAWNS & HEDGES

Assessing mowers

If you haven't started mowing yet, the first job is to drag the mower out of the shed where it has been rusting all winter. With a bit of luck, it will start. If not, get it down to the repairer pronto because there's bound to be a queue by now.

If you are a keen lawn-keeper but have an old mower, and want to be popular with your neighbours, let me diplomatically suggest that you consider renewing it. Manufacturers have made great efforts to tackle excess noise recently, and not without cause: noise is regularly listed as the biggest complaint levelled by neighbours who like to live in peace. Apart from noise level, the type you buy depends on the kind of lawn you want.

I'm not a great believer in bowling-green lawns in gardens. They are a lot of work and can make the plot look too neat and precious for my liking. I'd go for a good green hard-wearing lawn that sets off borders well but can also be used by the family and requires minimum labour. I encourage grass to grow as strongly as possible, and learn to live with a daisy or two. If you do dream of the perfect finish, you'll need a cylinder mower with as many blades as possible. It will give the finest cut and tend to remove the coarse grasses.

If you cut the grass less frequently or need a good general-purpose lawn, a rotary mower is fine. I always insist on a mower that picks up the cuttings, which look ugly and tread into the house if they're left to lie in swathes. On the other hand, there are mulching mowers which cut the grass very fine and blow it evenly downwards so that it is re-incorporated into the soil, improving its structure and returning the nutrients, thus saving many trips to the compost heap.

The best source of power depends on the size of your garden. Electric mowers are cheap, as easy to use as a vacuum cleaner and quieter than most, but have the disadvantage of a trailing cable which can be dangerous unless you use a residual circuit-breaker.

Battery models are a good choice for small lawns, now that the rechargeable batteries are smaller and lighter than earlier kinds and run for longer on a single charging. For bigger gardens, petrol power is the best choice and much more versatile, if more expensive and not as quiet as electricity; and some have electric ignition, which can save a lot of back-breaking effort when starting the engine.

Don't despise the good old-fashioned push mower if you have a small lawn and you're under 80. They're as cheap as electric models, up-to-date designs are a million times easier to use than the rusty old job father had, and the exercise is as life-enhancing as gardening itself. And they're the only type that are pleasant to listen to.

Trimming formal hedges

A formal hedge of box, yew, lonicera or santolina, needs clipping more often than other kinds and can begin to look shaggy and neglected if you don't start trimming it as soon as the danger of heavy frost has passed. Use a taut line if necessary as a guide to get a precise finish. It will need clipping again in August (see page 128).

VEGETABLES & HERBS

Growing French beans in pots

Dwarf French beans hate having cold feet, and if you put them outside a bit early or sow them too soon they will quickly turn up their toes. Even if they survive, they will stop growing and be reluctant to start again for several weeks.

They can be started in the greenhouse, however, with a few potted on to give the earliest pickings. Sow a variety like 'Daisy', two seeds to each 8cm (3in) pot of John Innes No. 1 compost, and give them a little bottom heat if you can, although this isn't essential. If both seeds germinate, remove the weaker seedling. Space plants as they grow to give plenty of light and to make strong bushy plants for hardening off and planting out in late May.

If you want to grow them to maturity in the greenhouse, transfer four or five of the young plants to a 20cm (8in) pot when they've made their first true leaf, or sow half a dozen seeds direct. Keep them in good light, and support them as they develop with some twiggy sticks or a few thin canes and raffia. Feed them every week once they come into flower, and you'll be picking tender beans well before outdoor crops are ready.

BELOW Gentle heat is enough to ensure a spring crop of dwarf French beans in pots.

Starting leeks

If you have a greenhouse, it's always worth growing an early variety of leek such as 'King Richard' by sowing indoors in March and then planting outdoors in early May. Sowings of maincrop leeks, such as 'Musselburgh' and 'Giant Winter' are usually made now in a seedbed outdoors. Any earlier, and you risk the plants running to seed later in the season.

Fork and rake the soil until you've got a nice fine tilth, and then make shallow drills 15cm (6in) apart. Sow the seeds thinly 1cm (½in) deep, and thin them to about 2.5cm (1in) apart as soon as they're large enough to handle. When they are as thick as a pencil, they're ready to transplant into holes made with a dibber, 15cm (6in) apart and the same in depth. Water the seedlings well before lifting, separate them and just drop one in each hole. Then pour water into each hole to settle the seedlings, but don't refill with soil – the stem of the plant will fill the hole as it grows and develop a pure white blanch where it is buried beneath the ground.

Sowing peas

If you cover a strip of ground with polythene or cloches you can sow peas as early as the beginning of March. Otherwise start this month, and make further sowings at three-week intervals up to the beginning of June. Always use a first-early wrinkle-seeded variety, which will take about 12 weeks to mature compared to the 16 weeks for maincrop kinds; the sweetest early pea I've yet found is 'Douce Provence', although 'Hurst Beagle', 'Hurst Greenshaft' and 'Kelvedon Wonder' are almost as tasty.

You can take out a single drill for a narrow row of plants if space is limited, although I prefer to make a wide drill the width of the spade and about 5cm (2in) deep. Scatter the seeds in this, aiming to get each one about 5cm (2in) from its neighbours – the actual distance isn't critical, but it's always worth taking a bit of time to space the seeds out as plants dislike overcrowding. Cover with soil, tamp down lightly and, if the weather's cold, cover with polythene. You'll have to keep an eye open though, so that you can remove the cover as soon as the first seedling shows through. If you use horticultural fleece instead, this can stay over the seedlings until they make their first tendrils, when it is time to remove the cover and push in a few twiggy sticks or stretch some netting between canes to provide support.

ABOVE Pliable stems from willow, hazel and other shrubs can be recycled as decorative pea supports.

Planning late crops

As the month progresses you can really get going with sowing summer vegetables outdoors, and right now I would sow spinach, carrots, turnips, radishes, kohl rabi, lettuces, spring onions, summer cabbages and cauliflowers. But don't forget to look ahead, even though it seems crazy to be thinking about Christmas before spring is really under way.

If you want big cauliflowers, savoy cabbages and Brussels sprouts for your Yuletide dinner, you'd better get to it because the seeds need sowing this month. You'll produce plenty of seedlings for the average garden from seedbed rows 60cm (2ft) long and 15cm (6in) apart. Sow autumn and winter cabbages, Brussels sprouts, winter cauliflowers, curly kale and sprouting broccoli, all at the same time, and add a few calabrese for eating in late summer too.

I like to transplant all these when the seedlings are still quite small, about 10cm (4in) high or when they've made 2–3 true leaves – never leave them until the stems darken and become woody, as they are unlikely to grow well then. The trouble is that autumn and winter varieties need quite wide spacings, anything from 45cm (18in) to 60cm (2ft) apart, but you can arrange some catch-crops of quicker maturing stuff in between. Fast carrots, beetroot, lettuces, radishes and salad onions, for example, should have plenty of room within 60cm (2ft) rows of transplants.

FRUIT

Choosing trained fruit trees

Fruit trees are at their most appealing now, when they are covered in blossom. More traditionally, apples and pears are planted in November, and early winter is the best time for bare-rooted trees (see page 170), but a good range of varieties is available in containers now. This means that you can plant them straight away, and may even get an apple or two this year (though you shouldn't count on it!).

The great thing about apple and pear trees is that you can do just about anything with them, short of growing them upside down. So even if you have a postage stamp of a garden, you can still grow your own fruitful orchard by training the trees in special ways. A hedge of cordons, or a fan or espalier against a wall, for example, will take up a strip of soil about 15–30cm (6–12in) wide and look terrific.

Of course, what puts most people off trained apples and pears is the thought of all that complicated pruning. But a fruit-farmer I know prunes his apples with an electric hedge trimmer and still gets a bumper crop, so you see it needn't be difficult. It's mostly done in the summer and is easy to understand (see page 130). Most container-grown trees are sold ready-trained, however, because it is the first year or two's training that needs the most care. All you need do now is decide on the tree shape.

To restrict growth and reduce the amount of pruning you need to do, trees are grafted on to a special rootstock. If you want a very dwarf apple tree and your soil is fertile, go for the rootstock M27. If you need a slightly more vigorous tree to cover a larger space, or your soil is not as good as you would like, stick to MM106. There's less choice with pears, and most are grafted on the semi-dwarfing Quince A rootstock. If your nursery or garden centre can't identify the rootstock, go to one where they can.

BELOW This dessert apple 'Sunset' has been grown as a single espalier or 'step-over' tree on low supports.

TRAINING FRUIT TREES

1 An espalier is a neat productive shape, perfect for growing beside a path. A fairly vigorous rootstock is best, together with tight wires or a timber framework to support the horizontal tiers of branches.

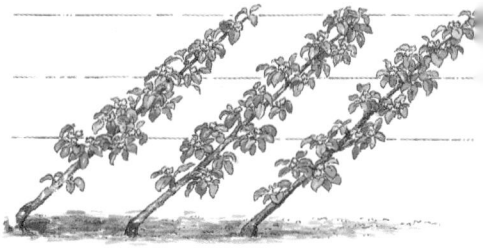

2 Cordons take up the least room, and several different varieties may be grown in a confined space to spread out the harvest. Sloping them at an angle increases the length of the single stem and encourages heavier crops of fruit.

3 A perfectly trained fan, normally used for plums, cherries and pears trained on walls, is very decorative and easy to manage. Choose a vigorous rootstock and train the branches from an early stage, tying them to long bamboo canes to keep them straight like the ribs of a fan.

MISCELLANEOUS

Feeding outdoor plants to stimulate growth

Signs of renewed growth in the garden means that plants will be hungry after their long winter's sleep. You have to speculate to accumulate, and now's a good time to shell out on fertiliser – and reap the benefits later in the year.

All plants need three main nutrients – nitrogen, potassium and phosphorus. Nitrogen helps to produce leaves, so it's especially important for leafy plants like spinach and hostas. Potassium is needed by all flowering and fruiting plants, while phosphorus helps root growth so is essential for all plants.

The chemical symbols and their percentages in the mix are marked on a bag of fertiliser. N is the symbol for nitrogen, P is for phosphorus and K for potassium. So Growmore, which has equal amounts of each, is marked N7:P7:K7, although the letters are sometimes dispensed with. A 'balanced' or 'general' fertiliser like Growmore is ideal for routine use, and if you want to buy only one kind, this is the one to go for. As an alternative you could use rose fertiliser, high in potassium, for most flowering plants in spring, and bonemeal (high in phosphorus) when planting in the dormant season.

Organic fertilisers

As a 'natural' gardening freak, I prefer to use organic fertilisers, and they are generally much easier to use. Because chemical feeds are concentrated, they must be applied in precise amounts, whereas organic kinds release their nutrients slowly so it's hard to overdo it and cause damage. Generally I use two handfuls of pelleted chicken manure per square metre before sowing or planting. Bear in mind that, because this kind of feed must be broken down in the soil before it can be used by plants, your soil needs plenty of it, which is why organic gardeners use so much manure and compost. Either dig the fertiliser into the soil before planting, or apply it as a mulch on the surface afterwards – or even better, do both, especially for fruit.

ABOVE All fruits, particularly greedy kinds such as blackberries, benefit from a rich mulch of manure or compost this month.

Growing your own manure

If you can't buy manure or make compost, why not grow your own? Wherever you have a bit of ground bare for six weeks or more, try growing a crop of 'green manure' such as clover, mustard, lucerne (alfalfa), lupins or beans. When you need the ground, cut down the plants and dig them in to recycle the nutrients they've brought up from below. They also improve the soil structure, making it more water-retentive. Field beans and winter tares can be left uncut to keep the soil covered in winter, preventing rain damage and erosion. Try a crop or two and see the difference they make to your soil.

PLANTS FOR
april

1 *Clematis alpina* 'Ruby' grows to 3m (10ft) tall by about 1.5m (5ft) wide, with slender climbing stems and elegant foliage. The pendent four-petalled blooms have a central tuft of stamens.

2 In mid-spring the vigorous arching stems of *Berberis* x *stenophylla* are wreathed in dense clusters of golden-yellow blooms. The hardy evergreen shrub can reach 3m (10ft) high.

3 The double wild cherry or gean, *Prunus avium* 'Plena', is a medium-sized deciduous tree with peeling mahogany bark on older specimens, and masses of drooping blooms.

1

2

3

4

4 The 10cm (4in) wide blooms of perennial pasque flowers, *Pulsatilla vulgaris*, range in colour from light mauve to deep red and sit snugly in a bed of ferny leaves and silky hairs.

5 Doronicums are dependable hardy perennials for supplying a bright splash of colour early in the season. Growing to about 60cm (2ft), they revel in full sun and also do well in partial shade in light soils.

5

As it did for many gardeners, 'Chelsea' – the Royal Horticultural Society's main annual show held in London – tended to dominate May for us. Geoff loved it. Because he fronted the *Gardener's World* filming, we could spend Monday there, before it was open to the public, feeling very privileged. One of his dates that week was lunch with the *Daily Express*, for which he did dress more formally. Seeing my nod of approval, he grinned: 'I clean up nice, don't I?' But he also did stints answering questions at the *Daily Express*'s garden. He enjoyed meeting what he called 'real' gardeners, hearing their views and finding out what they were doing, and spent several weekends each spring and autumn at various garden centres and at our own nursery doing just this. Some customers demanded to see his hands – just to make sure they had all the scratches and calluses working gardeners can't avoid, especially if, like Geoff, they don't wear gloves. But most knew instinctively that he was a hands-on gardener. They would comment on the way he'd pour soil and compost through his fingers, glad to see this earthiness.

The double late tulip 'Mount Tacoma' makes a strong impact in a cool green and white border with white violas and the prettily edged foliage of *Hosta crispula*.

May

key tasks for may

ANNUALS & BEDDING PLANTS

- ❍ Plan and plant out summer bedding, page 74
- ❍ Plant out dahlias and take cuttings of their young shoots, page 75

BORDER PERENNIALS

- ❍ Support tall herbaceous plants while they are small, page 77
- ❍ Plant hardy chrysanthemums for autumn flowering, page 77

BULBS

- ❍ Feed daffodils to build up next year's flowers, page 78
- ❍ Dig up and store tulips after flowering, page 78

CONTAINER PLANTS

- ❍ Deal with the first signs of vine weevils, page 80

SHRUBS, TREES & CLIMBERS

- ❍ Take soft cuttings of garden shrubs, and make a cuttings frame for them, page 80

LAWNS

- ❍ Feed lawns for good summer growth, page 81

VEGETABLES & HERBS

- ❍ Plant tomatoes under glass, page 82
- ❍ Sow some extra root crops for winter storing, page 82
- ❍ Sow and plant tender vegetables outdoors, page 82
- ❍ Beware of frosts and blackfly, page 83

FRUIT

- ❍ Nick and notch fruit trees to control growth, page 84
- ❍ Prune plums and cherries now the sap is rising, page 84

MISCELLANEOUS

- ❍ Make a compost container for home-grown fertility, page 85

ANNUALS & BEDDING PLANTS

Summer bedding

Towards the end of this month there's a busy week or two in store for bedding plant enthusiasts. The sooner the salvias, petunias, alyssum and begonias go in, the quicker they'll fill their spaces and cover themselves with flowers.

I know there's a sensitive school of design that claims annual bedding is brash and gaudy, while devotees hold that no other group gives as much joy all summer long. But gardening is about doing your own thing, so take no notice of what others think – thank goodness we all have different tastes. For sheer colour, bedding plants give maximum value until the first frosts consign them to the compost heap.

I wouldn't be without half-hardy bedding like petunias, busy lizzies and salvias, but I plant them in large informal drifts among the shrubs and herbaceous plants, and under roses – not too close, though, because you don't want to impede the growth of the shrubs. Towards the back of the borders, I leave a space for taller annuals like the sweetly scented white tobacco plant (*Nicotiana affinis*). And I find that cosmos, with its ferny foliage and constant succession of flowers, and tall mallows like *Lavatera* 'Silver Cup' are indispensable.

For later in the season, don't forget the taller asters and annual delphiniums, which start flowering in July. Annual nemesias are ideal in the middle of the borders, producing flowers in an amazing mixture of colours from crimson through pink, white and yellow, to blue. The shorter tobacco plants

RIGHT Single tulips, wallflowers and hardy pansies are all popular ingredients of colourful spring bedding.

are terrific there, too: many of the newer varieties have the advantage of presenting their flowers facing upwards instead of hanging down.

Then there are all those annual poppy mixtures, such as 'Summer Breeze', which produce a good succession of silky flowers in shades of yellow, orange and white, and also poor man's orchids (*Schizanthus*) with a range of fantastic shades and markings.

If you want a few special plants to catch the eye in a large expanse of low-growing bedding, buy a few tender perennials like cannas, marguerites, pelargoniums and fuchsias to use as 'spot' plants in the middle. At the front of all these, I grow bedding petunias – these incidentally are not affected by the virus that tends to hit the trailing types. And there are always new varieties of phlox and annual pinks, none of them to be missed.

BEDDING PLANTS FOR SHADE

Most summer bedding is best in the sun, but I've found a few plants that are excellent for deep shade. Mimulus, busy lizzies and lobelia do well, as do foliage plants such as the silver-leafed *Cineraria maritima* (*Senecio cineraria*), all kinds of coleus and the fibrous-rooted begonias, especially *B. semperflorens*. But don't expect quite so many flowers, and allow for most plants to grow slightly taller than they would in full sun.

Planting out summer bedding

First fork over the planting area, remove all the weeds and work in a little compost – the nutrients in this should be enough, but if you don't have any compost or your soil is very poor, a little organic fertiliser or a tomato base feed is needed. But the operative word is *little* – too much nitrogen will result in large plants with lots of green leaves and few flowers. Most summer bedding plants thrive in poor soil, so I try never to feed them at all. Plant them 15–23cm (6–9in) apart according to size, with 30cm (12in) between the very largest varieties.

You've nothing to gain by planting out too early. In cold conditions plants simply stand there waiting to get warm, and any check to their growth takes a while to get over so they lose the race against those planted a little later. Look for plants that are not yet in flower. Growers know that a few flowers will seduce you into buying, but a precocious start to flowering often means that plants will go out of flower sooner.

So bide your time, plant strong young specimens when the weather's warmed up, water well and then stand back. If you can find time to deadhead plants as they go out of flower, they'll produce even more colour. The very last job is to reckon up what you've spent, and resolve firmly that next year you'll raise your own!

Growing dahlias

From the land of the sombrero and the hot chilli pepper comes the dahlia, and it is no surprise that this can be one of the most dazzling, flamboyant flowers we grow. They'll give sunny life to the dullest border, but they're not all brazen hussies and some varieties are as demure as a vicar's daughter. All can be invaluable for a number of garden uses.

If you see them in flower you'll almost certainly want them all now, but bear in mind that they are the tenderest of plants which can be knocked back by the slightest frost. You can plant dormant tubers towards the middle of this month,

LEFT Hardy perennials such as *Euphorbia characias* and the young spring foliage of spiraeas and hardy geraniums begin to make an impact in the border this month, while tulips are still in full bloom.

but growing plants must wait until the first week in June because a late cold snap could see them off altogether. Buy tubers now by all means, and pot them up in 13cm (5in) pots of soil-less compost. Keep them in a warm place such as the greenhouse or a sunny windowsill, provided you can avoid cooking them in the mid-day sun. Water them so they're just moist and you'll find they'll shoot in next to time, usually producing at least 2–3 strong young growths. These shoots could provide propagating material for cuttings, or you can simply start hardening plants off in a cold frame for planting out early next month.

The soil needs to be dug thoroughly, with a good dressing of compost or manure worked well in and a rose or general organic fertiliser raked in the surface just before planting. All tall varieties will need strong stakes or canes, so knock these in position before planting giant varieties 75cm (30in) apart, other kinds 60cm (2ft) apart, using a trowel and firming them in with your fingers. Cover with 8cm (3in) of soil. Water them after planting and regularly afterwards, and tie in the stems as they grow. If you want enormous blooms for shows, you'll need to thin stems and remove all but the central bud; otherwise pinch out the shoot tips in June to encourage sideshoots and plenty of slightly smaller blooms.

Taking dahlia cuttings

Bought tubers planted in pots this month, together with your own stored tubers started earlier in the year, can all be used for propagation once their shoots are about 8cm (3in) long. Cut them off the plant with a sharp knife, leaving just one or two shoots on each tuber to carry on growing. Trim the shoots just below a leaf joint, and remove all but the top three leaves.

Dip the ends of the cuttings in hormone rooting liquid, and dibble them into 8–10cm (3–4in) pots of soil-less compost. Put a plastic bag over the top of each pot and put it in a warm spot out of bright sun. The cuttings should look quite perky after 7–10 days, when you can remove the bag. A week later separate and pot the cuttings up individually in 9cm (3½in) pots. Grow them on until the first week in June, when you should be able to plant out two or three extra plants from each tuber. These will flower, then make tubers of their own.

CHOOSING DAHLIAS

For me, the real worth of dahlias is as cut flowers and I always grow a row or two of mixed types in the veg plot for this.

When it comes to size and flower shape, they are a mixed bunch, so choose carefully. They range in height from 15cm (6in) to 1.8m (6ft), and the shapes vary tremendously. Perhaps the most popular are the fully double, flat-petalled decoratives, and the narrow-petalled cactus and semi-cactus types. Then there's the almost too perfect pompon and ball types. My own preference is for the open-centred singles, broad-petalled daisies in a whole range of wonderful colours. Even more beautiful are the collarettes, perfectly shaped singles with a central fringe of smaller petals, often in a contrasting colour.

METHODS OF SUPPORTING BORDER PLANTS

Large clump-forming plants such as peonies benefit from a stout support set in place well before the foliage develops.

You can buy interlocking wire stakes which can be joined together to make variably sized enclosures to surround the plants.

Tall-stemmed plants such as dahlias, delphiniums and hollyhocks are best secured to single bamboo canes or stakes with string, plastic twists or wire rings.

Thin canes and string is a perfectly adequate method for supporting bushy plants, but don't have the string so tight that it makes stems look trussed.

A panel of wire netting attached to a few canes is ideal for supporting plants with tall slim stems or flower stalks – border carnations, for example.

Twiggy sticks cut from hedges or left over after pruning provide what must be the simplest support method of all, and one that costs nothing.

BORDER PERENNIALS

Supporting border plants

Taller perennials need some kind of support, a job you cannot leave until the last minute. Once delphiniums or hollyhocks, for example, fall over, the stems will kink and never straighten again.

Choose a method of support that suits the particular plant. Just remember that the stems should not be too constricted – they need to spill outwards a little to look natural. Craftsmen gardeners used to support plants with peasticks. They'd put a few in around the plant, break the twiggy bits near the top, bend them in towards the centre and weave them together. It's a skill that, along with the peasticks themselves, you see only rarely these days, but you can make natural supports of this kind from your own prunings – a few twiggy sticks of philadelphus or deutzia, say, can be shoved into the middle of a border plant to support it; and dogwood and willow stems are pliable enough to be woven or tied together to make a sort of wigwam for climbing plants.

Planting out hardy chrysanthemums

My first job ever involved growing chrysanths for cut flowers and, for nostalgia's sake, I wouldn't be without a few in my garden every year. They provide a splash of colour in the borders during late summer and autumn. And now's the time to plant them.

Chrysanths hate wet feet but need a steady supply of moisture throughout the season, so dig the soil very thoroughly and add plenty of well-rotted manure or garden compost before planting, together with a light dressing of general fertiliser. They like slightly limy conditions, so if the soil's on the acid side use a little lime, but not if you've only just manured.

Plant cut flower varieties 45cm (18in) apart with 90cm (3ft) between rows, tying each plant to a strong 1.2m (4ft) cane. Then 'stop' the plant by pinching out the growing tip just above the first fully developed pair of leaves. This encourages more sideshoots that will bear the flowers. If you want cut flowers for the house limit the sideshoots to the six strongest, but if you want to win the show leave just four stems. Spray varieties should not be disbudded and can be left to their own devices to produce large sprays of smaller flowers.

Plant 'cushion' chrysanths in the same way but without the cane. Pinch out all the growing points until late July or early August, and you'll get big bushy plants which, by September, will be a mass of blooms.

BELOW The Welsh poppy, *Meconopsis cambrica*, in its desirable double form 'Flore Pleno', is happy in full sun or partial shade.

BULBS

Feeding daffodils

Daffs look wonderful in spring and no garden can afford to be without them. But when they've finished flowering, they're nothing short of ugly. The last thing you should do, though, is cut the leaves off or tie them into neat knotted bunches: the plants need the foliage for at least six weeks after flowering to give them a chance to build up their bulbs for next year.

For this reason you should give them a boost by feeding them as soon as the flowers fade, using a fertiliser high in potash – a rose or tomato feed is ideal. Do this whether you leave the bulbs in the ground or move them somewhere else. If your garden's small you may need the space for planting bedding, and in that case it's best to dig up the daffs carefully and replant them close together in a sunny corner, in a trench at the same depth as before. Mix the feed in the soil as it is replaced, and leave the bulbs until the foliage has died down. Then you can dig them up for drying. Store in a cool dry spot, and you'll have top-quality bulbs to plant again early next autumn.

If your garden is large enough, or you can't spare the time to shift bulbs each year, you can plan the planting scheme around them so that something covers the daffs after flowering. It's hard to time this exactly, but you can make sure that you see the dying leaves for only a short while. What you need are herbaceous plants that die down in winter and then produce lots of good leafy growth in late spring. Hostas are excellent, though they may be a bit too late in colder gardens. Try bleeding heart (*Dicentra*), which has superb foliage and grows fast, as does the forget-me-not-flowered brunnera. For shade you could use evergreen *Tellima grandiflora* or *Tiarella cordifolia*, two similar foliage plants that cover a lot of ground quickly and produce attractive sprays of small flowers.

Digging up tulips

Once tulips are over, it is a good idea to deadhead them to prevent them from setting seed. Most then need warm dry conditions – something our summers can't guarantee – while they are dormant. There are a few species, including the soft yellow *Tulipa sylvestris* and dwarf *T. tarda*, which survive happily in sunny well-drained spots. Some of the hybrids will too, if they are planted deeper than normal in gritty soil. Most tulips, however, are better if they are dug up and stored indoors. Start by lifting and heeling them in close together in a trench where they can get the benefit of full sunlight. If you haven't space in the garden, pack them in pots of compost and stand these in a sunny place. When the leaves have died down lift the bulbs and dry them in the sun, outdoors or under glass. After a week or so you can rub off the dry foliage and roots, and store the bulbs in a dry place until November.

RIGHT Flowering onions such as *Allium aflatunense* and its richly coloured hybrids are superb bulbs that need a little shelter; here they are imaginatively partnered by the profuse blooms of a wisteria trained horizontally on low supports.

CONTAINER PLANTS

Controlling vine weevils

The dreaded vine weevil is on the march across the country. The first sign it's arrived is when your plants suddenly wilt or keel over. Lift them up out of the pots and you'll find the roots eaten away and the compost full of creamy-white grubs.

They especially seem to like cyclamen, primulas and begonias, but their tastes are expanding. The adults, which are dark grey beetles about 2cm (¾in) long, are rarely seen as they are nocturnal. They do little damage, but if you see notches chewed from the edges of pot and container plants be on your guard. It's the grubs that are difficult to control. They hatch out in late spring, and then munch away underground until they emerge as adults in the autumn under glass, or the following spring outdoors. They resist most chemicals except some ludicrously expensive and dangerous kinds used by growers. The most effective control available to amateurs is a biological one, sold under several trade names. Basically it is a microscopic worm called a nematode, which attacks and feeds on the grubs. This can be bought packaged in granules for adding to a measured amount of water. You simply pour this in the infected pot, or apply once or twice as a precaution to all your container plants. The nematodes only work when temperatures are higher than 10°C (50°F), however, so there's no point using them before this month, and once they've cleared an infestation they'll die out. So get some this month, and another batch in late summer for total control.

SHRUBS, TREES & CLIMBERS

Taking soft cuttings

Even after all these years of gardening, I'm still amazed and delighted at the astonishing way shoots, lumps of root and even leaves are so ready to put out roots and produce another generation of plants. It's something you should be taking full advantage of towards the end of this month.

Most shrubs are becoming fine and bushy, with lots of sturdy young shoots that have grown this year and can be used for soft cuttings. You've got from now until the beginning of July to select them from somewhere on the shrub where the loss of a shoot or two won't be noticed. Normally you'll want just one plant, so take about six shoots to be on the safe side, and cut them off the plant just above a leaf joint so that each cutting is about 8–10cm (3–4in) long. Have a polythene bag with you and pop them inside; keep the bag closed and out of the sun. When you've finished, the sooner you can get back indoors the better – if you can't work on the cuttings straight away, put them in the main compartment of the fridge.

Prepare the cuttings with a sharp knife or razor blade. Start by trimming just below a leaf joint, where most of the root-forming hormones are located, to leave cuttings about 5–8cm (2–3in) long. Remove all but the top 2–3 leaves, then immerse them in a solution of copper fungicide, and dip the cut ends in hormone rooting powder or liquid. Dibble 4–5 cuttings to half their depth in an 8cm (4in) pot of cuttings compost or a 50:50

TAKING SOFT CUTTINGS

1 Cut off the soft tips of main stems and sideshoots, and keep all the cuttings fresh in a plastic bag until you are ready to prepare them for potting.

2 Trim the shoots to length, cutting the base just below a leaf joint or 'node'. Remove all the lower leaves, together with any stipules and flower buds.

3 Dunk in fungicide and then dip the cut ends in rooting hormone. Insert the cuttings, to the lowest leaves, in compost and seal in a thin polythene bag.

RIGHT A greenhouse packed with pelargoniums, coleus and gerberas, all competing for space with young begonias and carnation cuttings, would be a favourite target for vine weevils, so do beware.

mixture of peat-free compost and vermiculite, and water them in with more fungicide solution. Cover the pots with thin polythene, making sure this is resting on the top of the cuttings and held in place with an elastic band, and then put the pots in a shaded cold frame. They should root without further watering in 6–8 weeks.

Making a cuttings frame

I get a great deal of enjoyment from propagating plants, so I've made a special frame to take softwood cuttings rooted straight into the ground. Mine is made from an old wooden box with the bottom removed, but it'd be easy to knock up a simple frame about 60cm (2ft) by 45cm (18in), and 30cm (12in) deep to hold about 100 cuttings.

Start by cultivating the soil and working a good quantity of horticultural grit into the top 5cm (2in); level the soil and then spread a layer of grit over it with a layer of sharp sand on top of that, before putting the box in place. The cuttings are dibbled in about 2.5cm (1in) apart and watered in with a fungicide solution. Cover with thin polythene resting lightly on the cuttings and then use a piece of glass or rigid plastic for the lid, shading it with a couple of old onion bags from the greengrocer. You'll soon see rooting taking place when the cuttings perk up generally. Leave them 6–8 weeks, and then lift them for potting up or lining out.

LAWNS

Feeding the lawn

There's one plant in the garden we really take for granted. We tread all over it, we prune it every week, we kick it and scuff it, use it and abuse it, and yet it still comes up smiling. Grass is pretty hard to offend, but it'll repay you if you look after it: the energy removed by mowing, for example, needs to be replaced.

As I suggested in March (see page 47), a feed in spring and again in summer can work wonders. Alternatively, if you use the type of slow-release fertiliser that supplies nutrients over a long period, one feed early this month should normally be enough – autumn feeds are really only for deficient soils. As with any other fertiliser, the important thing to remember is to measure the amount you spread and stick religiously to the maker's instructions. Don't add a little extra for luck, because too much causes scorching, so it's always worth hiring or buying a special spreader to apply just the right amount. You can buy 'weed and feed' dressings that contain a herbicide, and for these it is even more important to keep closely to recommended application rates.

Most lawn feeds are very much of a muchness in terms of quality, and the only real choice is between liquid and granular feeds. Liquids act a bit faster, they're cheaper and they generally allow a greater margin for error, but it can be a fag going backwards and forwards with the watering can. Granular or powdered types last a little longer and are more easily distributed, but must be watered in afterwards. They always say apply just before rain on the pack. But that can't be guaranteed, and if it hasn't rained two days after spreading you'll have to water the lawn well in order to avoid scorching.

VEGETABLES & HERBS

Planting tomatoes under glass

If you have a greenhouse, you'll find that there's plenty to do in it from now on. Perhaps the most important task is to plant tomatoes and other tender crops as these will be safe now without any extra heat. You can grow them direct in the soil after digging in plenty of garden compost and a base fertiliser. There is a risk of attack from soil-borne virus diseases, although the chances are small – many gardeners have used the same soil for more than twenty years without a problem.

If a virus does strike, and you will recognize it from yellow streaks or mottlings on the leaves, the crop won't be wiped out, but next year you should use 'grow bags', or you can grow tomatoes individually in 25cm (10in) pots of soil-less compost, and save the cost of bags.

When you put in the plants, run a strong nylon string from a wire fixed to the glazing bars above each plant down to the ground. Leave enough string for the loose end to be 'planted' by passing it under the rootball. The tomato stem can then be twisted round the string as it grows. I feed at every watering after the first truss has set, but try to use as little water as possible because that will improve the flavour. And don't shade the plants unless the heat becomes extreme.

You should remove any sideshoots that grow in the leaf joints. (If you need more plants, the shoots can be rooted as soft cuttings under a plastic bag.) When the plants are flowering, spray them over at mid-day with water or tap the stems sharply with a cane to help pollinate the flowers. And then you just keep picking the fruit, pound after pound of it, well into the autumn.

BELOW When planting a tomato in the greenhouse, secure one end of the support string under its rootball.

Root crops for winter

There are two important vegetables for winter storing that are often forgotten at this time of year, probably partly because it seems too early to be thinking of winter: swedes and salsify. The swede's now a completely different vegetable from the one you hated at school. The flavour and texture of modern varieties has been improved no end, and swedes are as sweet and nutty as anyone could wish. Try a variety like 'Marian', which is resistant to mildew and club root – don't forget swedes are a form of brassica and share the same pests and diseases as cabbages. 'Ruby' has very large roots and a flavour rating second to none, while 'Lizzy' resists root cracking and bolting in a dry season. Sow direct in rows 23–30cm (9–12in) apart, thin the seedlings to 20cm (8in) apart, and grow on until lifting time after the first frosts.

Salsify and scorzonera are usually grouped together because they need the same treatment. Salsify roots are white and scorzonera black, but they taste much the same with a subtle, though superb, flavour and they're rich in minerals. They are gourmet crops which are unfairly neglected these days, partly I suspect because they take a little extra trouble to prepare for cooking. But they're very easy to grow in deeply dug soil, in rows 30cm (12in) apart with the seedlings thinned to 15cm (6in). Either lift them for storing in autumn, or leave them in the ground until needed.

Growing tender vegetables

Courgettes, French and runner beans, tomatoes and cucumbers are the aristocrats of the kitchen garden, and yet they're as easy to grow as radishes. If you've got young plants in the greenhouse or on the windowsill, you're laughing, but if you haven't, there's still time to catch up.

If frost is no longer a threat all these crops can be set out in their final places, but keep a few large flowerpots handy for covering them up, just in case. In colder areas, you'll have to wait a couple of weeks before planting out, but you can sow seeds outdoors now with a bit of protection to warm the soil. All these crops are moisture-lovers so, since you only get out what you put in, it's worth piling on the compost or manure – dig it in the top spit, together with a handful of general fertiliser such as pelleted poultry manure, and they'll be set up for the season.

ABOVE Early broad beans are here in full bloom, with rows of young lettuces, onions and peas well advanced for harvesting later in the summer.

Courgettes and bush marrows can be sown direct if you didn't manage to sow them last month under glass. Sow two seeds per station about 60cm (2ft) apart, and cover each station with a jam jar or cut-off plastic bottle. Take this off when the seedlings show through, and remove the weaker seedling. But if the weather is still cold, leave the jar on for a while to create a warm humid atmosphere and also to protect against slugs.

Treat French beans in the same way, sowing two seeds at stations 30cm (12in) apart. They crop better than runners in a really hot dry season, and are usually a better bet if there's a hose-pipe ban. But personally I think it's always worth growing runner beans, whatever the season, as I could happily eat them at every meal. Sow the seeds for runners in twos, each pair at the base of a 2.4m (8ft) cane. You'll have to slit a plastic bottle up the side to get it round the cane, and then leave it in place over the best seedling until it is large enough for the leaves to touch the sides.

It's too late to sow tomatoes for outdoors, but you can usually buy plants if you haven't started any under glass. If you go for a bush variety such as 'Red Alert', you can grow them 60cm (2ft) apart without any support, and they'll produce excellent crops if you mulch the plants with straw to keep the fruit clean; alternatively plant them through a sheet of black porous matting, which will also suppress weeds as well as stopping the soil from drying out.

Guarding against frost and blackfly

Don't let thoughts of summer crops lead you into thinking that all risk of frost has passed. If frost threatens, earth up potatoes or cover them with fleece; keep cloches handy for other early crops; and be prepared to cover cold frames at night.

Broad beans will be safe from frost, even though they should be flowering well by now, but their soft growing tips are a prime target for blackfly. Discourage these by pinching out the tips as soon as the lowest pods have set.

FRUIT

Nicking and notching fruit trees

Sometimes the buds on apple and pear trees can be infuriating. Varieties differ, but some can produce quite long lengths of bare shoot where the buds refuse to grow out. And without sideshoots, of course, you'll never get fruit.

One of the reasons is that the bud at the top of the tree sends down hormones which retard the growth of others. This is to ensure, in natural conditions, that the tree reaches up for the light as quickly as possible. The growth hormones are carried just below the bark so, if you nick out a tiny bit of the bark just above the reluctant bud as shown on the right, the retardant is diverted and the bud will grow into a new shoot.

The experts call this method 'notching', and it's particularly useful if you are training an apple or pear tree to a formal shape and happen to have a shoot missing just where you want one. There's also 'nicking', which is making the same kind of cut just below a bud to stop it growing. In practice, it's usually much easier to simply rub off a bud before it can grow, which you often have to do to wall-trained trees to stop shoots growing towards or away from the wall.

NICKING AND NOTCHING

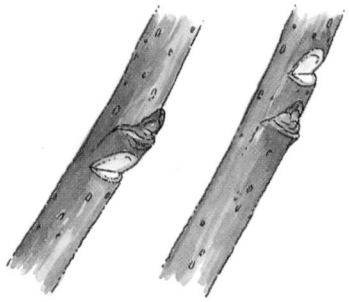

This simple method of switching sideshoots on or off depends on knowing what goes on under the bark of a stem. Removing a tiny bit of bark and the green cambium layer underneath it interrupts or diverts the upward flow of nutrients and hormones. So nicking below a bud stops it developing, while notching above it makes it grow.

LEFT Turning fermenting compost heaps once or twice helps to accelerate their decomposition.

Pruning plums and cherries

The regular pruning for plums and sweet cherries is straightforward, and all done in spring and summer. This is when the sap is rising and cuts heal quickly to reduce the risk of fungal spores entering the wounds. As soon as a new shoot has made six leaves in the spring, pinch out the tip. Then after the fruit has been picked, take out any dead or overcrowded shoots and shorten by half those you pinched back earlier. That's all there is to pruning plums and sweet cherries.

Acid cherries such as the self-fertile 'Morello' are quite different, though. These make their fruit on two-year-old wood, so you always have to look forward. Select a shoot for fruiting this year, but also allow a replacement for next year to grow alongside it. Then, instead of shortening the fruited shoot after harvest, cut it out altogether and tie the new one in its place.

You can prune flowering cherries at the same time, especially if you've just planted a weeping cherry, which has to be butchered now – you need a lot of courage but you'll get a much better tree in the end. Inspect each branch and discover where the new wood grew from last year: it'll be a lighter brown and the joint will be quite easy to see. Then cut back to leave 2–3 buds of this new wood, cutting back to an upward facing bud. That bud will be the one to grow out and, by the end of the year, you'll get a wider, and more graceful tree.

If you have fan-trained plums or cherries against a wall or fence (see page 68), you will simply need to tie in sideshoots wherever you have a hole, and in spring remove any shoots that are growing directly towards or away from the wall. Ready-trained fans are well worth their rather high cost because they'll save two years of careful pruning and shaping. As they grow, tie in the main branches to canes arranged in a fan shape on horizontal wires fixed to the wall and spaced 60cm (2ft) apart.

MISCELLANEOUS

Compost heaps

As well as providing food for all those soil organisms that are vital to a healthy, colourful and productive garden, organic matter is the first line of defence against drought. Once the soil starts to dry out in summer, it'll be very noticeable when you fork over the garden that the areas which have received a heavy dose of manure or compost are still satisfyingly moist; those which haven't will soon be in need of water.

So, if only because most of the ingredients are free and readily available, it's important to get a compost heap working overtime. Compost is second only to good farmyard manure, and it's easy to make. Of course, we've all made some pretty repulsive compost at some time, either wet and slimy or as dry as straw, but making good compost only comes down to the right technique.

Compost containers

It's best to have two containers, one for compost that is rotting down while the other's filling up. They don't have to be elaborate or expensive, and the cheapest way to make one is to bang four posts into the ground and then staple on wire netting to make an enclosure about 90cm (3ft) square and the same high. Then beg a large cardboard box or two, and line the enclosure with the cardboard. Cover the compost material with a bit of old carpet or cardboard, and you're on your way to making perfect compost.

If you'd like something a little more decorative, there are any number of wooden and plastic designs available. Make sure that there are no holes or spaces in the sides, and that there is a lid of some sort as it is important to keep in all the heat you can.

It is also possible to construct a fairly basic wooden container using old floorboards, as shown below.

Compost material

Almost any vegetable matter that has once lived can be composted, from weeds, vegetable waste and grass cuttings to woollen or cotton clothes and paper. But avoid roots of weeds such as ground elder or couch grass, weeds that are seeding, and cooked food which might attract rats. Leathery evergreen leaves will take longer to decompose, and the stems of shrubs and trees will take longer still.

Grass clippings are the very best composting material because they heat up quickly, which helps break down the rest of the contents. Unfortunately, because they're small and soft, they tend to pack down tightly if you put a lot in together, and they'll push out the air. Then they'll be rotted down by a different type of bacteria which can turn your heap into a vile smelly mess. What's needed is air within the heap itself, so mix the grass cuttings with coarser material such as large weeds or straw. Good gardeners don't have large weeds, so I keep a bag of fresh strawy manure by the container to mix in when coarse stuff is scarce.

After you've filled the container and the contents have been working for a month or so, turn them by throwing them out of the container and back again, fluffing them up as you go. You might have to do that twice, and it does need some energy, but it'll make sure you stay young and beautiful, and you'll produce compost fit almost to eat – within six months over the summer, and within eight or nine over the winter.

MAKING A COMPOST BIN

Strong boards and a few uprights can be transformed into a double bin with channels at the front, for slats to slide in and out so you can reach the compost at the bottom when it is ready. Completely fill one bin, cover its contents with an old blanket and the wooden lid, and leave it to rot down while you fill its neighbour.

PLANTS FOR

may

1 'Nora Barlow' is an old cottage garden variety of hardy herbaceous perennial *Aquilegia vulgaris*, with fully double flowers on strong leafy stems 60cm (2ft) tall.

2 *Allium aflatunense* is one of several ball-headed flowering onions and the source of various richly coloured hybrids such as 'Lucy Ball' and 'Purple Sensation'. The large rounded heads are carried on 75–90cm (30–36in) stems, and are excellent for cutting.

1

2

3 The best known of a small group of yellow-flowered peonies, *P. mlokosewitschii* (affectionately known as Molly the Witch) is a small herbaceous perennial, often less than 75cm (30in) high, but its cool yellow blooms make a strong direct impact in any border.

4 Viridiflora or green-flowered tulips are a great favourite with flower arrangers for their unusual colour combinations: 'Spring Green' is also a fine garden variety, with shapely blooms on sturdy 40–45cm (16–18in) stems.

5 *Viburnum sargentii* 'Onondaga' is a vigorous deciduous shrub, up to 3m (10ft) high, with maple-shaped leaves which are rich red when young and again in autumn. In the large lace-cap heads of flowers deep red fertile buds are surrounded by a ring of clear white sterile flowers.

3

4

5

Geoff genuinely felt that each month was the best one in the garden. But perhaps June was his favourite. 'Gardening is half achievement and half optimism,' he said, 'and in June we really have the best of each. The foliage is at its finest, borders are awash with flowers, with plenty to come; strawberries have started, raspberries are on their way and the vegetable plot is at its most mouthwatering.'

June was also the month when he finished pruning the spring-flowering shrubs. He was quite convinced that this shouldn't be done without the aid of a large teapot – a more vital tool, he once joked, than secateurs. 'You should take off a branch, then step back with a cup of tea and weigh up the consequences before you take off another.' Cups of tea were always an important part of gardening to Geoff. If possible, he liked to have them every hour, on the hour. Often I would carry two mugs down to meet him where he had said he would be, only to find that he had moved on – and because the layout of the garden is such that you can't see or hear far, the tea would be cold by the time I found him!

Poppies, campanulas and roses of all kinds are essential ingredients of the summer border, which begins to make a colourful impact this month.

june

key tasks for june

ANNUALS & BIENNIALS
- ❍ Sow biennials, including polyanthus, and winter pansies, page 90

BORDER PERENNIALS
- ❍ Increase your violas by mounding them, page 91
- ❍ Sow ripe hellebore seeds, page 91
- ❍ Tidy up oriental poppies after flowering, page 92

BULBS
- ❍ Plant anemones for autumn flowers, page 93

CONTAINER PLANTS
- ❍ Grow tender plants for an exotic display, page 93
- ❍ Plant up patio containers for the summer, page 94

SHRUBS, TREES & CLIMBERS
- ❍ Prune spring-flowering shrubs after blooms have faded, page 95

ROSES
- ❍ Train climbing roses, page 95

VEGETABLES & HERBS
- ❍ Guard against pests, especially carrot fly and cabbage root fly, page 97
- ❍ Plant cauliflowers in rich soil, page 97
- ❍ Sow Belgian chicory for forcing, page 97

FRUIT
- ❍ Control fruit pests before they become serious, page 98
- ❍ Train soft fruit as their shoots develop, page 98
- ❍ Train raspberries as a pillar, page 98

MISCELLANEOUS
- ❍ Tackle weeds, especially perennial kinds, page 100
- ❍ Check watering equipment and methods in case of drought, page 100

ANNUALS & BIENNIALS

Sowing biennials

With summer only just under way, we gardeners are already thinking about next spring, because if you want a colourful display then, you'll have to act soon. Forget-me-nots are so prolific that you can just pull them up after they have flowered and shake the dead heads over a bit of ground to produce a mass of seedlings for transplanting in the autumn. Biennials like wallflowers, sweet williams and Iceland poppies need a little more care. Sow them either in a nursery bed in the garden or in pots if you haven't the ground to spare. Use plastic pots of soil-less compost, and sprinkle a pinch of seed in each; stand them on a hard surface, on a porous mat like a piece of carpet underfelt, and keep them moist. When the seedlings are large enough, prick them out 5–8cm (2–3in) apart in the open ground or in seed trays, and grow them on until the autumn when they can be planted out where you want them to flower. Polyanthus and pansies need slightly different techniques.

Sowing polyanthus

These seeds need a little gentle heat – 15°C (60°F) should be sufficient – and at this time of year a cold greenhouse or frame will provide that. Sow them on the surface of very moist soil-less compost and cover with a little vermiculite. Put clear polythene over the pots and keep them in full light as this is essential for germination.

Once the seedlings are through, transfer them to plastic modules, trays of small pots about 4–5cm

ABOVE Campanulas, clematis and lady's mantle congregate round *Choisya ternata* in a mixed border of hardy perennials and shrubs.

(1½–2in) in diameter (see page 15), and grow them on by standing them on a piece of capillary matting to make sure they never dry out. After three weeks start feeding them with a general fertiliser, and by October they should be large enough to plant outside. For this, of course, you need a tough strain, and I can recommend 'Crescendo' for real winter hardiness.

Sowing pansies

The way to germinate pansies is just about as different from that for polyanthus as it could be. The seeds are sown in the same way and covered with vermiculite or a little seed compost sieved over the top. But they must be dark and cool to germinate, so cover the pots or trays with black polythene or kitchen foil to exclude light, and put them in a shady place outdoors. Seedlings take about a fortnight to emerge, so check them regularly after about ten days. Once they are large enough, transfer to modules or transplant them outdoors 15cm (6in) apart in rows. Grow them on until early October, when you can finally plant them out 15–20cm (6–8in) apart where you want them to flower.

Winter pansies are popular for good reasons: hardy types give a little colour during the winter and then, in spring, they really shine with masses of blooms. The Universal strain is well known, and is available as a fine mixture or in separate colours, but 'Allegro', an S_1 mixture and cheaper than the slightly more uniform F_1 hybrids, is an excellent alternative.

BORDER PERENNIALS

Increasing violas

By this time of year, the chances are that some of your violas will be getting a bit straggly and untidy. You can simply trim them back, but if you would like to increase the number of your plants, try taking 'Irishman's cuttings'. This process is also called 'mounding' or 'mound-layering', and is a logical short cut to propagating perennials that produce long stems.

Make a compost mix using equal parts of good soil, well-rotted garden compost and sharp sand (make sure it isn't builder's sand which will go rock hard). Add a little organic fertiliser, but no more than a handful, to a large bucket of the mixture. Then work the compost into the clumps of violas so that the straggling stems are well covered. Water occasionally, and in a few weeks you'll find the stems have rooted into the compost. Cut them off the main plant and then either pot them up or plant them in a corner where they won't get swamped by other plants.

Sowing hellebores

If you look at any catalogue of hellebores, you'll find that many of the varieties are in fact strains or seedlings. This is because the plants set seed quite readily, and most of the seedlings are worth growing – and will give you a whole range of fine colours. But they're best sown just before the seeds ripen, so you'll have to be quick off the mark.

Check your plants and remove any capsules from the flowers before they dry and split. Crack the capsules open and take out the

LEFT This arbour at Barnsdale is surrounded by a riot of roses, foxgloves and campanulas, as well as lilies on the point of opening – summer is in full swing.

RIGHT Vivacious but fleeting single scarlet oriental poppies complement the lavish longer lasting perennial flowers of valerian (*Centranthus ruber* 'Coccineus').

seeds. Sow them on the surface of deep 15cm (6in) pots filled with moist soil-less compost, and cover with a thin layer of coarse grit. Put the pots in a cold frame on a layer of sand or grit, and cover them with slates or something similar that will keep them moist, humid and cool.

Check the pots from time to time to make sure they don't dry out. The seeds should germinate from October to the end of the year, although this often depends on which species their parents have come from. The stinking hellebore (*Helleborus foetidus*) and the Corsican kind (*H. corsicus*) are fairly quick to appear, and can even flower the following year. But Lenten and Christmas roses (*H. orientalis* and *H. niger*) are slow growers and may not appear until next spring, after which they need growing on for 2–3 years before they'll flower. Once in final position, they prefer not to be moved.

Tidying oriental poppies

The huge blowsy blooms – either brilliant red or in varied shades of pink, orange and white – of oriental poppies (*Papaver orientale*) make them irresistible. But like several other early-flowering herbaceous plants, once they finish flowering they become a nuisance. The large, rather rank foliage looks good in early spring but begins to flop after flowering, smothering anything else in its path and looking untidy and ugly. Be ruthless and cut it off right down to the base. The foliage will always regrow, returning to its early spring freshness, and if you're lucky you may benefit from another blooming in late summer.

This is also a good time to sow oriental poppies in pots outdoors. Prick out the seedlings when they are small into separate 9cm (3½in) pots, and plant them out 30–38cm (12–15in) apart in the autumn or next spring, disturbing the roots as little as possible when you do so.

A full-grown oriental poppy is a huge plant, often up to 90cm (3ft) or more in diameter, so if you haven't room for this classic giant try the modern dwarf mixture 'Pizzicato'. Although this is a much smaller plant, the blooms are just as glorious, more than 10cm (4in) across with at least a dozen per plant in a range of colours.

BULBS

Planting anemones

Growers have got anemone production to such a fine art that the cut flowers seem to be available for most of the year. This is partly because the tubers are not too fussy about when they're planted. You can start them at various times to flower about three months later: plant them in April for summer flowers, in June to bloom in the autumn, and early autumn for late winter or spring flowers.

Anemones are particularly welcome towards the end of the season, so this month plant as many of the small dry tubers as you like, some in groups near the front of the border to flower there, and others in rows in the vegetable garden for cutting. Start some in pots at the same time, for windowsills or outdoors on the patio. There are two main kinds, both forms of the poppy anemone (*A. coronaria*): De Caen or Giant French make huge single flowers up to 8cm (3in) across in a range of bright colours with dark centres, while St. Brigid is similar but semi-double.

Soak the dry knobbly tubers overnight to give them a good start, and then plant them 5cm (2in) deep and 8–10cm (3–4in) apart. They were traditionally grown for cutting in the kitchen garden, where the soil was rich and well-manured, and this gives a clue as to the diet they enjoy. Work plenty of compost into the soil, especially if it is light and sandy, and add a handful of pelleted chicken manure before planting. Water well and then stand back for a glorious display.

Some growers lift the tubers after the leaves have died down and store them for replanting, but you can leave them in for another season. After that they tend to deteriorate, so plant some more every other year for a continuous supply. They can also be raised from seed, taking about 18 months to flower, but there's an F_1 hybrid mixture called 'Cleopatra', with blooms up to 10cm (4in) across, which takes just a few months to come into flower and can be grown outdoors like a hardy annual.

CONTAINER PLANTS

Growing tender plants in pots

All too often when I buy plants I don't know, I find, when I come to look them up, that they are too tender for my cold garden. And I wouldn't mind betting you do too. If a book says a plant is on the tender side, my solution is to grow it in a pot – then you can bring it inside in October and take it out again late the following May to give a repeat performance each year.

I always use large pots at least 30cm (12in) in diameter or small tubs, filled with a soil-based compost because that provides enough weight to anchor them down on windy days and also offers a buffer against forgetting to water them. I also include a slow-release fertiliser to save the job of fortnightly feeding. It helps to prolong flowering if you pinch off faded blooms, and if a plant is outgrowing its position, just pinch back the shoot tips to keep it in check.

You'll need to repot the plants each year, gradually moving them on into larger containers until they reach maturity. Then all you need do is revive the soil in the containers each spring by replacing the top 5cm (2in) of compost with a fresh supply. Alternatively, most plants root readily from cuttings taken in late summer, so you can replace the old ones after 3–4 years with younger ones.

There are some tender plants that I risk growing outside, but only if I have taken cuttings as an insurance policy. These include willow-leafed jessamine (*Cestrum parqui*), which has great spikes of yellow flowers (deep blue in 'Cretan Purple') and is

TENDER PLANTS TO GROW IN POTS

Plants I've grown successfully in pots, taking them outside for the summer, include angel's trumpets (*Datura* or *Brugmansia*); abutilon hybrids (which need pruning back quite hard in spring to induce new growth), with their bright yellow, red or orange chalice-shaped blooms; perennial cherry pie (heliotrope), which can be grown as a pyramid or standard – its fragrance is unique, so grow it near where you sit; oleanders, shrubby evergreens with heavy clusters of double flowers in various shades of peach, pink and crimson as well as white; pineapple sage, an attractive evergreen with mouthwatering fragrance and scarlet flowers in winter; and the Chinese hibiscus, an evergreen with spectacular trumpet-shaped flowers all summer.

ABOVE Containers of all kinds can be adapted for summer bedding plants, as here at Barnsdale where florists' buckets are packed with pelargoniums, marguerites and petunias.

too good to miss, and several fuchsias of borderline hardiness. I take cuttings in the plant's first or second season and, once they're growing well, I plant the youngsters in a well-drained gravel bed under my warm south-facing wall. They remain outside, while the parent stays in the pot and comes inside when the first frost threatens. That way I can find out just how hardy a tender plant can be, while keeping the big plant safe in its pot.

Planting up patio containers

Most gardeners need no encouragement to buy pots and plants to decorate patios and the paved areas outside the back door. Most of us have some hard areas of paving in the garden, and they can all be softened and brightened up with a real splash of summer bedding; after that's cleared, replant the containers with small evergreen shrubs and bulbs to continue the colour through winter into spring.

There are hundreds of different plastic containers available these days, most of them reasonably priced, although it must be admitted that some of them come in quite obnoxious colours. But it's easy to respray these with the colour of your choice by using aerosol spray paint sold for cars. Plastic is fine unless you want a more traditional look or intend keeping permanent plants outside in winter, when plastic offers little protection to roots in freezing weather. In this case you'll have to buy clay, stone or concrete containers, which often look much more attractive anyway.

The compost in containers always dries faster than the garden soil, so you'll need to water regularly. Soil-less composts are much more demanding than soil-based ones, although you can mix water-holding crystals into the compost to help delay drying out. Perhaps because I'm old-fashioned, I prefer to use soil-based John Innes composts because I find it easier to control the watering. It's really a case of getting used to it, but whatever else you do, never use ordinary garden soil, which will not grow good plants in containers.

Planting is a very personal thing, but I like to plan a bright medley of colours in the summer using pelargoniums, marguerites, felicia, fuchsias, verbena and bacopa, plus half-hardy annuals such as petunias, salvias and lobelia.

If you think mixing all these colours can be a bit garish, stick with just a few shades such as pale blue, pink and white. Try something like the pink marguerite 'Vancouver' in the centre, surrounded by the much shorter marguerite 'Sugar Baby' with its masses of white daisies. Mix that with mauve *Nemesia* 'Elliott's Variety' and pink *Diascia* 'Joyce's Choice', and you'll have a display guaranteed to soothe any savage breast. If you feel in a gaudier frame of mind and have a sunny spot, plant something brilliant like vivid 'Vista Red' pelargoniums in the middle, with *Verbena* 'Pink Parfait' – a delightful pink and red – and the brilliant orange-red *Arctotis* 'Red Devil'. Trail a bit of blue lobelia down the sides, and you won't be able to resist a quick samba round the patio every sunny morning.

At the end of the season you can lift all these, shake off most of the soil, cut back the straggly tops hard and pot up afresh. Water and bring them indoors into full light. Give them a weekly feed at half strength, and they'll reward you with more flowers within a couple of months.

SHRUBS, TREES & CLIMBERS

Pruning spring-flowering shrubs

Many shrubs that flower early in the year – weigela, mock orange (philadelphus), kolkwitzia and deutzia, for example – are best pruned immediately after they have flowered. In warm areas and seasons, that could be the second half of this month, but in colder parts they may not be over for another week or two.

Obviously you don't want to remove wood that has grown this year and will flower next. So look for older branches that have flowered and cut those out, either right at the base or down to a good sideshoot near the bottom. Lilacs, for example, should be carefully pruned down to the two new shoots below the flowers – these will carry next year's blooms. As a rule of thumb for spring-flowering shrubs, you should remove about a third of the branches to open up the bush to light and air, and to encourage the growth of new young shoots for future flowering. If space is precious harder pruning will not harm the plant, but you may sacrifice some of next year's blooms.

One exception to this is broom, both *Cytisus scoparius* and *C. praecox*. These won't grow out of old wood, so they should be cut back to leave about a third of the current season's growth. Bear in mind that these are short-lived shrubs and, however well you prune them, they're bound to become untidy and exhausted after 7–10 years. Then it's best to bite the bullet and throw them away, but only after first taking some cuttings, of course, or buying a new plant.

ROSES

Training climbers

Keeping on top of training climbing roses can be a painful and frustrating battle at this time of year, although it's worth it in the end. The trouble is that you have to get the thorny branches into the

CLIMBING ROSES FOR NORTH- AND EAST-FACING WALLS

The main difference between ramblers and climbers is that ramblers are more vigorous, producing very flexible stems that are generally longer than those of climbers, but they normally only flower once, while many climbers will repeat flower all summer. My recommendation would be to choose climbers for walls or fences, and leave ramblers for training up posts or to ramble through trees. A great many varieties will be happy on a south- or west-facing wall, but east- or north-facing walls can be difficult. For scarlet try 'Danse du Feu' or the darker red 'Guinée' or 'Etoile de Hollande'; for yellow try 'Maigold', 'Gloire de Dijon' or the perfumed 'Golden Showers'; for pink I'd recommend 'Madame Grégoire Staechelin' or the thornless 'Zéphirine Drouhin'; the best white is undoubtedly 'Mme Alfred Carrière'. Roses on walls are susceptible to mildew because of the reduced air circulation, so avoid disease-prone varieties such as 'Crimson Glory', 'Dorothy Perkins', 'Handel' and 'Mrs Sam McGredy'.

ABOVE The Seven Sisters rose, *R. multiflora*, and *Clematis* x *durandii* are companion climbers behind white foxgloves.

TRAINING CLIMBING ROSES

The best way to train climbers growing on a wall is on horizontal wires 60cm (2ft) apart, or on trellis. Make sure the wire is strong, since there could be quite a weight of leaf and stem to hold, especially in wet and windy weather. When you tie the branches in, aim to pull them down more or less horizontally – this will encourage new shoots from the top of those you've tied in, and lots of bloom low down on the wall.

place where you want them, and hold them there while you tie them in. If you've tried fiddling with thin string while wearing thick gloves, you'll know what I mean.

My answer is to use sweet pea rings. These are small wire rings used to hold climbing sweet peas in place on their canes – they're easy to handle with gloves on, and will hold the branches in position long enough to enable you to tie them in with string after taking your gloves off. But even if I had to do it with my teeth, I'm sure I would – there are surely no better climbing plants.

VEGETABLES & HERBS

The warm weather doesn't just wake up plants and get them going. It also sends a signal to all the pests that might be lurking, telling them there could be rich pickings in your vegetable garden. There're two pests in particular you need to keep an eye open for this time of year.

Carrot fly

The female cruises around just above soil level, looking for the tell tale smell that attracts her to lay her eggs at the base of the carrot foliage – and not just on carrots, but on parsnips, parsley and celery too. The eggs hatch out into tiny grubs that make brown tunnels in the tops of the roots. There are chemical treatments you can use, and a few carrot varieties such as 'Fly Away' and 'Sytan' are 90 per cent resistant, but the best way to foil the fly is to hide its target. You can alternate rows of carrots with onions, which have a stronger smell that confuses the fly, or plant them among flowers, or you can cover or surround them with a sheet of horticultural fleece.

I prefer to grow all the susceptible crops together in a block, and surround this at planting or sowing time with a wall of fleece or clear polythene supported on short posts – the low-level carrot fly will bump up against this and then fly round. But remember that the larger your block of plants the higher the barrier needs to be, or gusts of wind could carry the fly up and over to drop inside. Panels 45cm (18in) high work for a block 1.2m (4ft) square, but you might need to go 60cm (2ft) high for anything bigger.

Cabbage root fly

Another kind of root fly attacks young brassicas such as cabbages, cauliflowers and Brussels sprouts, causing them to collapse completely. If you see a small transplant wilting and then dying, pull it up and you'll probably find the root has been invaded by tiny fat white grubs. By that time it's too late to take action, and it's best to take precautions at planting time by preventing the adult fly from getting to the soil near the stem, where she lays her eggs. Use a piece of old carpet or underlay, and cut this into 15cm (6in) squares. Make a cut to the centre of each square, where you make another small slit at right angles so that the square will sit neatly round the brassica stem. Then plant in the usual way, simply slipping a square round the base of each plant so that it fits tightly all round the stem and lies flat on the soil.

Planting cauliflowers

Although they're very popular for summer and autumn use, there's no doubt that cauliflowers are a difficult crop to grow well. For a start, they're some of the greediest plants and need transplanting to soil that has been deeply prepared with as much compost or manure as you can spare, not just to feed the plants but also to keep the roots moist at all stages of growth.

One of the most common problems is that the flowers – the bit that you eat – sometimes start to mature too early. They come to a tiny head and refuse to develop further. This is called premature curding, and the biggest frustration is that, by the time you see it, it's too late to do anything. The secret is to give the plants a good start: thin them early, water them well in dry weather, and keep them growing smoothly.

One of the great danger periods is about now when the plants are being moved from the seedbed to their final rows. There's no way to eliminate stress, but you can reduce it greatly by transplanting when the seedlings are still small. Move them just as soon as they're big enough to handle, and certainly before they're six weeks old. Make sure that the roots are kept covered while they're out of the ground, water them in thoroughly with a little feed added to the water, and then ensure they are never short of water afterwards.

PREVENTING CABBAGE ROOT FLY

It doesn't matter whether you buy special planting mats or make your own from old materials. They can be round or square, but the important thing is that they fit snugly round the plant to stop the adult fly laying her eggs at the base of the stem.

Sowing chicory for forcing

Round about Christmas I always like to have my own chicory roots for forcing to produce the best winter salad available. There are, of course, two distinct types of chicory. One is like a lettuce but with a slightly bitter refreshing flavour, and that's sown this month for eating fresh in late summer and autumn – 'Sugar Loaf' is a fine variety, or there's the red 'Rossa di Verona'. The other is the Belgian or Witloof kind, also sown now but in this case to produce roots for forcing in winter. Make sure you have the right one!

Start by sowing an up-to-date variety such as 'Apollo' or 'Zoom', which can be forced without blanching the shoots with soil. You'll need a fairly sunny position, and rich soil to fatten up the biggest roots, so add plenty of manure and a couple of handfuls of pelleted chicken manure per square metre. Sow in shallow drills 30cm (12in) apart, and thin the seedlings to 15cm (6in) apart. All that's needed before you dig the roots up in October or November (see page 170) is to water them in dry weather.

BELOW The decorative ferny foliage of carrots blends successfully with colourful multiflora petunias, a combination which hides the crop from the carrot root fly.

FRUIT

Controlling fruit pests

Many common fruit pests are difficult to control by conventional methods such as spraying because they arrive on the wing and are gone in seconds after laying their eggs. But trapping is a modern way that uses the flies' own lifestyle to lure them to their doom.

Take codling moths, for example. They're flying around on warm nights this month and next, looking for apple trees where the females can lay their tiny single eggs on the immature fruits and leaves. These hatch into those disgusting little maggots you generally bite in half if you haven't noticed the hole that they make at the top of the apple.

Trapping the females doesn't have much effect, but pheromone traps use the typical smell of the females to attract amorous males, which then get ensnared on panels of sticky grease. With reduced fertilisation, the females are unable to lay eggs and you'll cut the problem by 85 per cent. Just one trap for every five apple trees is enough.

There's a similar device for controlling plum fruit moth, which is a close relative of the codling moth and does the same amount of damage – the little blighters tunnel into ripening plums, causing them to drop prematurely or making them inedible at harvest time. In a poor season when a cold spring has thinned the crop, almost every plum can be ruined, so it makes sense to invest in a few of these tent-shaped pheromone traps and leave them suspended all summer from the tree branches to save the fruits of all your labours

RIGHT A wide selection of lettuces, including cos and loose-leaf types, promises a succession of colourful summer salads. Behind them is a bank of diascias for cutting, and a gooseberry trained as a standard.

Training in bush fruit shoots

If your garden is small and lack of space is a real problem you can, if you're canny, fit in a whole range of bush fruit by training the bushes into restricted shapes. These can be very decorative and no less productive than normal bushes.

A gooseberry, for example, can be grown as a standard, which is nothing more than a gooseberry bush grafted on a 90cm–1.2m (3–4ft) stem. These look great, even in a border and, since you can grow flowers or vegetables underneath, they really take up no room at all.

You can also grow gooseberries and red and white currants as cordons. These consist of single, double or triple stems, grown vertically and trained on canes tied to a post and wire support or on wires against a fence or wall. Kept neat, they can take up just 15cm (6in) of your valuable border. The main pruning is best done later, in August (see page 130), when sideshoots made this year are cut back to two leaves. But at this time of year new shoots are extending fast, and need to be tied back and into shape while they are still young and pliable.

Growing raspberries in a retricted space

If you're beginning to pick raspberries and find that you haven't got room for as many canes as you'd like, my solution is to grow them as a pillar. When the

canes grow they're tied to wires to form a column of foliage and fruit, as shown below. This arrangement produces a slightly lower crop than is normal in traditional rows, because the light only reaches the outside of the canes. But it looks neat and decorative, and takes up much less room. And, as with all these training methods, the fruit is more easily covered with netting or fleece to protect it against its two biggest enemies – frost and birds.

At the same time as you're harvesting the fruit, take along your secateurs and cut out late suckers that are congesting the plants at ground level.

GROWING RASPBERRIES AS A PILLAR

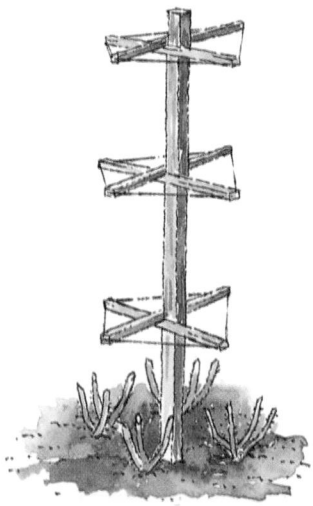

Drive a 2.4m (8ft) stake about 45cm (18in) into the ground; then nail six 60cm (2ft) 'arms' to the stake, in pairs to make a cross shape, one at the top of the stake, one in the middle and another about 60cm (2ft) from the ground. Staple wires to the ends of the arms to tie the canes to. Plant the raspberries 45cm (18in) apart in a circle around the pillar.

MISCELLANEOUS

Tackling weeds

I've proved that organic gardening is not just good for the environment: it works better too, filling your garden with wildlife, fine sturdy flowers and excellent crops of fruit and vegetables – all without chemical fertilisers or pesticides. But what about weeds?

Annual weeds such as chickweed and groundsel are no problem and certainly not a reason to spray, because you can pull them out easily by hand or use the hoe regularly. Awkward weeds like stonecrop (*Sedum*) in a drive would resist chemical control anyway, with the waxy waterproof coating to their leaves. The solution here is to use a flame gun, which works on portable gas cylinders and is simplicity itself to use – you can get one from a small tool-hire shop quite cheaply. The job might need doing every month for a while, but eventually you'll manage to get rid of the stuff.

Weedkillers won't touch tough customers like marestail and oxalis, which are particularly difficult, and here you must rely on that other well-known preparation, elbow grease. By hoeing regularly before the shoots are more than 1cm (½in) tall, you'll deprive the plants of light and without that they'll eventually die.

If you're starting with a new garden, however, and find it is smothered in pernicious weeds such as couch grass, bindweed or ground elder, then it's worth making an exception to the organic rule and spraying with a total weedkiller. One containing glyphosate will kill everything green that it touches, so do be careful, but it is inactivated when it hits the soil and is harmless to animal life.

For tough perennials like nettles and ivy the best bet is to spray now, and again in late summer. The weedkiller is taken down to the roots, but these can sometimes regrow so the second application, just when the plants are beginning to slow down, should complete the job. For weeds growing in borders among plants, you'll have to paint the weedkiller on the leaves – wear rubber gloves and diligently avoid the leaves of other plants. To treat bindweed growing among plants, try putting a cane near the weed and allow it to scramble up: this makes it easier to treat safely.

And finally, why would this hardened old reactionary advise using a chemical weedkiller? Well, otherwise you'd get thoroughly discouraged and just give up. And that does no one any good at all. But promise me you'll throw the sprayer away afterwards.

Watering techniques

Whatever the reasons and whoever's fault it is – and believe me, I've shaken the bones and danced round in circles a bit – we have to face the fact that water is likely to be in short supply in the foreseeable summers ahead. So it is vital to manage those resources we have as efficiently as possible.

The first and most obvious measure is to catch rainwater. A lot comes off the house and greenhouse roofs, so water butts are essential. You can buy little plastic inserts which fit to the down pipe, fill the butt to the top and then divert the rest to the drain. Better still, link

LEFT As temperatures rise under glass, tomatoes need regular watering and feeding.

other butts to the first with a series of simple connector pipes and fill them as well.

Next, it's worthwhile directing water just where it is needed. A sprinkler is very inefficient with big losses to evaporation: bear in mind that one hour's sprinkling uses as much water as an average family in a whole day. Much better to target plants that need it most – young transplants, leafy plants and vegetables or fruit that are in flower or ripening their crops. Use a hose which oozes water along its whole length so that, when laid among the plants, it delivers water straight to the soil with minimum evaporation. A soaker hose – a flat hose with rows of tiny holes along its length – can be turned upside down to do the same job.

Watering's best done in the evening, when the heat has gone out of the sun, by soaking a few plants thoroughly and then leaving the rest for the following evening. And make sure they are soaked. lightly sprinkling the ground makes matters worse by bringing roots to the surface where they'll dry out even quicker. Mulch the plants after watering. One way to trap water is to work plenty of organic matter such as compost into the soil, and then add more to the surface while it's still moist. Anything organic will help – grass cuttings, shredded prunings, compost, manure, leafmould, bark and so on.

Even your newspaper can make an effective and inexpensive mulch. When you've finished reading it, don't throw it away. Instead, get out in the garden with it, rake away a little moist soil, lay three sheets of newspaper on the surface and cover them with a thin layer of soil. You can even lay the paper in place and then plant through it when transplanting: the paper barrier will last all season and can be dug in afterwards to add a bit more organic matter. Black plastic between rows of vegetables is excellent and also inhibits weeds, cutting down on work and reducing competition for moisture. But ideally you should use one of the porous woven plastics that will allow the rain through when it eventually does come.

Proper gardeners never go away in summer – life's one long holiday already – but if you do, watering precautions become critical. First, chat up a neighbour who can come round and water hanging baskets, containers and plants in the greenhouse; or, alternatively, fit up one of those automatic trickle devices that deliver drops of water direct to the plants through individual nozzles. Weed the garden as much as you can, soak essential plants and then mow the lawn the morning you depart.

Indoors or in the greenhouse, take all the house- and pot plants and stand them in the bath or in large bowls. Lay a blanket or wet towels on the bottom with one end resting in a bowl of water. The towels will stay wet for a couple of weeks, drawing up water from the reservoir bowl as necessary, and the plants will have enough to drink while you're away. And remember to draw the curtains and shade the greenhouse to exclude hot sunshine.

PLANTS FOR

june

1 The large-flowered jackmanii type clematis 'Comtesse de Bouchaud' is a versatile variety. It grows to 1.8–2.4m (6–8ft) and blooms profusely even on a north-facing wall.

2 *Digitalis purpurea* 'Alba', the white-flowered form of the common foxglove, is a coveted hardy border biennial or short-lived perennial up to 1.8m (6ft) high.

3 The popular hardy deciduous mock orange, *Philadelphus coronarius,* makes a vigorous bushy shrub 3m (10ft) high, even on light dry soils. In early summer it's smothered with creamy-white, richly fragrant blooms.

1

2

3

4

4 Bearded irises are classic early summer flowers, very often flamboyantly bi-coloured, for growing in mixed borders or in beds to themselves. Although their flowering season is somewhat short, they are very hardy plants with hundreds of varieties that are divided into tall, medium and dwarf categories.

5 Available in a number of brightly coloured mixtures easily raised from seed, the sun-loving Iceland poppy, *Papaver nudicaule*, can be treated as a biennial or short-lived perennial; the 30cm (12in) blooms are produced over a long season.

OVERLEAF Many lovely plants combine well with roses, whether as ground cover or as edging, a role for which lavender is traditional. Here *Campanula lactiflora* 'Pritchard's Variety' complements glorious old-fashioned shrub roses.

5

With the heat of the summer came perhaps my least favourite – but also my most favourite – times in the garden. At weekends, when there was no extra help, the job of watering fell to me. It was time-consuming and fiddly: there were seven greenhouses, three tunnels, two conservatories and an alpine house to take care of, as well as all the individual gardens. Some had water butts, so cans had to be filled and carried, others needed what seemed like miles of hose. But it was an educational task; I learned a lot about plants as the weeks and years went by.

On the other hand, hot summer evenings, when we had the whole place to ourselves, were blissful. We'd walk through the garden at twilight, relishing the peace and quiet, the sights and the scents. The white flowers stayed visible the longest, seeming almost luminescent as darkness fell, while the scents of the flowers were at their strongest after sundown. Geoff would never grow scentless roses or sweet peas, however beautiful they were; he just couldn't see the point.

The well-known rambler rose 'American Pillar' flanks a stone path leading through mid-summer borders where hollyhocks and white mallows provide elegance and height.

July

key tasks for july

ANNUALS & BEDDING PLANTS
- ❍ Harvest flowers and dry them slowly, page 108

BORDER PERENNIALS
- ❍ Divide and plant flag irises, page 109
- ❍ Take cuttings of pinks and carnations, page 109
- ❍ Cut back flowered perennials to encourage a second flush, page 110

BULBS
- ❍ Divide congested clumps of daffodils, page 111

SHRUBS, TREES & CLIMBERS
- ❍ Prune clematis, take cuttings and watch out for wilt, page 112
- ❍ Propagate short-lived shrubs by taking soft cuttings, page 112

LAWNS & HEDGES
- ❍ Keep lawns in top condition, page 114
- ❍ Control leylandii hedges and take cuttings, page 114

VEGETABLES & HERBS
- ❍ Watch for tomato disorders, page 115
- ❍ Ripen and harvest shallots and garlic, page 115
- ❍ Plan for plenty of autumn vegetables by sowing now, page 115
- ❍ Cut back herbs for further young growth, page 116

MISCELLANEOUS
- ❍ Make the best of limited space with a deep bed, page 117

ANNUALS & BEDDING PLANTS

Harvesting flowers for drying

True everlasting flowers, such as helichrysum, helipterum and rhodanthe, hardly need drying because their flowers are naturally papery and long-lasting. They need picking just as they reach their best – which is fractionally before they're fully open.

Hang them upside down in a cool airy place to dry them slowly with plenty of circulating air. Whatever you do, don't try drying them in the kitchen or greenhouse as they quickly shrivel up.

Many other flowers can be preserved in the same way. The translucent white seedpods of honesty are always popular, but it's also worth having a go with achillea, amaranthus, delphiniums, gypsophila, golden rod, zinnias and, of course, lavender.

DIVIDING FLAG IRISES

1 Irises branch each side of the thick original main rhizome, which is sometimes rotten at its oldest end. Use these young laterals or side pieces for propagation. Cut each one off with a fan of leaves, using a sharp knife.

2 Throw away the old root. Reduce the leaves on the young rhizomes by half their length, and replant the young segments in groups of three or four to make good-sized clumps. Make sure they're not completely buried, especially on heavier soil.

Planting flag irises

Every cottage garden used to have its stand of blue 'flags' making a splendid show each year. While they've lost none of their hardiness or vigour, irises have come a long way since then and they're now available in almost every colour from deep purple through smoky browns to white and yellow, with many bi-colours too.

Given the right situation, they are among the easiest plants to grow. I don't remember ever having a single pest or disease attack mine, and they never fail to flower their hearts out. Their one demand is for a dry well-drained sunny spot. Their fleshy rhizomes form clumps that need to be baked in the sun to ensure a crop of flowers.

Before planting, dig in some compost or manure and, if your soil's heavy, add plenty of coarse grit; if this raises the soil above its surroundings, so much the better – it all improves drainage. A good dressing of general fertiliser completes the job. Scrape a shallow depression in the soil, and make a ridge in the centre so that the rhizome can rest on it with its roots lying either side. Plant it so it is half buried and water once. In windy sites it pays to support the leaf fans with short canes. Then leave the plants to their own devices.

LEFT A combined display of hardy perennial white leucanthemums (shasta daisies) with annual *Godetia* 'Grace'.

Dividing flag irises

Plants increase rapidly and should be divided every 3–4 years because the centres produce fewer flowers as they age. But the job's not difficult, and the best time for it is about five weeks after flowering ends. Start by cutting off the old flower spike, and then lift the clump and shake off the soil – you might want to wash the roots to see where to cut. Then cut the rhizomes and replant as shown above, planting in groups of three or four to make a good-sized clump.

Propagating pinks and carnations

There's little point struggling to grow plants that don't like the conditions in your garden, when there are lots of others that will grow there happily and unaided. If your soil's chalky, for example, you should be growing lime-lovers – and there are plenty of real beauties, few finer than garden pinks and border carnations. But be warned: they soon get thin and straggly unless replaced every 3–4 years.

I've never understood why so many gardening books recommend

PROPAGATING CARNATIONS

You can cut off the tips of shoots with a sharp knife, or more simply just pull out the end with the last few pairs of leaves. Peel off the lowest of these carefully so as not to break the base of the soft stem, and dip the cut end in rooting hormone. The 'pipings' will root in pure sharp sand or perlite if this is kept moist, but I like to use cuttings compost with extra grit for drainage. Cover pots with plastic bags to stop them drying out.

propagating them by layering, a method I find very fiddly, time-consuming and rarely successful. Taking stem cuttings or 'pipings' at about this time of year is so much quicker and more reliable. Just pull the top 8cm (3in) of the stem away from the plant. It'll come out quite cleanly, and then you can dip the end in rooting hormone and dibble it into a pot of soil-less compost. Cover the pot with a clear plastic bag and stand outdoors in the shade. If you have the space, you can even make a shallow depression in the soil in a shady part of the garden, fill it with sharp sand, and strike the cuttings in this.

Cutting back perennials

Raising a family is an exhausting business, and since plants produce offspring by the thousand it's little wonder they tend to flop a bit. Many of the early-flowering herbaceous varieties are now getting on with the job of making seeds but, unless you intend raising more plants this way, you'd be well advised to teach them a bit of family planning.

It's especially important with notoriously short-lived plants such as lupins, which last only a few years anyway and much less if you let them run to seed every year. As soon as the last flower has faded, cut the spikes off to allow the plant to put all its strength into enlarging itself, with the help of a little general fertiliser. Just leave one or two stems to produce seeds so that you can replace short-lived varieties every few years.

Early-flowering geraniums, violas and delphiniums can be sheared off right down to the crown, just above ground level. If you leave them the foliage will collapse and swamp other smaller plants around them. Take the old leaves to the compost heap, give the plants a sprinkling of fertiliser and a good soak of water if necessary, and they'll soon produce fresh young leaves. In warmer parts of the country, many will also produce a second, smaller crop of flowers as a bonus.

One disadvantage with this drastic method is that it leaves a bare patch in the border at a time of year when it should be completely overflowing. Obviously you can't plant anything permanent because the space will soon be filled again. So I keep a few pots of tender perennials or mixed hardy annuals which can be put in the empty spaces as temporary fillers.

LEFT There is a huge expanding range of modern double pinks, all supreme edging plants for sunny well-drained positions, and good for cutting too.

ABOVE Some osteospermums, such as this *O. ecklonis*, are reliably hardy perennials, whereas the marguerite behind needs over-wintering indoors.

Not all perennials benefit from cutting hard back, and the simple test if you are not sure is to part the old leaves and look down at the base of the plant. If you see new leaves at soil level, the old ones can go. But plants that tend to have a single stem at the base with branches above, such as penstemons or perennial cornflowers, also known as knapweed (*Centaurea*), should be just trimmed lightly.

Another example of this is the perennial wallflower (*Erysimum*), which can die out in two or three years on heavy soil – trim it lightly as I've suggested, and take some cuttings from the prunings to make sure you have replacements.

BULBS

Dividing daffodils

The bulbs in old clumps of daffodils multiply over the years, and eventually begin competing with each other to the point where they go 'blind' and refuse to flower. So split them up before this happens. Early in the month, when the foliage has died right down but while you can still see where the clumps are, lift large ones and split them into individual bulbs. Then either dry the bulbs off and store in a cool dry place for replanting in late August or September, or replant them immediately.

If daffodils that were planted last year failed to flower this spring, they might be too small, of course, and need another season to build up to flowering size. But they could also be planted too shallowly, and it's worth digging them up now for replanting either straight away or at the usual time in early autumn. Aim to cover the bulbs with at least twice their own depth of soil, more on light soils where they can go 5–8cm (2–3in) deeper.

SHRUBS, TREES & CLIMBERS

Looking after clematis

Nothing gives such a startling display of large flowers or masses of smaller ones over as long a period as clematis. But there are two factors which put gardeners off.

First is the dreaded clematis wilt. This is a fungal disease that makes clematis wilt from the top, progressing gradually downwards until the whole plant is affected. It is most noticeable in the summer, especially after humid weather. Chemical control is not much good, but there are measures which can help. Always plant clematis deeply, with about 15cm (6in) of soil above the top of the rootball. The fungus doesn't attack below ground, so even if you lose the top there will still be plenty of buds below the surface to replace infected growth. If you do see any signs of wilt, such as limp, drooping shoots, prune back immediately to healthy wood.

Pruning is the other big deterrent for some gardeners, because the rules can sound complicated. But I have found that there's a much simpler approach that works. If your clematis flowers before the end of June, prune it immediately after flowering by shortening sideshoots back to 2–3 buds off the main framework of branches. If it flowers after June, prune in the autumn or, in colder areas, in February by cutting hard back to just above a good fat bud within 15cm (6in) of the soil.

Propagating clematis

You can often take advantage of pruning to propagate clematis from cuttings. I've no idea why I have little success layering it: the books tell me that all I have to do is pin the shoots to the ground in autumn or late spring and they'll root in no time, but they never seem to. I find that taking cuttings any time in spring or summer is usually far more successful.

Unlike most plants, clematis are propagated by 'internodal' cuttings, as shown below – several can be cut from a single stem, since each needs only one pair of leaves. Once potted, cover the cuttings with very thin polythene, which should rest lightly on the leaves, and tuck it under the pot to make a good seal. Put the pots in a shaded frame or even outside in a shady spot, and the cuttings should root in 6–8 weeks.

Propagating short-lived shrubs

There's still time to take soft tip cuttings of shrubs and herbaceous perennials, and very often they root fast at this time of year while the temperatures are high. I try to make a point every season of propagating anything that seems to be short-lived or doubtfully hardy. Plants like lavender, which soon becomes gaunt and leggy, or grey-leafed shrubs like artemisias and euryops that often don't last long in heavy soils or cold gardens, all benefit from replacement every 3–5 years.

There's never a problem finding a home for surplus young plants – friends and relatives often welcome them or you can donate batches to local fund-raising events – so keep on taking cuttings whenever there's space in a frame or you see inviting young shoots. Soft tips just 5cm (2in) long are all you need. Remove the lower leaves, immerse the cuttings in fungicide and dip their ends into hormone rooting powder. Then insert them in pots of soil-less compost and keep them in a shaded frame. It takes no time at all, and ensures a continuous supply of young plants to replace any losses.

RIGHT The rose garden at Barnsdale where mat-forming edging plants, such as stachys, soften the angular paving, also includes border perennials and lilies in a framework of shrubs and trees.

PROPAGATING CLEMATIS

1 Cut between leaf joints to leave a long stem below the leaf.

2 Dibble the cuttings into soil-less compost so that the leaves are resting on the surface.

LAWNS & HEDGES

Keeping lawns in top condition

A hot dry summer will usually show up the inadequacies in your lawn. It's often the nicely manicured lawns made of the very finest grass species that suffer first in a drought and start turning brown, while those composed of tougher grasses, clover and even moss still look refreshingly green.

If your lawn regularly and quickly turns brown in dry weather it's a sure sign of stress, and you're not going to cure it just by watering – all this will do is waste water and stop the symptoms from showing for a little bit longer. The real cause is more likely to be a combination of poor soil preparation and over-enthusiastic mowing, and the best way to start putting things right is to raise the cutting height of the mower. Aim to mow less frequently, leaving the grass 2.5cm (1in) high or a little more, and it won't look so parched and scalped. Leave the grass box in the shed and allow the cuttings to fall on the lawn where they'll act as a thin mulch and gradually return humus and nutrients to the soil – if you invest in a mulching mower, this will chop the clippings very finely so they are virtually invisible and won't tread into the house. Then resolve to add some organic matter to the soil in the autumn, and again in the spring, by spiking the lawn and raking in some sieved garden compost to help retain moisture at the roots. If the season continues to be dry, give the lawn an extra feed in the autumn just before rain is forecast, and it'll soon look immaculate again.

Controlling leylandii hedges

Conifer hedges are much maligned these days, mainly I suspect because they tend to be of Leyland cypress, × *Cupressocyparis leylandii*. This is often sneered at because it's so widely grown, but if the truth be told, the reason that it's common is that it's such a good hedging plant.

It is, of course, a fast mover, putting on 60–90cm (2–3ft) of growth in most seasons, and you can't afford to let it get away from you. The plants won't produce new growth from old wood, so it's essential to begin trimming the sides as soon as they start to exceed the width you want. Plants can be as narrow as 15cm (6in) each side of the main stem if you clip them twice a year – early this month and again between late August and October.

You can trim the sides while the plants are still young, but leave the main leader at the top until it has reached about 90cm (3ft) higher than you want it. Then cut it back to 15cm (6in) lower than the required height. This will allow it to form a thick bushy top, which you'll be able to cut to a neat flat finish. By trimming it regularly you'll have a hedge that's almost as aristocratic as yew but a lot quicker.

LEFT An immaculate grass path emphasises lavish plantings in the Barnsdale borders and creates an illusion of distance.

Taking conifer cuttings

Whenever you're trimming any conifers at this time of year, decide if you want to grow more of them because the prunings will often supply perfect semi-ripe cuttings. These are the little sideshoots, about 5–8cm (2–3in) long, growing from the main stems and branches, and just becoming woody at their base. Pull them off, as shown below. There's no need to remove any lower leaves, but otherwise root them like other semi-ripe cuttings (see page 125).

TAKING CONIFER CUTTINGS

1 Pull sideshoots off downwards so that each has a little heel of tissue at its base.

2 Trim the ragged end of the heel with a knife and root like other semi-ripe cuttings (see page 125).

VEGETABLES & HERBS

At this time of year, when the vegetable garden is overflowing, one of the main jobs is to keep harvesting. Don't forget that the more you pick summer vegetables such as courgettes and runner beans, the more they'll produce.

Looking out for tomato disorders

In order to help the fruit finish ripening before the frosts, it's a good idea to stop tall outdoor tomatoes after three trusses. Keep an eye on greenhouse tomatoes too. Black marks at the flowering tip of fruits is not a disease but a physiological disorder called blossom end rot, and is the result of irregular watering. It's hard to stop completely, especially in hot weather, but it helps if you can shade the greenhouse lightly and keep the compost evenly moist at all times. Another problem is halo blight, which shows as small spots on the fruits, surrounded by a lighter ring. This is a water-borne fungal disease and can be prevented if you avoid splashing the fruits when you water or damp down.

Harvesting shallots

Shallots need to be ripened well in the sun. This helps ensure that the bulbs keep for a longer period in store, and I'm convinced it improves their flavour too.

In a warm dry season the bulbs can be left to ripen in the ground, especially if you draw a little soil away from the clusters to expose them to the sun. Otherwise lift them carefully with a fork when the leaves turn yellow, making sure you don't break the clusters up before they're ready or you'll leave wounds open to disease. If you make a temporary 'table' with a piece of wire netting nailed to four posts, you can spread out the clusters clear of the ground and surrounded by free circulation of air – but keep a piece of polythene handy to cover them over if it rains.

When the skins are papery and dry, you can separate the bulbs in each cluster and clean them up by removing the old leaves and scaly skin and rubbing off any clinging soil. Pack the bulbs in onion or Brussels sprout bags begged from the greengrocer, and store them in a frost-free place.

Harvesting garlic

Like shallots, garlic also needs to be ripened in the sun, but there's no need to wait until its leaves turn completely yellow before you harvest the bulbs. These can be dug up as soon as the tips start to turn colour. Dry them in the same way as shallots, or hang them in bunches in the sun until the skins are dry and flaky. Cut off the dead foliage and rub the bulbs clean before storing them in the same way as shallots. If the crop is good and the plants were healthy – their leaves free from the yellow spots and stripes of virus – save a few bulbs for replanting this autumn.

Planning vegetables for autumn

Despite the fact that the vegetable plot is yielding masses of delicious fresh produce every day, we can't afford to rest on our laurels and rely on a never-ending supply of runner beans. Control the euphoria for a bit, because autumn will be upon us sooner than you think. As soon as a bit of ground becomes available, revitalise it with a dressing of compost and a light dusting of organic fertiliser so you can bung in a follow-on crop.

Lettuces are welcome at any time, and you should be trying to aim for an unbroken succession of supplies. At this time of year they're quick to mature provided they get enough moisture – if you're unlucky enough to have water restrictions in your area, dig in as much compost, rotted manure or spent mushroom compost as you can to hold the moisture in the soil. And if you can sow in a shady place, that'll help too. This month I continue sowing 'Saladin' and 'Lakeland', which have large crisp iceberg-type heads.

For beetroot I stick to quick maturing 'Boltardy' because I find it's just as good for winter storage as for pulling young; sown now it'll provide delicious baby beet for autumn use. For rapid germination it pays to wash the seed capsules in a flour sieve under the tap to remove the germination inhibitor in the seed-coating.

Carrots will also produce delicious young roots this season, and any not needed immediately can be stored. For some years I've used, and been pleased with, the variety 'Berlicum Berjo', even if it does sound like a music-hall song.

Let me say a word for kohl rabi. It's a funny looking customer with leaves sticking out all over the swollen stem, the part you eat. Despite mouthwatering claims in catalogues, it's not the best flavour in the world eaten raw, but it makes a superb soup. Old-fashioned varieties tend to get pithy when they're bigger than tennis-ball size, but modern types like 'Rowel' and 'White Danube' stay sweet and fibre-free even when they become large – not that they'll have time to get enormous if sown this month. Sow them in a seedbed and transplant next month or, better still, sow direct and thin to final spacings of 23cm (9in) each way.

Turnips are so quick to mature that they can be left until the last week of this month or even early August, if you sow 'Golden Ball', a fast-maturing variety that can also stand some frost in autumn. There's still time to sow Florence fennel, which is delicious with roast meat and lasts well into winter if covered with cloches: use a modern variety like 'Zeva Fino' or 'Cantino'. Keep the plants well watered and if you're sowing in dry weather, water down the drill before you sow and then cover the seeds with dry soil – this prevents the surface crust that forms if you water after sowing.

Sow some spinach beet (perpetual spinach) in a shady spot, and also its close relative, Swiss chard, which happily stands the hardest frost.

Finally, one crop I wouldn't be without is land cress, sometimes called American cress. It has a delicious watercress flavour, but without the need for a running stream to grow in. Sow it in the coolest, moistest part of the vegetable plot where it's less likely to run to seed, and transfer a few spare plants to the frame or greenhouse in September to make the most delicious and nutritious winter soup you could ask for.

BELOW A neatly sculpted mophead bay tree crowns a bed of fennel and echoes the formality of annual herbs in rows.

Rejuvenating herbs

Years ago I used to wonder why gardeners bothered to grow sorrel, one of the ugliest herbs there is. It tends to run to seed quickly, and when it does the leaves seem to become tougher and more bitter. But I discovered that if it's cut back hard as soon as it starts to bolt, reducing the whole clump in fact to nothing more than a stump, a wealth of tender new leaves soon appears from the base, and these have a wonderful flavour.

Marjoram, mint and tarragon respond to a good haircut about now by producing new young leaves. When you cut them back, sprinkle some general fertiliser around the plants and give them a good watering to encourage faster regrowth. The new leaves are much tastier than the old ones, and by the time they're ready to be harvested you might have enough to lay up a good store of preserves such as mint jelly for the winter.

ABOVE Deeply dug organic vegetable beds are easily managed and protected when they are narrow and framed with edging boards.

MISCELLANEOUS

Building a deep bed

If you're serious about growing vegetables and you haven't got unlimited acres at your disposal, you'll naturally want to maximise your harvest per square metre. One of the best ways to do this is to grow your crops on the deep bed system, which can double or even treble yields. And if the mention of beds starts you thinking of snoozing, I'd better explain that there's nothing cosy about these. They need a bit of hard graft at first, but after this initial slog they get easier to work each year. They're cleaner, more encouraging to work on and, if they're well maintained, they look terrific.

This is what you do. Mark out a bed 1.2m (4ft) wide, with access from each side. You can make it as long as you like, but if you make more than one, leave a 60cm (2ft) path in between. It will repay you in dividends if you manage to double dig the bed. Ideally you should break up the subsoil but avoid turning it over or bringing it up to the top. As you dig, work in manure, compost, spent mushroom compost or some other humus (but not peat, of course). Make sure you mix it throughout all levels of the soil and not just in the bottom of the trench.

That part is hard work, but you only need to do it once because afterwards you'll single-dig the bed each year, working a bit more compost or manure into the top spit. After a while the soil becomes so easy to work that, for example, I don't have to put my foot on the spade at all – a gentle lean is all that's needed to slice into the soil. If you can't double-dig, initial single-digging is the next best thing and will still yield dividends.

There are several reasons why deep bed culture works. Except for the annual dig, you never tread on the soil because you do all the work from the side paths. That way the soil never gets compacted. Also, because it's deeply dug the plants' roots can get right down instead of competing with each other near the surface. This means you can space crops more closely together, and so grow more. Growing them close together has more advantages: there is less evaporation, so you need to water less, and there will be less room for weeds to grow. And on top of all this, if you edge the bed with 8 or 10cm (3 or 4in) treated boards and gravel the paths, it'll delight your eye every time you go out to pull a carrot.

PLANTS FOR
july

1 The vigorous woody twining stems of *Lonicera* x *brownii* 'Dropmore Scarlet', a hardy honeysuckle, will reach 4m (13ft) on a sunny wall or large host shrub. It is very long-lived, and produces an abundance of 5cm (2in) trumpet-shaped blooms in dense whorls from mid-summer until autumn.

2 This month and next are the peak season for *Phlox paniculata*, the hardy herbaceous perennial border phlox. It has tall stems 90cm (3ft) or more high and flowers in a range of colours, from purple and crimson through to the pure white blooms of 'White Admiral'.

1

2

3

4

5

3 There are several lovely forms of knapweed or perennial cornflower, with *Centaurea hypoleuca* 'John Coutts' among the finest. The hardy herbaceous plants are 50–60cm (20–24in) tall and, with their handsome long-lasting blooms, spread steadily without being invasive.

4 The common morning glory, *Ipomoea purpurea*, is a half-hardy annual climber up to 2.4m (8ft) high, with numerous large funnel-shaped flowers in shades of blue, white, pink and red. Each bloom lasts for a single day.

5 In full sun and well-drained soil, alstroemeria hybrids derived from *A. ligtu* and *A. aurantiaca* are reliable hardy perennials, easily raised from seed. They produce strong-stemmed flowers in a range of prettily marked colours.

August was birthday month – mine, one son's, Geoff's and, of course, his twin's. And the obvious place to celebrate with friends and family was in the garden, with a barbecue. Here Geoff took command of the cooking. He used a 50-gallon drum that he had cut in half, with reinforcing mesh as the grill, to do the job. But though he liked the idea of relaxing in the garden, he almost never managed actually to do so. The moment he sat down, he'd spot something that needed attention – a weed to be pulled up, a long stem to be tied back.

This was the time of year when the allotment bulged with rows of flowers that could be pillaged for the house. The rest of the garden was more tricky. Because I didn't always know which area was to be filmed in any one week, I could never simply go and pick where and what I wanted. But even though the finer arts of flower arranging were rather lost on Geoff – he really did prefer to see his flowers in the garden – he always made sure that he grew enough in the allotment for me to pick all through the summer.

There are many fine crocosmia hybrids, but few can match 'Lucifer' for bold foliage and dramatic intensity of colour in the late summer border.

august

key tasks for august

BORDER PERENNIALS
- ❍ Weed borders but watch out for self-set seedlings, page 122

BULBS
- ❍ Plant Madonna lilies to bloom next year, page 123
- ❍ Plant autumn crocuses and nerines, page 123

CONTAINER PLANTS
- ❍ Sow tender perennials for a late display, page 124

SHRUBS, TREES & CLIMBERS
- ❍ Summer-prune vigorous shrubs and climbers, page 124
- ❍ Take semi-ripe cuttings, page 125

ROSES
- ❍ Deadhead roses to stimulate more flowers, page 125

LAWNS & HEDGES
- ❍ Prepare lawn sites for sowing or turfing, page 126
- ❍ Seed a new lawn, page 126
- ❍ Trim hedges before growth slows down, page 128

VEGETABLES & HERBS
- ❍ Protect late sowings from sun and then from frost, page 128
- ❍ Sow Chinese vegetables for autumn and winter use, page 129

FRUIT
- ❍ Make new strawberry beds and propagate from old plants, page 129
- ❍ Summer-prune trained fruit, page 130
- ❍ Cut down spent raspberry canes, page 131

MISCELLANEOUS
- ❍ Take steps to discourage slugs, page 131

BORDER PERENNIALS

Looking out for seedlings

When you grow old-fashioned cottage garden plants, weeding ceases to be a chore and becomes a treasure hunt. It's essential that you do the job by hand or you may be guilty of hoeing out hundreds of free bonus plants.

Many flowering plants will seed themselves in the borders without your having to lift a finger. That has nothing to do with plants having developed a good aim; it's simply that, to be sure of success, they have been equipped with the ability to produce seeds by the thousand. Most of these will land in places that are unsuitable – sun-lovers land in the shade or vice versa, or small seedlings lose the battle against competition from larger plants. But just a few will finish up right on the perfect spot and thrive.

So when you're weeding, look out for seedlings of plants like aquilegias, Jacob's ladder, opium poppies and foxgloves. They may take a bit of recognising at first, but you'll soon get used to it. Some plants are renowned for their self-seeding: hellebores (see page 91), red valerian (*Centranthus*), sweet rocket (*Hesperis*), English or pot marigolds (*Calendula*), the prolific fried egg plant (*Limnanthes*) and Welsh poppies (*Meconopsis cambrica*) which tolerate fairly dense shade. Bowles' Golden Grass (*Milium effusum* 'Aureum') also seeds all over the place and always looks good wherever it falls, like a spring gloss of bright yellow between other plants in sun or shade. They're all worth saving.

ABOVE Bushy branching sunflowers such as these 'Sungold' are a perfect backdrop for late lilies and free-flowering marguerites.

My advice would be to collect everything and anything, provided you're prepared for a few disappointments. Most plants grown from seed are unique, like fingerprints, so there's always the chance you might find something new and exciting. Well-established annuals, hardy perennials and shrubs usually come fairly true to type every time, resembling the parent plants with only minor variations. But others, like aquilegias, poppies and hellebores, are very promiscuous and will cross-pollinate with just about anything. It pays sometimes to intervene before plants set seed, just to sway the odds a bit – for example, some forms such as mauve poppies and common purple foxgloves will predominate, but if you cull these before they set seed you'll raise the chances of getting something special.

BULBS

Planting Madonna lilies

It might seem a strange time to be planting lilies, but the lovely Madonna lily (*Lilium candidum*) is dormant just about now. Next month the bulbs start producing basal leaves which will stay there all winter, so now's the best moment to get them in. You'll probably have to buy bulbs by mail order from a specialist, but they're worth the effort. The lilies have been favourites ever since the days of ancient Crete and in medieval times were popularly associated with the Virgin Mary, hence their name.

The bulbs like a warm sunny position in well-drained soil, and always did well in cottage gardens where they were sheltered at the base by other plants. Unlike other lilies, it's important to plant them shallowly, just below the surface with a covering of no more than 2.5–5cm (1–2in) of soil. Give them a good dressing of compost and a handful of general fertiliser after flowering, and they'll keep on stunning you every summer with their pure white, heavily scented flowers on stems that are 1.2m (4ft) high or more.

Planting autumn-flowering bulbs

I like to plant autumn-flowering bulbs in late August or early September, but finding them in the shops is the difficult part of the job. The answer is mail order, and if you send for them early this month you'll still have time to get them in for flowering this year.

The well-known 'autumn crocus' is popular, although it isn't a crocus at all but a *Colchicum*; it's also known as 'meadow saffron', though it isn't saffron coloured either but rather pale lilac (in my view, this kind of muddle is one of the best arguments for sticking to Latin names). Whatever you call it, it's an eye-catching bulb, but it can look a bit naked without leaves and it also tends to flop in wet weather. Avoid both problems by planting it in grass or where it can show through other low-growing plants for support and modesty.

There are proper crocuses that flower in autumn. The most popular are the purple or white *C. speciosus* and the true saffron crocus (*C. sativus*). This has lilac flowers with darker veins and a purple eye, and vivid red stamens from which saffron spice is derived. *C. speciosus* will tolerate some shade, but the saffron crocus needs full sun. Plant all these kinds under a 10cm (4in) covering of soil.

Nerines are beautiful flowers from South Africa, and a good clump will make you the envy of your gardening friends. The flowers are produced before the leaves, like the autumn crocuses, the spikes bearing anything up to eight or nine blooms, with pink curling petals revealing purple stamens. You'll certainly need patience with these, because they're not too fond of cold weather. The only one that's frost-hardy is *Nerine bowdenii*, and even with this I would suggest that northern gardeners grow it in a large pot, and bring it in to a cold greenhouse or conservatory for the winter. Elsewhere you can plant the bulbs at the foot of a south-facing wall or fence in full sunlight. They need a real baking in summer if they're to flower well, so plant them with the top of the bulb level with the soil surface.

BELOW Humidity is important under glass, and most plants appreciate misting over at this time of year.

CONTAINER PLANTS

Sowing for late colour

If you've got opened packets of half-hardy annuals with some seeds left over from spring sowing, try using them up this month to provide a late batch of plants to flower in autumn and winter in containers. The naturally high temperatures and long day-length will bring them through in no time and they'll still be able to make small bushy plants for tucking into containers outdoors in sheltered sunny spots.

Alternatively you could also take some soft cuttings of ageratum, the dwarf *Begonia semperflorens*, busy lizzies, petunias and even lobelia, and insert several in a small pot to grow on unthinned and to flower late as excellent pot plants.

SHRUBS, TREES & CLIMBERS

Summer-pruning vigorous shrubs and climbers

Gardening advice is not always as realistic as it could be. I'm just as guilty as any 'expert' because we all preach perfection, even though many gardeners don't have the time to follow our advice to the letter.

For example, it is recommended that wisteria should be pruned every August by reducing sideshoots to 3–5 leaves. That's all right on small plants, but if yours covers the whole house it'll take for ever. And then you're exhorted to go back and do it again in February. Personally I'd prune large plants back wherever they're not wanted, and leave it at that. This is the time of year that one is in the garden and notices these things, and it's better to prune now than not at all. I honestly don't think that exact pruning makes that much difference to flowering, and if your wisteria doesn't flower it's more likely that it's facing the wrong way, or it may be too young.

Rambler roses are another sore point. They get very tangled and are much more difficult to prune than many books imply. So if you're growing something vigorous like an 'Albertine', you'll have to modify the instructions. Give the plant its head for the first few years, tying in the shoots to cover as much space as possible. Start pruning in the third year, remembering that the rose flowers on the previous year's wood. Try to prune those sideshoots that have flowered back to within a couple of inches of the stem. Then tie in the new shoots for flowering next year.

RIGHT While still relatively small, pampas grass (*Cortaderia*) is an excellent choice for providing clumps of evergreen foliage in a warm sunny border, where blue agapanthus is also very much at home.

In fact there's more latitude with pruning than many of us suspect. For example, I once bought a *Eucalyptus pauciflora* 'Nana', which I naturally expected to be dwarf with a name like that. But it actually grew to about 15m (50ft). Fed up with this spindly giant I took the saw to it one August, but only after noticing a fine crop of healthy shoots growing from the base of the trunk. Now I grow it as a shrub and prune it back every year – February is the time for this according to the books but, like a lot of pruning, it's sometimes best carried out when you see the plant really needs it, and have the time and inclination to do it.

Taking semi-ripe cuttings

This is a wonderful time of year for visiting friends and relatives – not for social reasons, but for pure selfish gain. Their shrubs will be fine and bushy by now, and they won't miss a cutting or two. Before you go plundering it's a good idea to be prepared, as the cuttings will need instant attention when you get home. The best way is to make a cuttings frame, as explained in May (see page 81), and then just grab a few plastic bags and you're ready.

Many of the shrubs that I've found difficult to propagate from soft cuttings in early summer – box, hebe, santolina, and so on – seem to root quite freely at this time of year, but it's semi-ripe material that you use now. Look for cuttings that are about 8cm (3in) long and just going woody at the base.

There's no need at this time of year to keep the pots in the greenhouse or propagator, and they're in fact much better outdoors as long as you protect them from drying out. They'll be perfectly safe in a shaded frame, but you could strike the cuttings direct into a bed prepared with plenty of sharp sand and then covered with a large glass or polythene cloche – shade it with diluted white emulsion and they'll root in no time.

ROSES

Deadheading

The sole object of any flowering plant is to produce seed. But if you prevent it from doing so, it'll go on trying until the frosts come along and curtail its efforts.

So the quicker you remove faded flowers from annuals, tender perennials and roses, the more they'll produce. It can be backbreaking and perhaps fiddly but, like weeding, it has the advantage of getting your nose right down there among the plants. Find out first, though, whether your roses produce attractive hips before you deadhead them, because if they do, you must obviously leave the dying flowers on.

Rugosa roses, for example, are noted for their huge hips like crab apples, while many *Rosa moyesii* hybrids, such as 'Geranium', 'Highdownensis' and 'Sealing Wax', have vivid red flagon-shaped hips. It would be pointless deadheading these, but most other roses will benefit, especially floribundas: they look tidier and will usually flower for longer. It's also a chance to do a bit of light pruning, so take your secateurs too, and cut each spent head back down at least to the first good leaf bud you come to – you can reduce the stem further if it looks rather long, always cutting just above an outward-facing bud or strong sideshoot. This will help shape up the plants as well as promote more growth.

BELOW The species rose, *R. moyesii*, is noted for its conspicuous red hips: 'Sealing Wax' has some of the largest and brightest.

LAWNS & HEDGES

Preparing to sow or turf a lawn

The two great talents you need for creating a wonderful lawn are a good eye and big feet – policemen should have the best lawns going. Whether you start with seed or turf, the preparation is really the secret of success and needs doing at least a month before you sow or turf, which is why I'm telling you about it now.

Start by digging over the whole area one spade deep, at the same time removing every perennial weed – docks, dandelions, daisies, buttercups and so on – together with all their root fragments. If there's a real mass of tangled weeds such as couch grass or ground elder, it could be worth spraying with glyphosate herbicide just this once. If you find the soil is really heavy and wet, make sure you don't have a 'hard pan' underneath – a solid layer caused by compaction – which you will have to break through.

Then simply dig in about a barrow-load of coarse grit per square metre to improve drainage, and as much manure or spent mushroom compost as you can spare. After that, leave the soil for a few weeks to allow annual seeds to germinate and for the soil to settle. When the weeds show themselves, hoe them off and you're ready to start levelling. And this is where your eye and feet come in.

Level with the back of a fork first and then go back over every square centimetre of soil, treading it down hard – provided the surface is dry it doesn't matter how firmly you tread, the grass will love it. It's a much more effective method than using a roller, which can ride over low patches leaving them soft. Then rake the soil level, stepping back from time to time to crouch down and squint across the surface: that way, the high and low spots are easy to see. When you're really satisfied, you can start sowing or turfing, either in September or in April, although spring sowing may involve more watering later.

Sowing the lawn

Don't be over-optimistic in your choice of grass seed. The finest mixtures look good on the packet, but need very regular attention: mowing twice a week, feeding, top-dressing, spiking and raking are all necessary to keep it in tip-top condition. If your children want to play football on it, forget the bowling green look and go for a tough rye-grass mixture – life is far too short to be forever nagging about the lawn.

Allow for 50g/sq.m (1½oz/sq.yd), although you can use less – it just takes longer to establish. Spread the seed thinly over the area, and go over it again with whatever's left until you've used all the seed. I find a good way is to put two 23cm (9in) plastic pots one inside the other, with the holes in the bottom misaligned; then you simply fill the top pot with grass seed and shake them over the soil surface. Rake the seed in using a spring-tine lawn rake, aiming to cover up at least half the seeds, and then stand back and wait for germination, which

RIGHT A well-tended lawn can be like a cool calm oasis when enclosed by meandering borders packed to the edges with vigorous flowering plants.

should take about a couple of weeks. If shortage of water might be a problem, have a hose and sprinkler to hand just to wet the surface from time to time.

If you feel all this is too much trouble and would prefer a faster result, see page 168 where I pass on the secret of laying turf successfully.

Trimming hedges

Because we all crave privacy and shelter from wind in our gardens, speed of growth is the name of the game when it comes to hedges. But by their very nature, most fast-growing plants that are suitable for the purpose just keep on going. So you need to keep an eagle eye on them while they're young and restrain them when necessary.

With most hedging plants, you simply let them go until they reach a little higher than the required height before cutting them back.

TRIMMING HEDGES

Fix a brightly coloured string to a couple of posts positioned at either end of the required cut, and trim by hand about 8–10cm (3–4in) in from the edge all along the line, using the string as a guide. Once you've established this finished level, take down the string and posts and finish the rest by eye with shears or a hedge trimmer.

Conifers can be allowed to grow 90cm (3ft) taller than needed, before pruning them back to 15cm (6in) below that height to develop a bushy top (see page 114). Beech and hornbeam are treated in the same way, but let them grow only 30cm (12in) taller than you want. Quickthorn and privet are best cut back hard after planting to force them to bush out right from the base. Privet is then trimmed two or three times in the summer, as shown on the left, while quickthorn is trimmed now if you want to have the pleasure of the flowers, or in spring if you want to keep it neater.

Formal hedges of box, yew or other evergreens will need attention even though you trimmed them to an immaculate finish in spring. Growth will be slowing down soon, so if you clip them now they should keep their strict outlines through the coming autumn and winter.

Whether you've got a new hedge or an established one, now is an ideal time for trimming. I like to cut my hedge by eye, stepping back every now and then just to make sure it's going right. After all these years I jolly well ought to be able to get the tops straight. But it's not easy, especially if you're using a power hedge trimmer.

I reckon cutting hedges with shears is by far the most accurate and satisfying way, but for a big expanse it's unrealistic. I use a petrol-engined machine, but there are many excellent mains electric models too; make sure you fit a circuit breaker to the socket before you use one, though – it could save your life. There are also battery machines which will do a good job for anything up to an hour or more before they need recharging.

VEGETABLES & HERBS

Protecting young seedlings

This is really the last chance to sow salads and a few other quick-maturing crops for harvesting later this year; but with temperatures normally so high this month, the sowings and seedlings need some shade to keep them comfortably cool. I provide the shade by draping a bit of 1.2m (6ft) wide windbreak material over the framework of my cloches. These consist of lengths of alkathene water pipe pushed into the ground to make large hoops spanning my 1.2m (4ft) wide beds (see page 35). In winter these are covered with polythene, but at this time of year I cover them instead with shading material which stays on until the weather turns cooler.

LATE SALAD CROPS TO SOW THIS MONTH

Restrict lettuces now to fast growing varieties such as 'Tom Thumb' or 'Little Gem', which should mature in about ten weeks. Try sowing some corn salad, which will carry on cropping through the winter, as will land cress. The endive 'Sally' is a great success if sown this month – the crisp self-blanching hearts staying in good condition until Christmas. Radishes are worth sowing too, both summer kinds such as 'French Breakfast' and 'Sparkler', and also cold-tolerant varieties like 'Robino' or 'Ribella', and winter 'China Rose' or 'Black Spanish'. And you may also try a hardy spring onion like 'Winter White Bunching'.

ABOVE Sheltered by a sunflower screen, rows of 'Primo' cabbages and 'Atlantic Giant' pumpkins almost fill the bed.

Then, if some of the crops fail to mature before cold weather sets in, I put clear polythene over the hoops for a more or less guaranteed harvest at the end of the year.

Before sowing try to rake some compost into the top 5cm (2in) of soil to assist water retention. I also use a sprinkle of pelleted chicken manure to feed the plants. Make sure the seeds have enough moisture to get them through the soil by taking out a shallow drill for sowing and watering it first. Allow the water to drain away, then sow the seeds and cover them with dry soil – then try not to water until the seedlings are showing through.

Growing Chinese vegetables

Many oriental leaf vegetables are used to cool summers and mild winters. It's easy to protect the sensitive varieties from the frost, but our hot summers often cause a lot of them to bolt to flower, which is why they're recommended for sowing after the longest day. They're particularly useful because they'll grow right through the autumn, only stopping when it gets really cold, and even then a cloche or two will keep them going.

I suggest you start with the familiar Chinese cabbage, essential for autumn salads and stir-fries. The newer F_1 hybrids 'Green Rocket' and 'Tip Top' make tall cylindrical heads packed with crisp leaves. Grow plants about 38cm (15in) apart each way, and make sure they never go short of water.

Chinese kale, also called Chinese broccoli, can be harvested about 10–12 weeks from sowing. You can space plants of a variety like 'Green Lance' as close as 25cm (10in) apart and you'll soon be cutting fat heads of flower buds a bit like calabrese – smaller sideshoots follow, but you can also eat the stems if you peel off the tough skin.

I wouldn't be without the spicy leaves of mustard greens or Chinese mustard, which are grown in the same way as Chinese kale. For a milder flavour, harvest them young by snipping leaves off with scissors; but if you prefer something a bit hotter, leave them longer and they'll really add some spice to your cuisine.

FRUIT

Planting strawberries

If you don't already have strawberries, now is the time to buy some – either as bare-rooted plants or you can pay a bit more and get pot-grown ones which get away much faster.

Once you have bought your plants, you'll need to make a bed to plant them in. Raised beds are now all the rage commercially, but have

STRAWBERRIES THROUGH THE SEASON

I reckon it's possible to start eating strawberries in May and continue until the first frosts. The basic sequence starts with 'Honeyoye' – buy twice as many of these as of later varieties, so you can cover half of them with cloches in February to get an even earlier crop. Follow these with the maincrop 'Tenira', not as heavy-yielding as the standard 'Elsanta' but much tastier. After this the perpetual variety 'Aromel' will keep supplies going until beyond late summer.

I also grow the French variety 'Mara des Bois', which is as large as ordinary cultivated kinds but has the distinct flavour of wild strawberries – and what's more, it produces one crop in the spring and another in the autumn. Finally, I wouldn't be without 'Cambridge Late Pine', which is an old strawberry raised just after the last war, and well worth keeping going: its flavour is unique, very sweet and aromatic.

PROPAGATING AND FORCING STRAWBERRIES

Use a wire 'hairpin' to peg plantlets down, either direct in the ground or in 8cm (3in) pots of compost. Once rooted, the plantlets can be detached from their parents.

been used in gardens for years and are still reckoned the best method. Make the beds about 1.2m (4ft) wide, dig them over thoroughly and incorporate lots of well-rotted manure or compost. This should raise the surface about 8–15cm (3–6in) above the paths, and you can either keep this in place with edging boards or simply mound up sloping sides with a rake.

Cover the beds with black polythene, buried at the edges, and plant through cross-slits cut in the plastic at 60cm (2ft) intervals. That way there'll be no weeding to do, no need to mulch with straw later on, and very little watering either, especially if you install buried irrigation. For this you need a 'leaky pipe', which oozes droplets of water along its length once it is connected to a hose. Run a pipe down each side of the bed, about 30cm (12in) in from the edge, before you set the black plastic in place.

Tidying and propagating strawberries

By this time of year your plants will have finished fruiting, and many young runners will have started rooting into the soil between the parent plants. If you don't want to grow more plants, you can use a rotary mower to cut down the main plant so that only the bare crown is left in the centre. If you do want to propagate more plants, use a pair of shears to cut down the parent plant to ensure you don't disturb the runners. Then select the best plantlets and pin them down as shown on the left.

Forcing strawberries

If you want to have the earliest possible fruit, transfer a few rooted plantlets to 13cm (5in) pots. Leave these outside where you'll notice them and remember to water if necessary. In December, turn them on their sides: they'll have stopped growing by then, and should not be allowed to get waterlogged or they'll rot off. After a good cold rest they'll be bursting to grow, so in February bring them indoors – into the greenhouse or on to a sunny windowsill. Remember you'll need to fertilise the open flowers by dabbing each one with a soft paintbrush, because there'll be few insects around that early. Even without any heat you'll still be picking fruit weeks ahead of outdoor crops, but a little warmth will bring them on even earlier.

Summer-pruning tree fruit

In Victorian times head gardeners were a feared and respected race, but I reckon they actually made the art of pruning seem more difficult than it really is in order to preserve their superior place. But nature gives you a helping hand along the way, so it's not nearly as difficult as some would make out – in fact, pruning apples, pears and soft fruit like gooseberries and red currants can be as complicated or as simple as you want to make it.

Trained forms – cordons, fans, espaliers and so on (see page 68) – are pruned now rather than in winter. Since cordons are the easiest

PRUNING FRUIT TREES

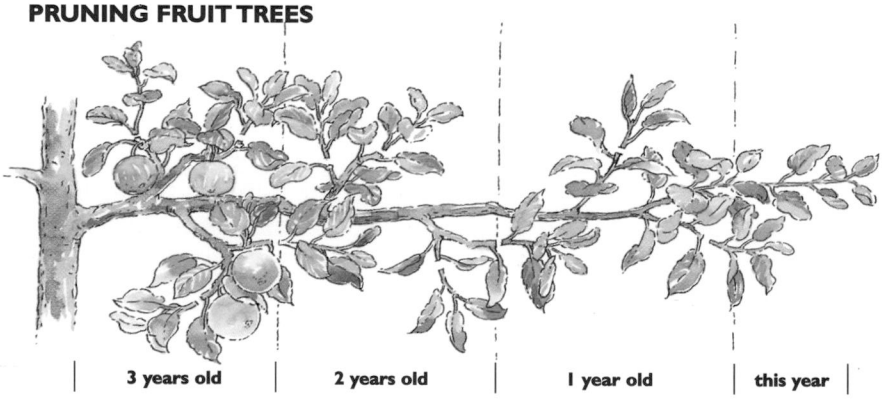

Each year the new growth of the main sideshoots can be pruned back to about 8cm (3in), cutting just above a bud to form new fruiting spurs.

Also shorten any new shoots growing from established spurs to 2.5cm (1in) long, again cutting just above a bud.

LEFT Many vegetables make decorative foliage plants, and few can rival the lush extravagance of courgettes or the towering magnificence of runner beans.

form to explain, let's start with these. They consist of one or more stems, on which you build up collections of short twiggy sideshoots called 'spurs', and it's on these that the fruit is borne. The main leading shoot will be needed to increase the length of the stem, so leave that alone until it reaches full height, then cut off the tip and turn it into a spur.

Espaliers and fans are no more complicated: each is a series of branches, and all you do is treat each branch as if it were a cordon. So once you've spent about 10 minutes on each tree, you can happily pass the rest of the day making apple pie – or eating it.

Dealing with raspberries

Once summer raspberries have been harvested, cut out the old canes and tie in the strong new ones 10cm (4in) apart.

MISCELLANEOUS

Discouraging slugs

One of the biggest threats to plants in any garden is slugs, which seem to be on the rampage for most of the year. Soft young leaf growth is the gourmet slug's version of a Waldorf salad, and as yet there's no final answer to the problem. But there's a lot we can do to give our plants a helping hand.

First, get nature on your side. If slugs are hungry, birds and black beetles and frogs are even hungrier, and these will eat both the slugs and their eggs. The eggs, and later on the baby slugs, are often just below the soil surface and regular hoeing will turn them up for the birds or carabid beetles. To catch the night-feeding adult slugs, put out a few boards or bits of tile or slate for them to hide under at daybreak; then simply turn them over to expose them to their enemies.

Cut-down plastic bottles are effective barriers – select vulnerable plants like young hostas, lupins and delphiniums, and all brassicas, and surround them with a plastic screen pressed a little way into the soil. I'm doubtful about the effectiveness of rough materials like toasted eggshells and gritty ash. A collar of lime works for brassicas, but for other plants it may change the acidity of the soil too much. Soot is an effective barrier and does nothing but good to the soil provided it is weathered for a few months. If you can bear to do it, picking up slugs and snails, or trapping them and then disposing of them can help a bit, but alas, there will be thousands, so you can never hope to win. Hunt them down at night with a torch – and don't give in to the temptation to throw them next door, because they have the homing instinct of pigeons.

I haven't mentioned pellets because I worry about the risk they pose to wildlife, although evidence of this is fairly rare. They are certainly the most effective control, but I never use them myself. If the problem gets really out of hand and slugs become a serious plague, you might have to admit defeat and not grow susceptible plants like hostas. Remember though, a cold winter may not thin the slug population much, but it does kill a lot of their eggs, which is something to be said in favour of hard frost.

PLANTS FOR

august

1 Commonly known as bergamot, bee balm or Oswego tea, hardy perennial *Monarda didyma* develops into a neat clump of 90cm (3ft) herbaceous flowering stems, in a number of warm colours.

2 The large hollyhock-like blooms of *Lavatera* 'Barnsley' open in profusion all summer and cover the 1.8m (6ft) hardy shrubs with masses of conspicuous 5cm (2in) flowers. These are pure white with a red eye, fading to a soft pink.

3 *Bracteantha* (formerly *Helichrysum*) *bracteata* 'Drakkar Mixed' is the familiar straw flower, with brightly coloured papery petals. Often used for dried indoor arrangements, it is sown under glass as a half-hardy annual and grows up to 90cm (3ft) high.

1

2

3

4 The late-flowering clematis 'Madame Julia Correvon' is a viticella hybrid. Very hardy, it grows to 4m (13ft) eventually; both foliage and blooms are larger than others of its type, and the flower display is long and generous.

5 *H. paniculata* 'Grandiflora' is one of the showiest hydrangeas. Very hardy and shade-tolerant, it is 3m (10ft) or more tall and wide, with vigorous open woody stems. Annual pruning and mulching promotes large blooms.

4

5

Early autumn was the time for new plants to go into the borders. Before they were planted, Geoff would read up everything he could about them. He was very particular about naming them correctly, as well as about giving them the best possible conditions. He might talk about plants using their common names, but he always knew the botanical ones. He once said that although a little learning can be a dangerous thing, a little Latin could be very helpful. If, for example, you knew that 'flore pleno' simply meant a double version of a flower you were half way to visualizing it. The only trouble with having studied Latin myself was that his botanical Latin sometimes clashed with my classical Latin – in the pronunciation of such names as 'Senecio', for example. However, as I adjusted to his over the years, I found my Latin vocabulary broadening – for instance, I hadn't realised that 'flavus' meant yellow.

Ornamental grasses make forceful statements in a large border, where dwarf pampas grass, *Cortaderia pumila*, flowers behind the sword-like leaves of phormium and the arching heads of *Pennisetum alopecurioides*.

september

key tasks for september

ANNUALS & BEDDING PLANTS

- ❍ Take cuttings of bedding plant, before the first frosts, page 136
- ❍ Prepare tender perennials, including dahlias and fuchsias, for over-wintering, page 137

BORDER PERENNIALS

- ❍ Overhaul borders, planting and dividing hardy perennials, page 138
- ❍ Collect and sow ripe seeds, page 139

ROSES

- ❍ Take cuttings of roses, page 139
- ❍ Save and sow seeds from rose hips, page 139

BULBS

- ❍ Plant bulbs outdoors for next spring and summer, page 140
- ❍ Force hyacinths for Christmas, page 141

LAWNS

- ❍ Give lawns a little early autumn care, taking out weeds and 'thatch', page 142

VEGETABLES & HERBS

- ❍ Store squashes for winter, page 142
- ❍ Prepare onions for lifting, and plant new sets, page 142
- ❍ Plant and sow spring cabbages, page 142

FRUIT

- ❍ Protect, pick and store tree fruits, page 144

MISCELLANEOUS

- ❍ Consider buying a greenhouse before winter sets in, page 144

ANNUALS & BEDDING PLANTS

Taking cuttings of bedding plants

Tender perennial bedding plants, usually grown as summer annuals, are all likely to be hit by the frosts quite soon. Pelargoniums, petunias, marguerites, fuchsias, abutilons, diascias and those wonderful South African osteospermums are all at risk, but there are ways to ensure their survival unscathed over winter. If you haven't room to keep the old plants safe under glass until next spring, try taking cuttings, which is very easy to do at this time of year.

Choose a strong healthy young shoot about 8cm (3in) long, and trim it just below a leaf joint with a sharp knife. Remove the bottom leaves, leaving two or perhaps three at the top, and cut off pelargonium stipules, those small green 'leaves' underneath each leaf stalk. Pelargonium cuttings can be dibbled into compost straight away, but other kinds are best plunged into a fungicide solution, and their cut ends then dipped in hormone rooting powder.

Insert the cuttings to half their depth in cuttings compost, or you can make your own from equal parts of peat-free compost and vermiculite. Arrange the cuttings around the edge of 10cm (4in) pots or, if you have a lot, use modules – these are like large seed trays divided into separate cells, and you just put one cutting in each cell.

Place in a shaded frame for a few weeks until rooted, and then pot them up individually into 8cm (3in) pots. As soon as frost threatens, bring them inside, into a conservatory or spare room kept at least frost-free and ideally at 7°C (45°F). Don't put the pots on a windowsill, because it will be too cold: instead, arrange a table near the window and draw the curtains at night for protection.

Keep the cuttings fairly dry during winter and don't feed at all. They'll tick over until the end of February, when you can bring them into the kitchen or sitting room where it's warmer. Start to feed with liquid fertiliser, and they'll grow into fine young plants for putting out in late May or early June.

Over-wintering tender perennials

All those glorious perennials need last-minute care to make sure they are safe all winter until you coax them back into growth next spring.

Dahlias should really be left outdoors until the frost blackens their foliage before you dig them up for storing in a frost-free place. Lift the tubers, shake off as much soil as you can, and then trim off all the old stems. Tip the tubers upside down to drain for a week, then pack them, right way up, in cardboard boxes, and store them in a cool greenhouse or a spare room.

Perennial salvias such as *S. patens* can be lifted after the frost has finished off their tops, and will keep safely in a little moist compost under the greenhouse staging. The more familiar scarlet salvias will also keep from one year to the next if you pot them up and keep them just moist in good light.

The dusky maroon *Cosmos atrosanguineus* can be treated like a dahlia, or in milder counties you could risk it outdoors under a thick mulch of bark. Marguerites (argyranthemums) can be potted up like houseplants and will often flower into the winter, or you can store them like pelargoniums, only not quite so dry.

ABOVE A small border can support an amazing variety of plants, with productive kinds such as artichokes and perennial onions tucked among summer flowers, provided the soil is regularly fortified with compost or well-rotted manure.

Potting up fuchsias

Tender fuchsias that have been bedded out or used for hanging baskets can be treated in two ways. Either fork them up and pot them in fairly small pots, and then bring them into a heated greenhouse or a cool well-lit room to carry on growing. Otherwise cut the tops back by half, pot them up and leave them in a cold but frost-free place. Don't let them dry out, but avoid over-watering. In the spring trim them back further to leave about 2.5–5cm (1–2in) of last year's shoots (see page 41).

BORDER PERENNIALS

This is a good time to start overhauling borders, because you will still be able to see where everything is and how much space it takes up. Start with the herbaceous perennials this month, move on to evergreen shrubs next and get on to the deciduous shrubs after their leaves have fallen.

Planting new perennials

Garden centres often stock a good range of perennials in 10cm (4in) pots at this time of year. If they're reasonably priced you can buy four or five to plant in groups to join up quickly and make large clumps.

Revive as large an area of soil as you can: work in well-rotted manure, garden compost or spent mushroom compost for all but acid borders. New plants will also benefit from a little general organic fertiliser or pelleted chicken manure. Prepare the whole area, not just planting holes because these can act as sumps and drown the plants.

When you knock the plants out of their pots, check to see if the roots are running round the bottom in a tight coil. If they are, ease them out a little so that they start to grow out and search for water and food. After planting, even if the soil is quite wet, water the plants in. This gives them a good start and also helps to settle the soil around the roots – they shouldn't need any more water until the spring.

Dividing old perennials

Most herbaceous plants thrive on being lifted, split up and replanted every 3–5 years. But it's worth looking them up in a book, because some, including the ice plant (*Sedum*) and yarrow (*Achillea*) like this treatment every year, and a few, particularly gypsophila and peonies, prefer to stay put. Others, such as alstroemerias and Japanese anemones, take a season or two to settle down after being disturbed.

Some perennials might have outgrown their allotted space, while others will have an ugly bald patch in the centre of the clump with all the young growth on the outside. These should all be lifted with a fork and put on to a large piece of polythene. You can often break or cut off a few juicy young bits from the outside of the clump with a spade. These are then transplanted into soil revitalised with plenty of good compost, while the tired old centres are thrown away. Or you can split clumps with two digging forks inserted back to back to divide them into smaller pieces.

LEFT Against background hints of early autumn mists, the Rugosa rose 'Roseraie de l'Hay' draws to the end of its long flowering season, while *Cosmos* 'Sensation', always at its best in autumn, blooms profusely.

Collecting seeds

Collecting seeds is the cheapest way to produce hundreds of extra plants, and it's great fun to do. Choose a dry day and look for flower heads containing brown dry seedpods. Cut the whole head and put it into a paper bag – don't forget to label it clearly. If the seedheads are even the slightest bit damp though, lay them on newspaper to dry.

After a week or so, tip the contents onto a sheet of paper. Often the seeds will have fallen out, but if not, break open the pods and shake them out. However careful you are, you can't avoid a mixture of seeds and chaff, which must be separated because it's the chaff that harbours diseases. Use a flour sieve or the point of a knife, or simply blow the chaff away gently.

Most hardy perennial seeds can be sown straight away on top of moist compost and covered with a shallow layer of coarse grit. Put them in a cold frame and they'll either germinate in a few weeks' time or next spring. Half-hardy seeds should be stored in labelled envelopes in a cool dry place for sowing next spring in gentle heat.

SELF-SET SEEDLINGS

Many plants shed seeds naturally to produce seedlings for the following year, and it's a pity to waste them. Some, like opium poppies for example, can be left where they grow to flower in natural groups. Others such as hellebores are best lifted and transplanted at the seedling stage, or they'll create too much competition for their parents.

ROSES

If you're particularly fond of one or two roses in the garden, why not try and propagate a few more from cuttings or seeds? They may not come true, and some varieties are reluctant to form roots, but if you're prepared for the occasional loss, it's worth having a go.

Taking rose cuttings

You can take cuttings any time from now until about Christmas but, like all hardwood cuttings, you'll be more successful while the soil still has some summer warmth left in it. Look for strong healthy stems about pencil-thick, and cut them low down on the bush. Deal with them as shown on the right.

You can avoid the need for weeding by preparing an area as big as you'll need in advance, digging it a spade deep and working in a little sharp sand and good garden compost on heavy soil. Once you've buried the cuttings, cover the area with woven plastic mulching sheet, making slits to let the rose cuttings poke through to the light. Bury the edges of the sheet in the soil to secure it. After that there's nothing to worry about until transplanting time, about a year later.

Roses from seed

Most species of rose come true to type from seed. Just gather a hip or two, split them open and remove the seeds. Sow these straight away in a pot or tray of well-drained seed compost, and cover with a layer of grit. Put a piece of wire netting over the pot to deter mice, and place in a cold frame. Seedlings may appear this coming spring, or next.

TAKING ROSE CUTTINGS

1 Cut stems of at least the thickness of a pencil, preferably just above a new shoot.

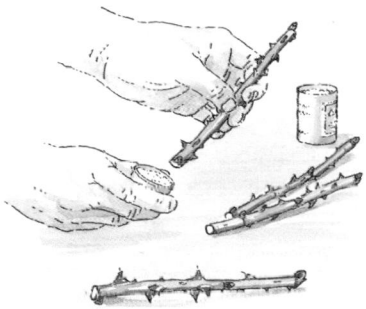

2 Trim the bottom to just below a bud, and the top to just above one, leaving the cuttings about 20–23cm (8–9in) long. Dip the bottoms in hormone rooting powder

3 Cover the bottom of a slit trench with coarse sand, then bury the cuttings, leaving about 8cm (3in) above soil level.

BULBS

Planting spring bulbs

There's a whole range of bulbs on offer about now that are almost guaranteed to provide a bright and cheering show for you next spring. The ones to start off with are daffodils: if they have the chance to make a really good root system before the worst of winter, they'll reward you with better and earlier flowers. The flowering season is said to last for a hundred days, starting with the earliest, the small cyclamineus varieties which appear in February, and ending with Pheasant's Eye kinds such as 'Actaea', which are usually still flowering in May.

As with all bulbs, it's essential to plant them at the right depth because shallow planting is one reason why they can go blind after the first year. As a general rule, get all bulbs in so they are covered with 2–3 times their own depth in soil.

Tulips are best left until last – planting them in early November (see page 166) helps protect them against slug damage and the fungus disease tulip fire.

Crocuses are popular favourites that go in now, as soon as possible, and there's a huge selection to choose from, either as single colours or (more cheaply) as mixtures; one of the earliest is *C. tommasinianus*. All are best planted in large informal groups in the sun; cover them with about 5cm (2in) of soil.

There are several ornamental onions (*Allium*) which make a bold display, generally with rounded flower heads. Short-stemmed *A. moly* and *A. ostrowskianum* are for the front of the border, but there are other later-flowering kinds that are much taller. For example, *A. giganteum*, *A. rosenbachianum* and *A.* 'Gladiator' can reach 1.2–1.5m (4–5ft) and look splendid in the middle or back of the border. Leave them undisturbed and they will form quite large clumps.

Anemone blanda is one of the best and most reliable of the small spring-flowering bulbs, and ideal for a shady spot under deciduous shrubs. It makes large clumps of brightly coloured daisies in shades of blue, and there's a pure white form too. The crown imperial fritillaries (*Fritillaria imperialis*) have been grown in cottage gardens for centuries and are not to be missed. They produce large yellow or orange flowers on tall stout stems, but cover them with at least 10cm (4in) of soil or they may not flower in future years. Smaller fritillaries such as our native snake's head (*F. meleagris*) are superb in retentive soil in sun or part shade.

Work in a bit of garden compost and a light dressing of organic fertiliser before planting in the ground or in containers. The answer to the problem of untidy bulb foliage after flowering is to tuck the bulbs among herbaceous plants such as hostas, rodgersias and brunneras. When the bulbs are

NATURALISING SPRING BULBS

1 Instead of arranging bulbs formally in neat groups, scatter them in natural drifts on the surface of the grass and plant them exactly where they have fallen.

2 Lift large turves with a spade and plant several bulbs underneath each one, or use a cylindrical bulb planter to excavate a plug of soil. Plant the bulb and replace the plug.

PLANTING DEPTHS FOR BULBS

As a rule of thumb, the ideal planting depth for any bulb is roughly three times its own size from tip to base, although a little more or less isn't critical.

in flower the herbaceous plants have lost their leaves, but once the bulbs have finished, up come the hostas etc., unfurling their leaves and covering untidy foliage.

Alternatively, sow some of the hardier annuals over the bulbs: calendula, convolvulus, echium, eschscholzia, godetia, iberis and nigella are ideal. These will take over in late spring and flower until about July or August, often seeding themselves afterwards.

Starting bulbs in pots

I'm hopeless at remembering where I planted my last lot of daffodils so, instead of putting my new ones straight into the borders, I pot them up during the first part of this month, and plunge the pots in compost outdoors until the spring, as shown below.

They can stay in the plunge bed until the tips poke through in the spring. By that time, those in the borders will also be showing, so you'll know exactly where to plant the new ones. When you do, plant them deeply so that you bury the white blanched part of the stems that was covered with compost.

Planting summer bulbs

Although attention is concentrated on bulbs for spring right now, don't forget the summer-flowering ones, including galtonias and camassias, that should also go in now. Summer hyacinths (*Galtonia*) produce 90cm (3ft) tall white spires that make a fine sight in the borders, while camassias make clumps of grassy foliage, from which arise 75cm (30in) tall spires of starry flowers in shades of blue and also white. They both like rich retentive soils, bulk up quite fast, and can be split and replanted every few years.

Forcing hyacinths indoors

If you're after hyacinths for Christmas, make sure you buy specially prepared bulbs. Plant them early, certainly by the middle of this month, in separate pots or together in boxes, and put them into a shady corner covered with a good depth of moist garden compost; alternatively a cool but frost-free garage will do. The idea is to try to encourage plenty of root growth before the shoots appear.

Bring them inside into a cool room after about twelve weeks, or when the buds can be seen. When they begin to colour up transfer them to bowls, using three or five bulbs per bowl. If you do it that way, you can make sure that all the flowers are at the same stage of development for a balanced show that will perfume the whole house by Christmas week.

ABOVE An inspired partnership between autumn-flowering bulbs, *Nerine bowdenii* and *Colchicum speciosum*: both are stars of the warm sunny border at this time of year.

PLUNGING BULBS

Once potted up, hardy bulbs are best kept in a corner where it is cool but frost-free. Covering them with a thick mulch stops them freezing, and also ensures complete darkness to coax them into growth. I make a plunge bed of old compost, and cover the pots so that the bulbs are buried at the same depth as if planted outdoors.

LAWNS

Early autumn care

At this time of year, especially after a dry summer, lawns may need a spot of intensive care. Start by taking out deep-rooted weeds such as dandelions. Tackle them with a daisy grubber, one of those new tools that twist them out, root and all, or cut them out with a knife, getting down as deep as you can, but don't use a weedkiller. For weeds in large patches, use a large pruning knife or one with a curved end. If this leaves a bald patch, you can re-seed straight away by adding grass seed to a mixture of soil, garden compost and sharp sand.

Dead growth or 'thatch' may have accumulated at soil level, and where this has happened it should be scratched out with a rake.

BELOW Dead 'thatch' builds up around grass roots after a summer of mowing, and needs to be raked out vigorously.

VEGETABLES & HERBS

Storing squashes

Marrows, pumpkins and all the other winter squashes need proper seasoning before they can be stored indoors. Cut them when they are full size and a good colour, and then lay them out in the sunshine to harden for a fortnight, or in the greenhouse or a sunny window if it's wet. After this treatment they will keep in good condition in a frost-free place well into winter.

Courgettes can be stored until Christmas or so if you leave a few fruits to grow as large as small marrows. Raise them up off the ground on bricks or a piece of wood to get a sun-tan, turning them from time to time between now and the end of October. When the skins are hardened they will keep just like proper marrows and, what's more, the flavour improves with every week in store.

Preparing onions for lifting

Maincrop onions that are starting to turn yellow at the tips should be prepared for lifting now. Insert a digging fork under the bulbs and lift them slightly to loosen the roots without breaking them. This will hasten ripening, but don't bend the tops over as this can invite disease.

Planting autumn onion sets

At the same time you can plan for the next crop by planting autumn onion sets. Varieties such as 'Radar', 'Swift' and 'Unwin's First Early' mature in late June or July, so they are way ahead of the main crop, and you can even use them sooner direct from the ground. Plant them between now and early November, 8cm (3in) apart in drills just deep enough to cover the top of the set. Use about half the fertiliser application normal for summer-grown crops, and then give them a boost next March with a dressing of high nitrogen feed.

Planting spring cabbages

Spring cabbage plants sown in a seedbed last month can be planted out now, especially if you have cleared maincrop onions for storing. Simply clean and weed the bed, rake in a half-dressing of general fertiliser, then level it off and it will be ready for the young plants, spaced 15cm (6in) apart in rows 30cm (12in) apart.

Next spring you can use every other plant for spring greens, and then give the rest a feed to encourage them to heart up for later. There's still time to sow another batch of a fast variety like 'Duncan' or 'Pixie' for continuity, either in a seedbed for transplanting next month or where they are to grow, thinning the seedlings to the right spacing.

Flea beetles often attack these young cabbages, drilling tiny holes in their leaves, but here's a way to get rid of them without killing all the beneficial insects too. Take a 10 x 15cm (4 x 6in) board and coat one side with petroleum jelly or fruit tree grease. If you pass the board over the affected plants, the beetles will jump up and stick to the grease – hence the 'flea' in their name.

RIGHT The allotment garden at Barnsdale shows how much can be packed into a small space without compromising good looks: sweetcorn, tomatoes, beans and onions make maximum use of a narrow bed.

FRUIT

Protecting tree fruits

It's not a bad idea to take steps this month to protect your ripening apples, pears and other tree fruits from hungry birds. Just one peck is enough to start them rotting or to attract wasps, who promptly set upon the fruit to complete the job. In the banana plantations of Central America the trees are almost constantly festooned with polythene bags, and that's one safe bet for controlling birds. If you have the time, put a perforated clear polythene bag over the top of each ripening fruit, secure it with a twist tie, and you will be guaranteed to get there first. If you grow trained trees, it's not too difficult to cover the whole tree with netting, while on larger trees you could try hanging a few strips of brightly coloured polythene in the branches as a deterrent.

Picking and storing tree fruits

Early apples such as 'Discovery' and 'Katy' should be eaten straight from the tree, of course, because they don't store very well. But sometimes that's easier said than done, especially if birds and wasps are going for them. To foil this, I pick my apples when they're ready to eat and store them in the same way as later varieties. You can keep them in the traditional way, by wrapping them individually in paper and then laying them out in single layers in open trays in a cool shed or garage.

Another way is to put about 1kg (2lb) of undamaged apples into a polythene bag and close the top. There will be a build-up of carbon dioxide – the gas used by fruit farmers to prolong the life of fruit in cold stores – in the bag. But you don't want too much of it, so make two pinpricks in the bag and then store in as cold a place as possible (but not freezing), where the fruit should last for a couple of months.

Harvesting and storing perfect pears is a work of art. William Robinson, the great Victorian gardener, reckoned there was just one day in the year when pears would be perfect for picking. That's perhaps a bit extreme, but they're certainly difficult to time. If you like them on the hard side, it's no problem; but if you prefer them soft and juicy, you need to pick them just before they are fully ripe andthen store them on their ends in open boxes in a cool place. Bring a few at a time indoors to finish ripening for two days, to eat at their succulent best. And how do you know that perfect day when they are ready to pick? Experience – so keep experimenting!

LEFT Even early apple varieties will keep for several weeks in the cool darkness of a polythene-lined underground store.

MISCELLANEOUS

The benefits of a greenhouse

I wouldn't be able to achieve half what I do in the garden without my greenhouse. I raise all my own bedding and vegetable plants there. I overwinter tender perennials, and in summer I raise crops such as tomatoes, aubergines, cucumbers, peppers and melons, as well as flowering pot plants.

A greenhouse will pay for itself in about two years – but if you include entertainment and enjoyment, it won't owe you anything after the first month. But don't wait until the spring before getting one. Wise gardeners get one jump ahead and you could make a start straight away with protection for chrysanthemums, dahlias and

EARLY BLOOMS UNDER GLASS

As soon as you have your greenhouse, raid the perennial border for astilbes, hostas, dicentras, pulmonarias and hellebores. Young divisions of these can be potted up in containers as small as will take them comfortably. Stand them in an unheated greenhouse, or in a cold frame for bringing indoors in late February, and they'll give you a really early spring display long before outside plants have woken up. If you also buy a couple of patio roses and pot these up in the same way, they'll make an extra-early show. But don't keep the plants in the warm too long after flowering; they'll be better off planted outside once more.

ABOVE Although essentially practical, some greenhouses are attractive structures, and this octagonal cedar-wood design will double as a small decorative summerhouse.

fuchsias, and a sowing of winter vegetables such as hardy varieties of lettuces and carrots.

Choosing a greenhouse

Choice depends on your budget. Buy as big as you can afford, but remember you do get what you pay for. Small polythene ones cost a fraction of a smart aluminium house, while the permanence of glass is comforting and presents fewer problems to growing plants than plastic. Make sure there's enough ventilation: at least one roof vent per 1.2m (4ft) run is necessary, preferably side vents too, so a 2.4 x 1.8m (8 x 6ft) house should have at least two vents in the top and two in the sides. I would also recommend the built-in base most manufacturers offer – this gives a good professional finish and makes erection easier.

PLANTS FOR
september

1 The dwarf guelder rose, *Viburnum opulus* 'Compactum', forms a dense 1.5m (5ft) deciduous shrub, with showy flattened heads of white lacecap flowers in June, and red berries and leaf tints in autumn.

2 *Imperata cylindrica* 'Rubra' or Japanese blood grass, here seen with *Sedum* 'Vera Jameson', is a deciduous 45cm (18in) grass for good soils. Noted for its bright red autumn leaf tips, it is not quite hardy and benefits from winter protection.

3 The sea holly hybrid, *Eryngium* x *tripartitum*, is a branching and colourful hardy herbaceous perennial. Its 75cm (30in) stems grow from a basal rosette and are crowned with steely-blue rounded flower heads.

4 Like all its *Allium* relatives, the leek (*A. porrum*) has dramatic ornamental flower heads if plants are left for a second season.

5 *Caryopteris clandonensis,* a hardy perennial shrub, grows up to 1.2m (4ft) tall. It flowers well on most soils, especially light sandy ones, and needs hard pruning every spring.

OVERLEAF Maples are supreme trees and shrubs for autumn tints: here the rich incendiary red of *Acer palmatum* 'Osakazuki' is all the more vivid against the buttery yellow foliage of the snakebark maple, *A.* 'Silver Vein'.

1

2

3

4

5

Recording had finished by the beginning of October, leaving Geoff the time for major appraisals in the garden. Throughout the year he kept copious notes which he used as the basis of his articles and books, but also as a fount of ideas for new projects. We would walk round the garden while Geoff bounced his ideas off me, describing in detail what he could see in his mind's eye: he really was able to visualise the completed plan perfectly in 3-D.

Much as Geoff enjoyed the daily demands of the garden, especially the propagating, what excited him more than anything was the start of a big new undertaking. He'd make plans in great detail so that when they went into action, everything seemed to fall seamlessly in place. Coming home one day from the school where I taught, I found that what had been the cottage garden had disappeared from outside the kitchen window. Inspired by Beth Chatto's garden in Essex, he had decided to make a Mediterranean garden. Within a month it had taken shape and been planted. Within a couple of years it looked as though it had always been there.

Dramatic colour compositions and contrasts are typical of October: bright michaelmas daisies and the opulent foliage of purple sage blend with the changing tints of background shrubs and trees.

october

key tasks for october

CONTAINER PLANTS

- ❍ Plant up outdoor containers for winter and spring, page 152

SHRUBS, TREES & CLIMBERS

- ❍ Plant new trees and shrubs now to minimise the stress to the plants, page 153
- ❍ Take hardwood cuttings while the soil is still warm, page 156
- ❍ Move large shrubs, page 156

LAWNS & HEDGES

- ❍ Plan space for hedges, page 157
- ❍ Choose deciduous or conifer hedges, page 157
- ❍ Plant hedges of all kinds, page 158

VEGETABLES & HERBS

- ❍ Harvest root crops for storing, page 159
- ❍ Plant garlic before the weather turns cold, page 159
- ❍ Protect late vegetables against frost, page 160

FRUIT

- ❍ Harvest maincrop apples, page 160
- ❍ Protect apple and pear trees against winter moth, page 160
- ❍ Prune blackcurrants, page 160
- ❍ Invest in a fruit cage to protect next year's crops, page 160

MISCELLANEOUS

- ❍ Start digging, but take it gently, page 161
- ❍ Encourage earthworms, page 161

CONTAINER PLANTS

Containers for winter plantings

I've seen summer displays in plastic buckets, china chamber pots, and discarded boots or shoes. But for winter use, choose containers made of clay, stone or wood, which offer more protection. Make sure that they're frost-proof and, even if they are, give them the best chance of survival by avoiding waterlogging: if water freezes in a pot, it could expand and crack it. And even the hardiest plant can be vulnerable if the roots get frozen. This could seriously injure plants, especially evergreens which do not go dormant in winter and can suffer badly from dehydration if the contents of the pot are frozen solid. So before the hard frosts arrive, wrap containers all round with a few layers of bubble polythene or sacking, tied in place with string. Wet soil won't do the plants any good either, so check that there are plenty of drainage holes, and stand the containers on a few pieces of slate or tile to keep the holes clear of the ground.

Planting up pots for winter and spring

Start by putting a good layer of pebbles or broken clay pots in the bottom before filling with compost. I like to use a very free-draining mixture, which is very important for anything that's going to stand outdoors all winter – soil-based John Innes No. 1 or 2 composts are ideal. If you're replanting a pot already filled with a JI mixture, just stir in some garden or mushroom compost, plus a handful of general fertiliser. For new pots, start with

ABOVE The varied succulent stonecrops such as *Sedum telephium* 'Autumn Joy' are important flowers both for late colour in borders and containers, and as a food source for the last butterflies.

the drainage layer and then cover this with fresh potting compost, at least 15cm (6in) deep and about 23cm (9in) from the top.

Bulbs are obvious winners for early colour. Plant daffs 5–8cm (2–3in) apart, and then cover them with an 8cm (3in) depth of compost. On this set a tier of tulip bulbs, about the same distance apart – even if you inadvertently plant one right on top of a daff, the lower bulb will soon find a way through. Cover these, and then plant some bedding.

To add a bit of height, I like to use a bushy evergreen in the centre, something like a small *Viburnum tinus* or a variegated elaeagnus, such as *E. pungens* 'Maculata' or *E.* × *ebbingei* 'Limelight' which can be planted out in the garden in late spring when you change the planting scheme. Around this centrepiece you could plant wallflowers, forget-me-nots, winter pansies and bellis daisies: bear in mind there won't be a lot of growth between now and spring flowering time, so choose good bushy plants and set them in the container so that they're almost touching.

Finally push in a few small bulbs like crocus and muscari, and you'll have all the ingredients for a stunning show from early winter through to mid-spring.

SHRUBS, TREES & CLIMBERS

The best time for planting

Up to the early 1960s, nurserymen (there were no garden centres in those days) grew their plants in the field and lifted and sold them to us through the autumn and winter. Then came plants in containers, and we began to buy most of our plants in the spring when the weather warmed up a bit. But in fact the traditional autumn planting of trees and shrubs is still best, and essential for bare-rooted ones. Planting is a cause of stress for plants: they are seriously disturbed and have to get used to new conditions above and below ground.

So it's sensible to plant deciduous trees and shrubs at a time of least stress, between now and early spring. Growth of shoots comes to a standstill, and there's little or no water loss – lack of water is the biggest cause of failure at other times of year. The plants can put all their energies into making new roots while the soil still has much of its summer warmth. What's more, after losing their leaves, deciduous trees and shrubs actually have a natural surge of root growth.

Evergreens are slightly different. Instead of shedding their leaves all in one go, they drop them continuously, a few at a time, so growth never stops. So even in winter there'll be some water loss from the leaves, though with lower temperatures it'll certainly be less than in summer. This means that for evergreens, as well as deciduous plants, the best time to plant is now, when the soil's still warm, shoot growth is at its slowest, and there's little likelihood of drought.

There are exceptions to the general rule that autumn is the best time for planting trees and shrubs. The plants which are best left until spring are those that don't like wet conditions – most of the grey-leafed species, such as santolina, and certainly any with woolly leaves, such as stachys; any species of borderline hardiness, such as French lavender; and those that move reluctantly, such as silver birch.

Planting deciduous trees and shrubs

If you observe a few basic rules, you shouldn't go far wrong. Always prepare as wide an area as possible to avoid the possibility of isolated holes filling with water and drowning plants. Dig thoroughly, adding plenty of organic matter such as compost, manure or one of the bagged planting mixtures, and add some bonemeal. Plant at the same level as the tree or shrub grew before, firm gently afterwards. Stake trees securely with supports that come about a third of the way up the stem and attach them with adjustable tree ties.

Use a general fertiliser in spring, keep an eye on watering during the first summer, and control the weeds because competition from these can really set back growth. The best way to do this is to surround the base of the tree or shrub with a square of woven planting fabric.

LEFT Bold planting on a grand scale emphasises the passage of seasonal colour at Barnsdale. Massed groups of michaelmas daisies flower early in autumn, followed by the bright-tinted foliage of acer and sumach, with the vivid red stems of dogwood continuing the sequence.

PLANTING A BARE-ROOTED TREE

Prepare the hole and hammer in a short support stake (about one-third of the tree's height) then place the bare-rooted tree in the hole. Use a cane to check that the old soil mark on the stem of the tree will correspond with the new soil level when the hole is filled in. Fix the tree to the stake with a proper plastic tree tie and attach the tie to the stake with a short nail. The tie can be adjusted as the tree grows, and removed altogether after three years.

PLANTING A CLEMATIS

Plant clematis so that the top of the compost that surrounds the rootball is about 15cm (6in) below soil level, in case it is attacked by clematis wilt. Lean the plant towards its support or host and, until it is established, leave in a cane to support its leading stem.

TREES FOR SMALL GARDENS

I firmly believe an important choice like this should be left to you, but for what it's worth, here are my top four small trees.

Acer griseum is perhaps the best specimen maple for small gardens. It has amazing bark which becomes bright cinnamon in colour and peels in a most attractive way.

Amelanchier lamarckii begins with young bronze foliage as a background to delicate sprays of white flowers in spring; then, in autumn, the leaves turn red in sunshine and yellow in the shade, so you often get both colours together. It's truly an inspiring sight.

Cercidiphyllum japonicum, the katzura tree, has no flowers but the foliage is nothing short of superb. In spring it starts out bronze and then turns to delicate shades of green and pink; in the autumn the leaves go red, orange and yellow, filling the garden with an enticing smell of burnt toffee just before they fall.

If you want fruit as well as blossom and colourful leaves, don't forget the crab apple (*Malus*). One of my favourites is 'Evereste', with green leaves and masses of tight red buds in spring, opening to white flowers that are followed by a multitude of orange fruits in autumn. 'Golden Hornet' is popular, with white flowers and yellow fruits. The best of all reds is surely 'Profusion', which is wreathed in wine-red flowers, dark red fruit and crimson foliage; the best for making jelly is 'John Downie'.

Planting evergreens

On the whole evergreens are planted in the same way as deciduous trees and shrubs, but because they never really go dormant, it's particularly important that you don't damage their system of fibrous roots, and you should always remove any hessian wrapping. This will rot away naturally, but it's best to give the roots free rein right from the start. Unlike deciduous plants, evergreens benefit from the addition of a general fertiliser to the soil when planting, and a further handful sprinkled around the plant afterwards. It's unlikely at this time of year that the roots will dry out, but you might need to water in a very dry autumn. An occasional spray over with water in a mild dry winter is helpful, as is a screen of windbreak material arranged on one side to protect the plants from cold drying winds.

Taking hardwood cuttings

Cuttings from many shrubs root easily at this time of year while the soil is warm enough to encourage rapid rooting, and this is certainly the cheapest way to fill your garden with trees and shrubs. The shoots you need are those which have grown this year and are near enough pencil-thickness or more. Take them as low down on the plant as possible, because the hormones that aid rooting tend to sink to the bottom of the plant this late in the season. The basic procedure is the same as I showed you for rose cuttings on page 139. Trim the shoots, leaving a cutting 15–45cm (6–18in) long depending on the size of the parent plant and the distance between leaf joints; dip the bottoms in rooting hormone; and bury all but the top 5–8cm (2–3in) in a slit trench.

This time next year you'll be able to transplant them. Remember to be fairly ruthless about cutting the young plants back to leave about 10–15cm (4–6in) of growth: this will encourage them to bush out. In cold gardens, you can do exactly the same inside a cold frame to give that extra bit of protection and rather more success.

HARDWOOD CUTTINGS

Leave all the buds on a hardwood cuttings if you want stems to develop from below ground. Gooseberries and other soft fruit that are to be grown on a 'leg' or clean stem should have all but the top few buds removed before the cuttings are planted.

SHRUBS TO GROW FROM HARDWOOD CUTTINGS

Berberis, buddleia, cornus, cotoneaster, elderberry, escallonia, forsythia, garrya, jasmine, kerria, laurel, leycesteria, olearia, philadelphus, roses, spiraea, tamarix, weigela and willow. Also take large quantities of privet and box cuttings for hedging.

And don't forget fruit such as gooseberries, blackcurrants and red or white currants, as well as quinces, figs and grapes.

Moving a large shrub

After several years' growth shrubs and trees will usually have developed big root systems, so moving them can be risky unless you take great care. It often helps to prepare them a season in advance by trimming the roots (see page 47).

This month you can really get down to the job. Evergreens are best moved now, while deciduous plants can be moved successfully any time between now and early March. Start by digging a trench all round the plant, slightly beyond the one cut earlier if you've already trimmed the roots. Dig right to the subsoil, and then cut underneath to form as large a rootball as you can manage to handle.

Once you're half-way under the plant, you should be able to tilt it enough to work a piece of sacking or polythene underneath. Then dig under the plant from the other side until you meet the sacking, which you can pull right under by tilting the plant again. Tie the sacking so the rootball's completely contained.

Now all you have to do is lift it out, which is easier said than done. If you tie a stout post firmly to the sacking, two strong people should be able to manage it without too much grunting.

Remember to dig the hole in the new spot first. Then plant as I describe on page 155, setting the shrub in position and securing it, if necessary, with ropes, which can stay in place for at least a year to prevent rocking and breakage of the young roots.

MOVING A LARGE SHRUB

1 Cut all round the shrub, digging out a trench and trimming roots as you go. Then excavate from one side until the shrub can be tilted away from you.

2 Tuck a piece of strong sacking under the rootball. Dig under the other side and pull the sacking through so that the shrub sits in the centre.

3 Knot the ends of the sacking round the stem and, for large shrubs, slide a pole under the knots to make lifting easier when you transfer the shrub to its new home.

LAWNS & HEDGES

Planning for hedges

However friendly your neighbours might be, you probably don't want them breathing down your neck all the time. So why not plant a boundary hedge, and let your privacy creep up on them? It will provide a soft leafy barrier and make a perfect home for wildlife.

And if you live in a windy spot, there's no doubt a hedge makes a far better windbreak than a fence or wall. When the wind is filtered through the foliage, it is slowed down to an acceptable speed; when it meets the solidity of a fence, however, it whips over the top and eddies down the other side, sometimes actually increasing in speed and turbulence.

The big problem for small gardens is that a hedge will take up more room than a fence. You need to allow 60–90cm (2–3ft) width at the least, and an informal hedge would take more. But there's no reason why it should not act as a support for a variety of climbing plants, making a fine background for a border.

Choosing deciduous hedges

A formal hedge is clipped closely and can be confined to quite a small strip, whereas an informal one is left to grow naturally and so takes up much more room. Your hedge can be just one plant, such as quickthorn, berberis, escallonia or viburnum, or you can simply plant a mixture of shrubs in a row. If you have the room and want to attract wildlife, you can't do better than a mixed hedge of native species such as quickthorn, hazel, blackthorn and ash – grow native roses through it, together with blackberries and clematis, and you will create a breath of fresh country air.

Most informal plants can also be clipped neatly. Quickthorn, also known as hawthorn (*Crataegus monogyna*), for example, can be cut back to make a hedge no more than 45cm (18in) wide, and this will encourage close bushy growth that attracts nesting birds. One of my own favourites is beech, which makes a fine green formal hedge in summer and retains its russet-coloured leaves all winter; the old leaves are pushed off by the new ones in spring. If your soil is the least bit waterlogged though, grow hornbeam instead.

Choosing coniferous hedges

In a formal garden you might prefer a conifer. Yew (*Taxus baccata*) is undoubtedly the aristocrat – it will grow only 23cm (9in) or so a year while young, but it has the great advantage of being able to regrow from old wood. As well as the dark green yew, there are also golden forms. *Thuja plicata* (western red cedar) shoots up about twice as fast and also regrows from old wood: I particularly like 'Atrovirens', the brightest green variety.

Leyland cypress is the fastest growing of all, and worth considering for a boundary hedge or windbreak. But beware, there are several clones or varieties and it's vital to choose a drought-resistant one that will not turn brown in dry summers, which could be a disaster because new growth won't regenerate from the old wood. I would go for the slightly greyish 'Haggerston Grey' or the slower growing 'Castlewellan Gold'.

Planting hedges

If you prepare the soil well with plenty of organic matter, you shouldn't have problems with drought damage. Cultivate a strip 90cm (3ft) wide, preferably 1.5m (5ft) for large boundary hedges, and continue all along the planting line, working in a barrowload of compost or rotted manure per metre (yard) run. Rake in a couple of handfuls of bonemeal per square metre, level the ground and then peg out the centre line of the hedge, positioning the string just to one side to leave room for the plants themselves.

Deciduous hedging species may be bare-rooted and quite small, but they transplant well at this stage. With conifers, buy pot-grown plants about 30cm (12in) high – smaller, cheaper plants are often no more than rooted cuttings and take a good deal of nurturing in the early stages. Buy 10 per cent more than you need, and grow the extras in pots so that you have replacements just in case. And buy all the conifers at the same time if you want consistent colour.

If you live on an exposed site, protect young conifers from wind damage with a screen of plastic mesh on strong posts for at least the first year. Make sure all new hedges get regular watering next season, and feed them just once with a general or rose fertiliser in March.

ABOVE Brilliantly tinted autumn leaves temporarily decorate a trim formal hedge. With growth slowing down, mowing and hedging are almost over by now.

BELOW Young bare-rooted deciduous species such as beech can be planted now in well-dug soil to create a new boundary hedge.

PLANTING A HEDGE

After trenching the site, replace and level the soil. Stand the plants along the centre line, deciduous species about 45cm (18in) and conifers 90cm (3ft) apart. Plant them firmly at the depth at which they previously grew, and water in with dilute liquid feed.

VEGETABLES & HERBS

Lifting and storing root crops

I leave a few vegetables in the ground to survive the rigours of winter. Parsnips, scorzonera, salsify and celeriac, for example, are much tastier after a nip of frost, although it's worth checking now and again to make sure there's no damage. And if hard frost threatens, make life easy by digging up a few of each kind and keeping them under cover.

Carrots, beetroot and turnips, however, should all be lifted and stored as soon as you can. Fork them up carefully to avoid damaging them, set any spoilt samples to one side for immediate use, and then store the perfect roots in boxes of just-moist sand or garden compost. If you don't have either, ordinary garden soil or bark chippings will do. Put them in as cold a place as possible, but make sure it's frost-free, and raise the boxes off the ground to ensure good ventilation.

Potatoes should be forked up carefully, left on the surface to dry for an hour or two, and then put into paper bags: again, only store the perfect tubers. Take care to lift all of them, even the smallest, because if you don't they'll regrow next year like weeds just where you want to grow something else. However, if any do grow again, leave them until they're worth digging up as first earlies – you'll find they nearly always come before any that you've planted.

Planting garlic

Even though you might associate garlic with warmer countries than ours, the crop produces much better yields if it is exposed to a couple of months of really cold weather early in its life. That's why it's always best to plant the cloves now, rather than in the spring. If your soil's unworkable at this time of year, start the cloves in small pots or modules, and keep them growing in the cold frame until you can plant out the young plants in the spring.

Buy seed bulbs if you can. The garlic you buy at the greengrocer will almost certainly grow, but it may be infected with virus, which will reduce yields. Gently break whole bulbs into the separate cloves, and keep the fatter ones for planting – the long thin central cloves are better used in the kitchen. Prepare a sunny spot in the same way as for shallots (see page 32), and then take out shallow drills 15cm (6in) apart. Space the cloves (pointed ends uppermost) 5–8cm (2–3in) apart in the drills, and then cover so the tips just show; on light dry soils you can bury the cloves up to 5cm (2in) deep. And then just leave them alone – each clove will develop into a fat bulb next summer.

ABOVE Each fat garlic bulb can be split into a dozen or so cloves for planting individually this month, outdoors or in a frame.

PLANTING GARLIC

If you can't work outside, start garlic cloves in modules, planting a clove in each cell with its point just above the surface. Don't be tempted to keep them warm: the cloves need cold exposure and are best stored over winter in a cold frame.

Protecting late crops

Now's the time to dust down all the cloches you can muster, and put them over the last of the summer vegetables. French beans, tomatoes and courgettes can all be encouraged to run on a bit and ripen those last few fruits, while protecting lettuce, spinach and other leaf crops improves their quality just that little bit. If you haven't any ready-made cloches and there's a threat of frost, cover the rows with one or two thicknesses of fleece or 3–4 pages of newspaper, which will keep out about 2°C (4°F) of frost. And hold down the edges with a few bricks or stones in case the wind gets up. If you have some clear polythene, you can improvise cloches with old wire coat-hangers, opened out and bent into hoops to place over the rows every 90cm (3ft): lay polythene over these and you have a very effective tunnel cloche that could save the crop.

If you have cloches in position, you can sow pea 'Douce Provence' and broad bean 'Aquadulce Claudia' for early harvesting next year.

BELOW Maincrop apples such as 'Spartan' should be ready for picking and storing.

FRUIT

Harvesting apples

Maincrop varieties such as 'Spartan', 'Sunset' and most of the russets and cookers will be ready to harvest about now. Picked when they are ripe and sound, they will keep well for two or three months if they are stored in the same way as earlier types (see page 144).

Guarding apples and pears against winter moth

To protect next year's crop, put grease bands around apple and pear tree trunks (and their stakes) to trap the grubs as they head down to their winter quarters underground.

Pruning blackcurrants

It used to be recommended that blackcurrants should be pruned at the same time as you harvest the fruit, to save coming back to do another chore. But recent research has shown that pruning so early in the season removes part of the plant's food factory and can reduce subsequent crops.

So prune now, once the leaves have turned colour, by removing a proportion of older stems right down to the ground, or low down on the bush at a joint where a strong sideshoot is emerging. The cut shoots can be used as hardwood cuttings by trimming them to about 23cm (9in) long and just pushing them into the ground. But don't do this if you've seen big-bud disease on the bushes or suspect they may have reversion disease (the leaves will be narrow and look like stinging nettles).

Alternatively, you can grow blackcurrants as biennial croppers by cutting all the stems down to the ground every other year. This is an ideal method if you're short of time or have problems bending and finding which shoots to remove. With liberal feeding, this method can produce very heavy crops, but obviously you would need twice the number of plants to provide a crop every year.

Caging soft fruit

I have something of a love-hate relationship with the birds in my garden. While they're singing sweetly or demolishing snails and greenfly, they can do no wrong. But when they turn to my fruit bushes, I have been known to curse.

I invested in a fruit cage, and then planted it up with all those soft fruits that are prone to attack and difficult to protect in other ways – strawberries, for example, are vulnerable but can stay outside because they're easy to cover with netting at the appropriate time. And talking of time, now is the right moment to install a cage: fruit might be a little scarce, but in a few weeks finches could start attacking the buds on gooseberries and other bushes, which will certainly reduce their crops later on.

The type of cage you buy depends on what you can afford and how much fruit you have. The least obtrusive and longest lasting are made of tubular steel with a permanent side net, and a separate roof net that should be taken off soon in case snow should build up and bring the whole lot down. But the net goes back in early spring to protect those fattening fruit buds. A self-closing door is useful to prevent birds slipping inside and getting trapped while your back's turned.

MISCELLANEOUS

The art of digging

The soil is moist but not sodden at this time of year, and the weather is cool but not icy – perfect conditions for the major task of digging, but don't rush it. Just as soon as bare soil's available, I like to start winter cultivation: that way I can take my time, and avoid overdoing it.

Existing borders need little deep cultivation, and it's new beds, any areas that are to be replanted and, above all, the vegetable plot that will need more thorough digging. The first job, I reckon, is to cover the vacant soil with clear polythene sheeting. Any day now, we can expect the winter wet to set in and that can hold up work for weeks, but if you keep the soil covered you'll be able to dig exactly when you want to.

There's no point trying to be macho about the job. Use a spade that's the right weight for you and see if you can run to stainless steel, which is so much easier to use. If you can't manage a spade, use a fork. Then every few minutes, stop for a breather and clean off any soil sticking to the blade. It's a good excuse to straighten your back, and makes life much more pleasant.

Double- and single-digging

Double-digging two-spades deep is usually only for masochists or gardeners with a new plot, but if you're making a deep bed, or you find that the builders have compacted the surface before bulldozing a hundred tons of topsoil over it, I'm afraid you'll have some hard work ahead – but only once. After that, normal single-digging is usually enough. Dig to the full depth of the spade and throw the soil forwards as you go. This leaves a shallow trench in front of you, and a freshly dug sloping mound ahead of that. This is the moment to add manure – well-rotted horse or farmyard manure if you can get it – and compost: garden compost, spent mushroom compost or composted straw. Place these on the slope, rather than in the bottom of the trench – that way, they'll spread through all levels of the dug soil.

Above all, try to work up a rhythm that is smooth and gentle. And stop just as soon as you feel your back has had enough – there's all winter to get the job done, so there's no point risking injury.

ABOVE Fresh ground is best double-dug to provide the perfect conditions for success in the seasons to come. Brussels sprouts are protected from birds and frost with fleece.

Keeping worms working

Whereas slugs are to be firmly discouraged, earthworms need positive discrimination to keep them happy and working hard on our behalf. Every year worms bring tons of soil to the surface, improving aeration and drainage, and we all know that wormcasts are wonderful stuff – when worms digest soil they grind it down and form it into pellets that are coated with mucous which actually contains plant growth hormones. Their other major act of charity is to drag organic matter into the soil where they grind it down; bacteria then breaks it down further, and plant foods are released.

It's obvious we need to encourage them, and that's done by providing plenty of organic material. Garden compost and rotted manure are ideal. My advice is to dig these into the vegetable plot, but just leave them as a mulch on the soil in the borders to give the worms something to do in the long nights.

PLANTS FOR
october

1 With its prettily mottled leaves which die down during the summer, hardy *Cyclamen hederifolium* (*C. neapolitanum*) is perfect for naturalising beneath trees and shrub. Its pink or white 10–15cm (4–6in) blooms appear any time from August to December.

2 Angel's trumpets (*Brugmansia*, formerly *Datura*) are tender vigorous semi-evergreen shrubs 3m (10ft) high and wide, with 15cm (6in) long flowers. They are best grown in large containers for summer display outdoors, and brought under cover this month.

1

2

3

4

3 The Japanese anemone, *A. x hybrida*, is a hardy 1.5m (5ft) late-flowering herbaceous perennial with an outstanding white form 'Honorine Jobert'.

4 *Sorbus aucuparia* 'Fructo Luteo',one of the rowans, is a fine hardy deciduous tree up to 6m (20ft) high, with vividly coloured spring and autumn foliage and creamy-yellow berries.

5 The rich autumn tints of Boston ivy, *Parthenocissus* (*Ampelopsis*) *tricuspidata*, commend this hardy deciduous 15m (50ft) climber for all walls, even north facing ones.

5

What Geoff called our plant-hunting trips took place towards the beginning of the month, during the half-term break of the school where I taught. Geoff had specially equipped our Land Rover with shelves that fitted across the windows, the right size to take two decks of plants. We would pick an area of the country, arm ourselves with a copy of *The Plant Finder* (published annually under the auspices of the Royal Horticultural Society), and set off, navigating our way from nursery to nursery, and staying at B & Bs on the way.

Geoff would talk to the owners of specialist nurseries, and buy plants that they recommended. He loved to experiment, to try growing plants that were new to him, to learn more about them. By the time we came home we could hardly see out, and there was scarcely enough room in the car for the one small suitcase that I had been allowed to take with me.

A cold November morning reveals the formal outlines of this potager, where dwarf hedges, simple box topiary and standard roses provide a permanent framework for the ever-changing crops.

november

key tasks for november

BULBS

- ❍ Plant tulips early in the month, page 166
- ❍ Plant lilies between now and April, page 167

ROSES

- ❍ Plant roses after their leaves have fallen, page 168

LAWNS

- ❍ Lay turf on prepared soil, page 168

VEGETABLES & HERBS

- ❍ Force Belgian chicory for eating at Christmas, page 170
- ❍ Lift and heel in winter leeks before the ground is frozen solid, page 170

FRUIT

- ❍ Plant new apple and pear trees, page 170
- ❍ Carry out winter-pruning, page 171

MISCELLANEOUS

- ❍ Collect autumn leaves and stack them to make leafmould, page 172
- ❍ Protect plants against frost and alpines from the rain, page 173
- ❍ Insulate the greenhouse ready for winter, page 173

BULBS

Planting tulips

Save planting tulips until all the other spring bulbs are safely in, and you'll stand a better chance of escaping the fungal disease tulip fire. But don't wait too long: the first half of the month is the best time; and make sure you choose sites where the tulips will be happy.

Find the sunniest spots you can, and if your soil is heavy lighten it by adding coarse grit, and plant the bulbs on a layer of grit to protect the base plate from sitting in water. Then, if you want your tulips to be a permanent feature, you'll need to arrange for plenty of sunshine to bake the bulbs. In mixed borders that can be a problem because the foliage of other plants is certain to shade them, and most eventually die out in these positions.

A traditional way round this is to grow tulips as part of the spring bedding scheme and, mixed with wallflowers and forget-me-nots, they take some beating. After flowering the bulbs can be lifted, packed close together in a corner to dry off and stored until they are replanted next autumn. Another way is to plant them among sparse-leafed plants that will not cast too much shade – flag irises, for example, enjoy similar conditions and will cause few problems. The bulbs can then stay there for years.

You can also grow them in pots. Either use the plunge bed system (see page 141) or plant in groups of six or seven in 20cm (8in) pots, and keep them over winter in a cool shady part of the garden. You can then plant them, pot and all, where you need a splash of colour or wait

RIGHT From late summer until mid-spring naturalised species of hardy cyclamen revel in well-drained leafy soil.

until they flower and stand them in groups on a path or patio. After flowering, move the pots out of sight and allow the foliage to die down naturally before drying and storing the bulbs.

Planting lilies

From now until the end of April, whenever the ground is workable, lilies can be planted outdoors, 15cm (6in) deep in groups. On heavy soil, plant the bulbs on their sides on a layer of sharp sand and pack a little more sand around them to improve drainage. (See also page 180.)

LONG-LASTING TULIPS

Both Darwin and Cottage varieties, often lumped together in catalogues as 'May-flowering', are robust, and available in a wide selection of colours. Plant them in large informal drifts rather than in rows like soldiers. If you want some of the earliest to flower, look for species such as the bright yellow *Tulipa tarda*, or *T. turkestanica* with its cream star-shaped flowers.

One of the oldest varieties still in cultivation is the tall, bright red *T. praestans* 'Fusilier', which flowers in late April and has been grown since the 1600s. And don't miss out on early 'Keizerskroon' with yellow-edged red petals, which has been here since 1750, or 'Couleur Cardinal' with red and purple flowers, which dates from 1845.

ROSES

Planting roses

You can buy bare-rooted roses now. They'll be a bit cheaper than container-grown plants and have a much better chance of establishing well. And there's no better time to plant than now, when they have lost their leaves. They're glorious plants and I wouldn't be without them, but they can be an awful lot of trouble. To ensure they live for a long time and really give their all, you must start right, taking extra care when planting, and then continue on the straight and narrow.

First, prepare the ground thoroughly. Roses need to be well fed because they flower more or less throughout the summer, and you're going to hack them back each year. So cultivate as large an area as you can, make each hole big enough to take the full spread of the roots without vicious bending, and work in rotted manure, garden compost or one of the tree and shrub planting mixtures that you can buy. No fertiliser is necessary at this stage, but remember to give the plants a feed in spring – use a special rose fertilizer that has all the nutrients in the right proportions.

Many roses you buy now will be pruned back to leave shoots about 15–20cm (6–8in) long, and they can be left like that until the spring pruning. If they haven't already been cut back, do it before you plant because you'll find it's easier while you're standing up. Chop each stem back quite hard, reducing shoots thicker than a pencil to about 8cm (3in) long and thinner ones to 2.5–5cm (1–2in). Always cut back to just above a bud and remember that it will grow in the direction it's facing, so the usual advice is to make a sloping cut above an outward-facing bud.

PLANTING ROSES

Plant the rose deep enough for the joint between the stems and the rootstock to be about 5cm (2in) below the surface when you refill the hole with soil. If you can't quite tell this point, go by the old soil mark on the stem, and make sure this is buried out of sight. Firm the soil gently with your foot after refilling, and mulch the surface with compost, rotted manure or bark.

Rose replant disease

If you're thinking of removing old roses and planting new ones in the same bed, you may have problems because the new roses are likely to sulk and eventually die from a disorder known as rose replant disease, about which very little is yet known. If you must plant in the same place, dig out as much soil as possible and exchange it with fresh from another part of the garden. For just one or two plants, you might then get away with it if you use plenty of manure or garden compost, but planting in another spot is much the best bet.

LAWNS & HEDGES

Laying turf

Lawns made with turf are more expensive than those grown from seed, but more or less instant. Buy the best turves you can: cultivated ones that are guaranteed weed-free will cost about twice as much as coarse weedy 'parkland' turf from cow pastures, but will save hours of heartache and remedial work later.

In most parts of the country this is about the best time of year for laying turf, since the soil's still warm and it's most unlikely the turf will dry out after laying – only delay if the ground is frozen or too wet to walk on. If you've prepared the ground as I suggested in August (see page 126), all you need do now is hoe off any weeds and rake the surface level again, adding a little general fertiliser as you go.

Start by laying out the edging turves all round. Use a full turf at each corner, standing outside the area you've just levelled and tamp the turves down with the back of a rake. Then rest a wide plank such as a scaffolding board on the longest straight row of turves and stand on this while you continue laying across the ground. When you get to the end of a row, place the last turf over the edging turf and trim the excess with a knife so that it fits snugly.

You should only need to water if it's exceptionally dry: sprinkle the grass little and often to keep it fresh and moist until it's established.

RIGHT Autumn leaves are a precious free resource; to protect the turf, don't leave them for too long before gathering them.

VEGETABLES & HERBS

Forcing chicory

If you sowed Belgian or Witloof chicory seeds in June (see page 97), the roots should be ready for digging up and forcing, as shown on the right, by now. Each root will produce a fat white shoot or 'chicon' after five weeks or so, three weeks if you keep them at about 13°C (55°F). The chicon is the bit you cut off to eat, while the root is then thrown away.

Winter leeks

Winter leeks, such as 'Musselburgh' and 'Giant Winter', have dark strong leaves and improve in flavour after a good frost. They should be the right size by now, and I like to lift a couple of dozen or so at a time and either heel them in in a trench of compost near the back door, or keep them in a bucket of compost in the shed. Here they will happily last for months and are conveniently to hand when the ground is frozen. I also transplant a few groups to the back of the borders, where they will soon root again and produce superb round seedheads next summer.

BELOW Lift and heel in a supply of leeks where they will not freeze in the ground in hard weather.

FORCING CHICORY

1 Start by carefully digging up the roots, which are shaped rather like a parsnip. Trim them by cutting off the dead foliage and shortening the other end to leave each root about 15–20cm (6–8in) long. Store the roots in a box of moist sand or old potting compost until needed.

2 Every few weeks you can take out a batch of roots for forcing. Place them upright in a deep box or pot – five will just about fit into a 20cm (8in) pot. Pack moist sand, soil or compost around them, and stand the container somewhere warm and dark.

FRUIT

Choosing apple and pear trees

Both apples and pears are best planted in late autumn or early winter, especially if they are bare-rooted. Container-grown trees can, in theory, be planted any time but they too are easiest to care for if put in now. If you have a large garden, you might have room for a full-blown tree: a large standard of either an apple or a pear can spread 6m (20ft) or more. The specially trained varieties on dwarf root stocks, as I explained in April (see page 68), are usually easier to cope with, particularly as you'll need to grow at least two different varieties which flower at the same time to get a good transfer of pollen from one to the other, and so ensure a heavy crop on both. Look especially for varieties that have a good flavour, that crop well and are relatively disease-resistant.

Planting fruit trees

Both apples and pears need a sunny position, preferably with some shelter from frost – pears are especially vulnerable as they flower earlier. Prepare as large an area as possible, at least 90cm (3ft) across each way. Dig two spades deep, breaking up the subsoil and working in plenty of compost or rotted manure. Dig out a hole large enough to take the rootball comfortably at the level of the old soil mark – you can test this by standing the tree in the hole and laying a spade across from one edge to the opposite side to see if it lines up with the mark on the trunk. Remember to drive in a stake, if it is needed, before planting.

Place the tree in the hole and cover the roots with some of the excavated soil, working it down between the roots by jiggling the tree up and down a few times. Continue refilling the hole until you are half-way, and then tread it firm; return the rest of the soil and firm again. Fix the tree to its support with tree ties, water the soil thoroughly if the weather is dry, and finally mulch with an 8cm (3in) layer of compost or rotted manure to control weed growth.

Winter-pruning fruit trees and bushes

Pruning at this time of year largely consists of removing larger branches to open up the centres of bushes and standards, whether these are apples and pears or soft fruit such as red currants and gooseberries. All of them tend to produce too many branches and shoots in the middle of the plants, where they cross and overcrowd the centre blocking out the sunlight and inviting diseases.

You can tackle all kinds in the same way: cut out branches which are dead or diseased, and any that cross or grow inwards, so that the centre is opened up to allow air to circulate and the sun to reach ripening fruit. With bush fruit you can also shorten the longer remaining branches by about a third to allow you to pick more easily.

If you grow your fruit in space-saving trained forms, you'll find that most of the essential pruning is done in summer, just when the weather's at its most inviting. All you need to do now is shorten the main stems and branches of trained forms such as espaliers by one-third of the current year's growth to encourage sideshoots to form.

Tying down fruiting shoots

There's one bit of training that doesn't need any cutting tools at all. Trimming back fruiting branches often results in a mass of new shoots just where you might not want them, and they're also likely to reduce the crop of fruit. These days growers tend to tie the shoots downwards, restricting the sap flow and encouraging further fruit buds. This method works for apples and pears, and is also the best way to deal with those long whippy branches that plum trees make.

All you need to do is tie a length of string near the end of the branch and pull it downwards until it forms a gentle arch, with the tip lower than the other end. Secure the string to the trunk or to a stake hammered into the ground. This needs to be done before winter sets in, while the branches are still supple; if you wait until the branch hardens up you risk breaking it.

ABOVE The extraordinary inflated seedpods of bladder senna, *Colutea arborescens*, hang in clusters all autumn.

FROST-TOLERANT APPLES AND PEARS FOR COLD AREAS

Eating apples: 'Ashmead's Kernel', 'Greensleeves', 'Jonagold', 'Katja' ('Katy'), 'Orleans Reinette', 'Suntan'.
Cooking apples: 'Blenheim Orange', 'Golden Noble', 'Howgate Wonder', 'Lane's Prince Albert'.
Pears: 'Beurré d'Amanlis', 'Conference', 'Doyenné du Comice', 'Gorham', 'Louise Bonne of Jersey', 'Onward'.

MISCELLANEOUS

Leafmould

Good gardeners look upon waste as an asset rather than a liability and, treated properly, autumn leaves are worth their weight in gold. I like to leave mine for a while to make a fiery tapestry of colour on the lawn, but when they lose their autumn hues they are gathered up and then left to rot down to make leafmould.

Leafmould is a wonderful crumbly brown material that looks like peat but contains much more goodness. It was greatly valued by old head gardeners as the 'magic ingredient' in potting composts, and it can still be used to replace peat in home-made mixtures. In the vegetable plot I also use it to run down seed drills if the soil's heavy and wet – it's pretty pointless sowing in wet cold soil but there are times when it's important to get on. A sprinkling of leafmould down the drill before and after sowing solves the problem, and the seeds nestle in a cosy haven, germinating strong seedlings that are raring to go.

ABOVE A wire-netting enclosure is all that is needed to transform autumn leaves into valuable leafmould. Make a new one the following autumn as full decomposition takes more than a year.

Making leafmould

You can simply rake up the leaves with a spring-tine, rubber or plastic lawn rake, or in larger gardens you might find a push-along sweeper useful. However, they'll rot down quicker if they're cut up into small pieces, and you can do that easily by running the mower over them on the lawn or by putting them through a shredder.

An easy way to store the leaves while they decay is to make a wire-netting enclosure by banging four stakes into the ground at the corners and then wrapping these round with wire netting. Unlike compost, which is decomposed by bacteria, leaves are rotted mainly by fungi which are not nearly so fussy and need no extra heat, additives or complicated containers to get them going. Just tread the leaves down firmly as you go and leave them for at least a year.

A quicker way to rot them down is to mix them with some lawn mowings – you'll do that anyway if you mow them up off the lawn. Make sure the leaves are damp and you'll find that the grass will heat the material and speed up decay, especially if you store the leaves in bags. You can buy special ones with holes in the sides, stiff enough to stand open so you only need one pair of hands to fill them. Otherwise use plastic bin-liners with a few holes stabbed in the sides. Tie the tops of the bags, store them in a corner, and they'll make superb leafmould ready for use about the middle of next year.

Protecting plants against frost

Unfortunately you never know if the weather will be hard until it's too late, so take precautions now and protect any plants of borderline hardiness. Those that die down for the winter can be covered with a little loose straw, bark, bracken or conifer branches to keep the worst of the cold away. Evergreens can be covered when a really hard frost is forecast, but what you use makes a lot of difference: hessian sacking and old net curtains are ideal, or try 2–3 layers of fleece.

Polythene doesn't work if it's just draped over the plants because any leaves touching the material will still suffer, but it will do the trick if you can rig up a support to keep the sheeting off them. The tops of climbers that grow against a wall or fence can be protected with polythene if you pin a sheet to two poles long enough to reach above the plant to be protected. When hard frost is due, unroll the sheeting and simply lean the poles against the wall to form a tent over the plant; then roll it up again in the morning. It's well worth a little bit of effort to sleep easy at nights.

Protecting alpines

Alpines can cope with cold weather – in their natural surroundings most are tucked up in winter under a blanket of snow – but in our milder, lowland climate those with grey hairy or woolly leaves need a bit of coddling to protect them from wet weather, which can rot them or causes diseases such as grey mould. If you can provide good drainage with plenty of grit in the soil and as a mulch round the plants, you're half-way to success. It's also a good idea to cover the plants over for the winter with a bit of glass or plastic to keep them dry. You can do this quickly and cheaply as shown below. That way they're sheltered from the heaviest rain but there's still plenty of ventilation around the sides, which is vital for these cold-loving species.

Insulating the greenhouse

It's also worth trapping all the warmth you can in the greenhouse by insulating it. Bubble polythene fixed to the inside of the glass will retain a lot. If there's nothing growing under the staging – so light won't be needed there – cut polystyrene sheets to size and push them between the glazing bars to keep ground frosts out.

There's a heater in my greenhouse, but it's only set to come on when the temperature drops to a couple of degrees below freezing and is rarely used. And meanwhile the greenhouse is usually filled to the brim with container plants that would be at risk outside, as well as bulbs of all kinds and spring-flowering herbaceous plants that will produce fine early blooms with just that amount of protection.

Watch the watering, though. Many plants will need very little while it's cold, and too much dampness under glass can encourage fungal diseases. Check regularly during winter, and if you find any infected leaves remove them pretty quickly before the problem can spread. And be sure to ventilate as much as you can on mild days – even a crack of air for an hour or so will help refresh the atmosphere and keep disease at bay.

And if you have an outside tap, make sure it's either cut off and drained for the winter or lagged with foam insulation.

PROTECTING ALPINES

Make three large wire staples out of pieces of bent coat-hanger, and push two into the soil to provide legs to support the glass; the third one goes over the top to hold the glass in place.

BELOW Take no chances with outdoor container plants as winter approaches: snugly wrapped in sacking or similar insulation, their all-important roots will be safe from freezing.

PLANTS FOR

november

1 The large leaves of crimson glory vine, *Vitis coignetiae*, a self-clinging hardy climber up to 25m (80ft) high, make a rich display in autumn.

2 The dense white 3m (10ft) plumes of pampas grass, *Cortaderia selloana* 'Sunningdale Silver', last well into winter over its tussocks of hardy evergreen foliage.

1

2

3

3 Even in the depths of winter, *Lonicera fragrantissima*, one of the honeysuckle family, produces its sweetly scented blooms on bare spreading branches up to 1.8m (6ft) high.

4 Hardy spray chrysanthemums are indispensable border perennials with flowers in a wide range of mellow colours. They bloom over a long season, often after the end of autumn in sunny sheltered sites.

5 The single 8cm (3in) nodding bright yellow blooms of *Clematis orientalis* 'Bill Mackenzie' develop into large silvery seedheads, which last for months on vigorous stems 3m (10ft) or more high.

4

5

This was the only month in which Geoff felt that he could leave the garden long enough for us to go away together on holiday. Unlike in November, we went further afield, to get sunshine rather than plants. But in fact Geoff never minded the weather – indeed, he loved it in all its guises: wet and windy, hot and still, silent and snowy. In spite of being a Leo, what he liked best was a crisp, cold, sunny day. Those were the days when I might catch him singing – anything from snatches of Frank Sinatra to a whole chorus from *The Messiah*. Singing was a shared interest – we met each other while carol singing, and for several years we travelled to the Albert Hall to sing in a 'Messiah from scratch' concert at Christmas. Geoff was such an unmaterialistic man that he was hard to give Christmas presents to, but records were always welcome – he loved listening to classical music and jazz – along with books and antique gardening tools. He was fascinated by old implements and methods, in why and how things were done. His interest in gardening was as broad as it was deep.

There is unexpected charm and beauty in the depths of winter: dormant apple trees trained formally on a series of arches are transformed into an inviting tunnel through the fresh snow.

december

key tasks for december

ANNUALS & BEDDING PLANTS

❍ Sow pelargoniums early or buy 'plugs' to flower next summer, page 178

BORDER SCHEMES

❍ Plan for winter colour in borders, page 179

BULBS

❍ Start potting up lilies in batches, page 180

SHRUBS, TREES & CLIMBERS

❍ Prune deciduous trees to shape, page 180

❍ Shorten or tie in long stems to prevent wind damage, page 182

VEGETABLES & HERBS

❍ Choose mini-vegetables for small gardens, page 182

FRUIT

❍ Prune and plant blackberries, page 183

MISCELLANEOUS

❍ Make a hotbed to force early crops, page 183

ANNUALS & BEDDING PLANTS

Growing pelargoniums from seed

I could never wax too lyrical about geraniums, or pelargoniums as we should call them to avoid confusion with hardy border geraniums. They've been the standard cottage garden pot plant since the year dot, and were often called 'window plants' because every cottage sported a few of them in flower on the windowsill. And they're terrifically versatile, flowering inside all winter and then, if you bed them out in borders or put them in containers, flowering outside all summer too.

If you're growing pelargoniums from seed, you need to sow them about now, and no later than mid-February. While growing from seed is fascinating, it does have two disadvantages: you need a propagator as the seeds won't germinate unless they are given a temperature of at least 18°C (65°F), and preferably higher; and it is expensive. Most seeds tend to be F_1 hybrids and so you only need two or three to fail, plus the cost of heating, to find that your plants are worth putting in the safe overnight.

You can, however, get the seedsman to grow them for you, so removing most of the risk. The majority of suppliers offer seedlings or young plants for potting on, and you can buy a pack of forty 'plugs' – tiny plants with an already established root system – for the cost of a couple of packets of seeds. But don't relax just because you've avoided the early sowing: if you're going to do it this way, you must send off for the plugs soon because they're usually grown to order.

LEFT All kinds of perennials can be coaxed to flower out of season under glass, including *Viola* 'Blackberry Cream'.

BORDER SCHEMES

Planning for winter colour

If you look out of the window on a winter's day and see nothing but bare twigs, mud and rotting herbaceous vegetation, it's time to get things in hand. And there is little better to do on a raw, bitterly cold day than make plans. Even in the depths of winter, a garden should provide a view to lift the spirits and put a smile on your face, and this isn't difficult to achieve in a border, especially if you use the three-tier approach. This involves making a composition with a tree or two, a lower tier of shrubs or herbaceous plants, and underneath that a layer of low-growing plants.

The top tier

The best, and as far as I know, the only tree that will flower on and off throughout the cold weather is the autumn cherry (*Prunus* × *subhirtella* 'Autumnalis'). It is a small tree with semi-double white flowers, and there's an equally lovely blush-pink version called 'Autumnalis Rosea'. Or you could go for an evergreen such as *Cotoneaster* × *watereri* and its variety 'John Waterer', both with masses of long-lasting berries – they're really large shrubs, but can be pruned to make small trees.

The middle tier

There are lots of medium-sized shrubs which are interesting all through the winter. Dogwoods have brilliant winter-bark colours that are a special delight on sunny days. I'd certainly include the bright red-stemmed *Cornus sanguinea* 'Winter Flame' ('Winter Beauty') which has the bonus of fiery autumn foliage. Prune it hard in spring to encourage the bright young shoots. Don't miss out on daphnes, which produce flowers in February and continue until April, filling the garden with delicious perfume. *D. mezereum* is a small shrub with reddish-pink flowers and scarlet berries, while *D. odora* 'Aureomarginata' has soft reddish-purple flowers and, later on, creamy-yellow variegated foliage – this variety is actually hardier than the plain green form. The evergreen foliage alone of skimmias would justify planting them, but they also bear clusters of tight buds throughout winter. My favourite is *S. japonica* 'Rubella', which carries large eye-catching clouds of red buds all winter until they open into white flowers in spring.

The bottom tier

Underneath the tree and shrubs, you can grow dwarf shrubs and herbaceous plants. Winter-flowering heathers, mainly *Erica carnea* varieties, go on right through from late January to April, and they don't need an acid soil which is good news for many gardeners. 'Myretoun Ruby' is one indispensable variety, a superb deep rose-pink that looks stunning beneath the autumn cherry. For an earlier show grow the rich carmine-red 'Eileen Porter', which will flower all winter.

Bergenias, sometimes known as elephant's ears, keep their round leathery leaves all winter, and some have the added bonus of superb winter colouring. *B. cordifolia* is one of the best species, especially the richly coloured 'Purpurea'; also consider the modern hybrids 'Abendglut' and 'Bressingham Ruby' which both have bright red flowers in early spring and glowing red winter foliage.

And of course, you can't be without the Christmas rose, (*Helleborus niger*), a lovely evergreen that produces delicate white flowers from late December to March. Around and beneath all these plants you can cram in bulbs such as February-flowering snowdrops, *Anemone blanda*, winter aconites, irises such as *I. histrioides*, scillas and the earliest cyclamineus daffs.

BULBS

Starting lilies in pots

I like to plant lilies in the garden about now. But very often they're not available this early, and by the time they do arrive the soil is likely to be too wet. So the solution is to pot them up temporarily until conditions improve, but there's no reason why you shouldn't leave them to flower in pots too.

Varieties such as the beautiful Asiatic or Mid-Century hybrids, especially short-stemmed kinds like 'Casa Rosa', 'Harmony' and 'Apollo', make an excellent display on the patio; the very dwarf Little Rascal and Pixie types, only 30cm (12in) or so high, are ideal container varieties. Sweet-scented *Lilium regale* was traditionally grown in large pots indoors for mass displays on special occasions.

If you're going to plant lilies out next spring, pot them up individually in ordinary 10–13cm (4–5in) pots and then keep these in a cold frame. Use extra-deep pots if possible for permanent potting, so bulbs are covered 15cm (6in) deep.

If you pot a few every month between now and early April, you should get a sequence of flowers up to the autumn. Remember to water and feed them regularly, and continue this after flowering until the leaves die down. Then renew the top 5cm (2in) of compost every September if you want to keep the plants flowering in pots.

PLANTING LILIES IN POTS

Put a good layer of grit, gravel or broken crocks in the bottom of each pot, and cover this with 5–8cm (2–3in) of soil-based compost such as JI No. 2 or No. 3. Spacing depends on the size of the bulbs: you might get five smaller ones in a 20cm (8in) pot, but only three of other varieties. Fill the pots almost to the brim with compost, and keep them in a cold frame or in the garden, plunged up to their rims in soil.

SHRUBS, TREES & CLIMBERS

Pruning deciduous trees to shape

As soon as their leaves have fallen, deciduous trees can be pruned. This is the time of year when you can shape them up; and in small gardens you might also need to reduce their size slightly and thin the branches to make sure they don't cast too much shade. Before you get too secateur-happy, though, remember that hard pruning stimulates vigorous new growth, and simply sawing off thick

RIGHT Bright hoar frost embroiders shrubby branches and fern and epimedium leaves to create a magical winter scene around a weeping purple beech, *Fagus sylvatica* 'Purpurea Pendula', with its characteristic high-grafted mushroom-shaped head.

RIGHT Even on a shaded house wall, pyracanthas produce huge crops of brilliant berries, golden yellow in the case of 'Soleil d'Or', while 'Mohave' is rich orange-red.

branches will result in a mass of weak sappy shoots next year.

The main rule is to open up the centre of the tree and remove branches that are crossing, damaged or overcrowding those you want to keep. Always cut back to a joint so that the shoot you trim back to can take over as a leader. Even then, keep an eye on the tree next spring and remove excess new shoots by rubbing them off while they're still small. Never remove more than about a third of the growth in any one year – and take your time: it takes seconds to cut bits off but years to grow them back again.

Preventing wind damage

If you're out and about with secateurs, take a look at your roses and other tall-stemmed shrubs, especially if they're growing in an exposed part of the garden. If the plants start rocking about in the wind, they'll work a hole in the soil around the stem. This will allow water to stand on the roots, which can cause rotting – in a snap frost it can also freeze the roots, which won't do the plant any good at all.

If there are long stems that look a bit vulnerable on buddleias or climbers such as vines, honeysuckle and ivy, cut them back by half, or tie them in before they get damaged by the wind. This also applies particularly to climbing and rambling roses, as well as to those vigorous shrub varieties that can make quite a lot of growth. It is only a holding measure, and you can finish pruning them properly in late winter or early spring. Don't waste the prunings, because there's still time to root them in the way I explained on page 156).

VEGETABLES & HERBS

There are often days when the sun shines, even if they are bitingly cold. Seize these moments to go out and check the kitchen garden; and, once out, you might even feel like doing something.

After a hard frost you should check any new plantings to make sure they haven't lifted, and firm them in if necessary. You could cut down the tops of Jerusalem artichokes, but leave the stems about a metre (3–4ft) long if they make a useful windbreak. You could also prepare a runner bean trench, one spade deep, and start filling it with weeds or vegetable waste, refilling it with soil in late March or April.

Planning to grow mini-vegetables

If you are armed with seed catalogues, the long evenings of December will give you wonderful opportunities to think ahead and make new plans for the garden. I always think that seedsmen are really selling us optimism. But you've every reason to be optimistic about growing crops even in a tiny veg plot if you use the latest 'mini' varieties. These can be grown closer together than normal kinds and are harvested while they're young and tender. What's more, they fetch a premium in the shops, so you'll be saving even more than you do with standard vegetables.

It's worth growing these varieties even if you've got a bit more room because, although they've been bred for harvesting while young, they can also be grown on to yield a more mature crop. That means you can gather them selectively over a longer season, with those left in the ground developing to full size. Nothing is wasted that way.

But to grow any crop well at close spacing you need very fertile soil, and I like to raise my mini-veg in deep beds that have been dug and manured to get the soil into fine fettle (see page 117). Then, every time you sow or plant a new crop, all you do is top-dress the soil with a general fertiliser and some garden compost. When you sow, you simply scratch shallow parallel drills with the tip of a garden cane and sow thinly in these; cover the seeds by drawing the back of a rake down the row, and tamp down lightly.

Most mini-veg can be sown in rows 15cm (6in) apart, with the seedlings thinned to suitable distances apart, from 1cm (½in) for leeks or 2.5cm (1in) for turnips, for example, up to 15cm (6in) for savoys and mini-cauliflowers. Try to arrange crops of similar height and shape side by side so that they don't shade each other and compete too much for light – they'll be jostling for space as they grow. One big advantage of this is that the soil surface is soon covered, which keeps weeds in check and also reduces evaporation in hot weather.

VARIETIES OF MINI-VEG

Kale 'Showbor' 15cm (6in) apart; savoy cabbage 'Protovoy' 15cm (6in); cauliflower 'Idol' or 'Lateman' 15cm (6in); carrot 'Amini' 1cm (½in); parsnip 'Lancer' 5cm (2in); beetroot 'Pronto' 2.5cm (1in); kohl rabi 'Quickstar' 2.5cm (1in); turnip 'Tokyo Cross' 2.5cm (1in); leek 'King Richard' 1cm (½in).

FRUIT

Growing blackberries

Now that it's getting harder to find a hedge, let alone a bramble twining through it in the wild, growing blackberries in your own backyard is an appealing option especially as the latest generation of compact varieties, 'Loch Ness' and 'Waldo', are thornless and produce large fruits with an excellent flavour.

You can grow these more choice varieties against a wall or fence, or free-standing on a post and wire support. Use 2.4m (8ft) fencing posts at the ends, with intermediate posts of the same height about 1.8m (6ft) apart. You'll need some strong wire stretched horizontally every 30cm (12in) from 90cm (3ft) to 1.8m (6ft) above the ground.

Now's the time to plant new canes, as well as to prune old ones. Plant canes 1.8m (6ft) apart in deeply dug soil with plenty of added compost or rotted manure, and after planting prune them hard to 30cm (12in) from the ground.

Blackberries fruit on canes they've produced the previous year, so pruning involves cutting out all those canes which have fruited, and then replacing them with the new ones produced this season. In the first year, train the canes into a fan shape on the wires, but leave a space in the centre. Then the new shoots produced the following season can be trained into this space while the older canes are fruiting. Once these have finished, they are cut out and the new ones that were bundled in the centre can be spread out in their place. That's all the care they need, apart from a lavish mulch after pruning each year.

MISCELLANEOUS

Making a hotbed

Gardeners a century ago were pretty lavish in their ways, but some of their less excessive ideas are still valuable today. The cold frame was one of them, and it should be used more widely; another Victorian brainwave was the hotbed, made inside a deep cold frame. It's something else that I think is due for revival, because it makes the best use of fresh horse manure that would otherwise have to be left in an unproductive heap for a year while it rotted down.

Fresh horse manure is certainly readily available in most parts of the countryside, if you keep an eye open for roadside signs. And even big cities have their share of stables where you are able to purchase a few steaming bags of the stuff.

To make use of it straight away, build a hotbed. You can make it in the open as a heap about 1.2m (4ft) square and 90cm (3ft) high, with the sides kept nice and square and the top quite flat. For best results, pile the manure into a wooden compost container which will help keep the heat in for much longer. Cover with a 15cm (6in) thick layer of 5 parts good soil, 3 parts mushroom compost and 2 parts coarse grit, all mixed well together.

Put a wooden cold frame over the top and leave for about 10 days while the fierce heat builds up and then starts to cool a little. At that point you can sow early lettuces, carrots, radishes, turnips, summer caulis and spinach for early harvest. When these have finished, plant the bed with bush tomatoes, melons, courgettes, aubergines, peppers or cucumbers to follow on in the summer. The heat produced at first will ensure fast early crops, the moist fertility will sustain the later summer ones, and at the end of the season you'll have a heap of well-rotted manure for the garden.

BELOW Making a hotbed in a stout wooden container confines the precious heat of the fermenting stable manure.

PLANTS FOR
december

1 One of the more vigorous bushy species, semi-evergreen *Cotoneaster* x *watereri* has distinctively textured leaves and heavy trusses of bright berries in autumn and winter.

2 Male forms of *Garrya elliptica*, the hardy evergreen silk-tassel bush, have conspicuous silvery-grey winter catkins. These are longest in the variety 'James Roof', which grows slowly into a dense 3m (10ft) shrub.

1

2

3

4

5

3 Very hardy and reliable even in exposed positions, the evergreen oleaster, *Elaeagnus* x *ebbingei*, is best known in this lustrous bushy variegated form 'Gilt Edge'.

4 Winter-flowering jasmine, *Jasminum nudiflorum*, is a favourite deciduous shrub for training on walls, where its leafless 3m (10ft) arching shoots bear a succession of bright yellow flowers until March.

5 Asian mahonias are vigorous hardy evergreen shrubs which prefer slightly shaded positions. *Mahonia* x *media* 'Charity' is a fine hybrid in this group, with long leaves and large upright-arching racemes of slightly fragrant blooms.

climate and the gardener

It is often said that the further north you go, the later spring arrives, and that on the whole gardeners in the North do things two or three weeks later than those in the milder South. But in reality the differences are not quite so clear-cut. For example, some of the earliest lettuces and tomatoes come from Lancashire and Sussex, two counties almost at opposite ends of the country. East Kent can experience frosts quite late whereas many London gardeners leave their geraniums out all winter, and in parts of Scotland frost is almost unknown. In fact, the difference between east and west can be as important as the north–south divide, while altitude and exposure are other potent influences on sowing, planting and harvesting dates.

Every garden is different and has its own local microclimate, which will only be revealed after a season or two of trial and error. In this book, recommended times for doing various jobs are based on years of experience at Barnsdale, a relatively 'late' garden in the east of the country. In Oxford you might manage things a week or so earlier, in Manchester a bit later, but the best guide is to watch and listen to your neighbours, who will know roughly when the first and last frosts are likely.

Observation and experiment are as important for successful gardening as following a monthly guide such as this, but there's always an element of unpredictability in our climate. Keep cloches and other forms of protection handy for a while after planting out, and take a few cuttings or make a second sowing as an insurance. Get to know the warmest and coldest parts of your garden, and keep an eye open for natural cues to do things. Nature does sometimes make mistakes, but when birds start nesting, hedgerow buds break or squirrels busy themselves storing food, you can be sure it's time for you to be doing something similar.

glossary

annual a plant which germinates, flowers, sets seed and dies within a year. The process can be spread over two calendar years, as when a hardy annual is sown in autumn to flower the following spring.

biennial a plant which makes most of its growth in the first year, and flowers and sets seed the next, after which it usually dies. Many vegetables are biennials, but most bedding plants grown as biennials are in fact perennials.

blind strictly used to describe a plant which has lost its growing tip, but often applied to bulbs that fail to flower because they are too young or overcrowded.

bottom heat warmth applied from below in a propagator or from a heated mat, to stimulate seeds to germinate or cuttings to root faster.

cane shorthand for a bamboo garden cane, but also used to describe the long annual stems of soft fruit such as raspberries and blackberries.

capillary matting woven material laid on greenhouse staging and kept moist so that pots and trays in contact with the matting can absorb moisture as needed.

catch crop a fast-maturing vegetable such as radish, lettuce or early carrots grown in ground that would otherwise stand empty for a few weeks between the harvesting and sowing of other crops.

cordon a plant such as an apple tree or tomato grown as a single stem and prevented from producing branches; cordons may be single, double or triple, and vertical or oblique (grown at an angle).

crown often used to refer to the upper portion of a perennial woody or fleshy rootstock of a plant which dies down in winter – rhubarb, peonies or asparagus, for example.

deciduous describes a shrub or tree which loses its leaves every autumn and is dormant until new leaves develop in spring.

dibber a valuable tool, made from a piece of dowel or a broken spade handle, used to make planting holes in the ground; the verb is to dibble.

disbud the removal of buds, either completely as when young strawberry plants are prevented from flowering, or selectively as when some flower buds on dahlias and chrysanthemums are removed to increase the size of remaining flowers.

drill a shallow channel scratched or drawn in the ground for sowing seeds or planting bulbs.

emergence the appearance of seedlings at the surface of the soil or compost, often the moment when less heat and more light are needed.

evergreen describes shrubs and trees that keep their leaves all year, a few old ones being shed continuously; in cold winters some of these plants may be semi–evergreen.

floret a small flower, one of several in a truss or spike – a delphinium floret, for example.

germination the moment when a seed starts growing; more heat may be needed than later, together with air, moisture and often darkness.

hardwood used to describe cuttings taken from the ripe woody stems of trees and shrubs in autumn.

hardy able to tolerate freezing, a relative term because there are various degrees of hardiness, and plants may be very hardy, fairly hardy and so on; half-hardy plants are sown in warmth and planted out after the last frosts.

heel a small piece of mainstem bark which is removed when pulling off a semi-ripe cutting, and which aids rooting.

heel in to temporarily bury and firm in the roots of trees and shrubs when planting is delayed; the last leeks and parsnips in spring are often moved and heeled in to allow cultivation of their bed.

herbaceous not woody; an herbaceous plant is one with soft top-growth, although the term usually refers to perennials that die down in winter.

humidity the amount of moisture in the air, an important quality under glass for cuttings and many soft leafy plants.

hybrid a plant which is the result of fertilisation between two different parents ('cross-fertilisation'); the first generation are known as 'first filial' or F_1 hybrids, the next generation as F_2. Random mixed fertilisation results in S_1 hybrids.

leader the main shoot at the top of a tree or the end of a branch.

mulch a surface layer of organic material, paper or plastic, used partly to feed plants and also to conserve soil moisture and suppress weeds; horticultural fleece is sometimes called a 'floating mulch'.

node the joint on a stem where a leaf stalk appears; the portion of stem between two nodes is called an internode.

offset a young plant or bulb produced at the side of its parent by division, and often removed as a method of propagation.

perennial a plant which grows and flowers each year; it is a relative term, many trees living for centuries, whereas the normally biennial foxglove may survive as a short-lived perennial for a few seasons.

pip a gardener's term for a small bulb, attached (as in garlic) to the main bulb by a short root, or formed in a seedhead, as often happens with leeks and other alliums.

piping a pink or carnation cutting produced by pulling the growing tip out of the lower stem.

pot up to transfer a seedling or plant to a pot for the first time; to pot on is to move the potted plant on to a larger container when its roots need more room.

rhizome a swollen underground storage root, as in many forms of iris.

root plate the disc at the base of bulbs and corms, from which the roots grow – easily damaged by rough handling.

runner a stem running above or just below ground, rooting at intervals and producing small new plants – strawberries, violets and buttercups all produce runners.

self-fertile able to produce seeds from its own pollen and cropping well when grown on its own.

semi-ripe (semi-hardwood or half-ripe) a type of cutting produced from a sideshoot which is just starting to ripen and turn woody at its base.

sideshoot a shoot growing from a main stem or branch, called a 'lateral' in technical books; a sideshoot growing from a sideshoot is a secondary sideshoot or a sub-lateral.

softwood used to describe a type of soft cutting prepared from the young growing tips of stems and sideshoots.

standard a form of tree or rose with all the branching growth at the top of a straight bare stem 90cm–1.8m (3–6ft) tall.

stipule the small leaf-like piece of tissue found at the base of leaf stalks on pelargoniums and some other plants.

stock plant a plant of any kind kept specially for providing cuttings and other propagating material.

stool as used by gardeners, this describes the rootstock of plants such as chrysanthemums when they are dormant; stools are usually kept for cuttings.

strike to treat a cutting so that it produces roots; a struck cutting is one that is rooted.

sucker an extra stem growing direct from the roots, unwelcome in grafted roses but also a means of propagating plants such as sumachs.

tilth the fine crumbly surface layer of soil after cultivation and preparation for sowing or planting.

top-dress to spread fertiliser, manure or some other 'dressing' on the soil surface without any cultivation.

vermiculite a treated mineral in the form of light translucent flakes, sterile and water-retentive, and useful for adding to compost or covering seeds.

index

Page numbers in *italic* refer to captions to photographs
Page numbers in **bold** refer to artwork illustrations

A

Abutilon 94, 136
Acanthus 17
Acer 21, 146, *146*, 155, *155*
Achillea 29, 42, 60, 138
Achimenes 30
aconites, winter 43, 179
Ageratum 124
Akebia 65
Allium *78*, *86*,140, 146, *146*
alpines 18, *18*, *60*, 60-1, *61*, 63, 173, **173**
Alstroemeria *119*, 138
Alyssum *60*, 74
Amelanchier 155
Anchusa 17
Anemone 16-7, 29, *38*, 93, 138 140, *163*, 179
Angelica 49
angel's trumpets 94, *162*
annuals 14, 23, 28, 40, 58, 59, **59**, 90, 108, 136, 141, 178
apples/apple trees 68, *68*, 130, 160, *160*, *176*
  choosing 170
  nicking and notching 84
  pests 98, 160
  picking and storing 144, *144*, 160
  planting 170-1
  pruning 68, **130**
  varieties 68, 144, 155, 160, 171
Aquilegia 42, 63, *86*, 122, 123
Arabis *60*, 63
Arctotis 95
Artemisia 112
artichokes 49, *137*
asparagus 49, 50
Aster 74
Astilbe 144
aubergines 33, 144, 183
aubrietia 63

B

balloon flower 29
bamboo canes 41
Barnsdale 6, *6*, 9, *10*, 11, *12*, *18*, *26*, 56, *60*, *92*, *94*, *112*, *114*, *142*, *155*
beans 50, 142
  broad 49, 83, *83*, 160
  French 66, *66*, 82, 83, 160
  runner 41, 82, 83, 115, *131*
bedding plants/bedding 14, 28, 40, 58, *59*, 74, 108, 178
  buying as plugs 59-70
  for shade 75
  sowing in modules 14
  summer 74-5
  taking cuttings 41, 136
bee balm 132
beech 128, 157, *158*, *180*
beetroot *6*, 49, 50, 67, 159
  varieties 49, 116, 182
Begonia 30, 74, 75, 80, *81*, 124
bellis daisies 153
Berberis *70*, 156, 157
bergamot *132*
Bergenia 179
biennials, sowing 90
bindweed 100
birds 9, 10, 56, 144, 160
blackberries *69*, 157, 183
  varieties 183
blackcurrants 34, 156, 160
blackfly 83
blackthorn 157
bladder senna *171*
bleeding heart 42, 78
blossom end rot 115
bogland 11, 15
bonemeal 43, 69, 155, 158
borders *63*
  cleaning up 60
  planning for winter colour 179
  starting to plant 60
  supporting border plants 77, **77**
Bowles' Golden Grass 122
box 66, 125, 128, 156, *164*
  dwarf 48, *48*
Bracteantha (Helichrysum) 108, *132*
brambles 45, 183
broccoli 67
  Chinese 129
broom 95
Brugmansia (formerly Datura) 94, *162*
Brunnera 17, 78
Brussels sprouts 67, 97, 161
buddleias 30, 156, 182
bulbs 28, 30, *30*, 40, *48*, 58, 59, 63, 74, 78, 90, 93, 108, 111, 122, 123-4, 136, 140-1, 153, 166-7, 179
  digging up tulips 78
  dividing daffodils 111
  feeding daffodils 78
  forcing hyacinths 141
  forcing spring 30
  naturalizing spring **140**
  planting anemones 93
  planting autumn-flowering 123-4
  planting depths for 140, **140**
  planting gladioli 63
  planting lilies 123, 167, 180, **180**
  planting snowdrops 43, **43**
  planting spring 140-1
  planting summer 141
  planting tulips 166-7
  plunging 141, **141**, 166
  in pots for winter and spring 153
  starting bulbs in pots 141, 166
  starting off tender 30
  treating flowered 63
busy lizzies 14, 74, 75, 124
butterflies 58

C

cabbage root fly 10, 97, **97**
cabbages 10, 21, 49, 50, 67, 82, 97, 142
  Chinese 129
  varieties 21, 42, 49, **129**, 142, 182
  savoy 67, 182
Calendula 122, 141
Camassia 141
Camellia *36*, *64*, 65
Campanula 29, 42, *88*, *91*, *92*, *103*
cannas 63, 75
capillary matting 14, 29, 91
carnations 77 , *81*
  propagating 109-10, **110**
carrot root fly 10, 97, *98*
carrots 10, 15, 49, 50, 67, 97, *98*, 116, 145, 159, 183
  varieties 15, 49, 116, 182
Caryopteris 30, *146*
Catalpa 21
Catananche 17
caterpillars 9, 10, 56
cathedral bells 59
catmint 48
cauliflowers 21, 50, 67, 97, 182, 187
  varieties 21, 182
Ceanothus 17, 30
cedar 157
celeriac 159
celery 51, 97
Centaurea 111, *119*
Centranthus *92*, 122
Cercidiphyllum 155
Cestrum 93-4
Chaenomeles *53*, 65
Chamaecyparis 30
Chelsea Flower Show 72
cherries *70*, 84
  flowering *47*, 84, 179
  'Morello' 84
cherry pie (heliotrope) 94
chicory 51
  forcing 97-8, 170, **170**
  varieties 98
Chinese vegetables 129
chives 49
Choisya *91*
Christmas roses 92, 179
chrysanthemums 12, 29, 44, 77-8, 144, *175*
Cineraria (Senecio) 75
Cistus 63
Clematis 4, 64-5, *91*, 157
  looking after 112
  planting **155**
  propagating 112, **112**
  pruning 30, 112
  varieties 64, *64*, 65, *70*, 96, *102*, 133, *175*
  wilt 112, 155
climbers 14, 20, *24*, 58, 74, 108, 122, 182
  growing annual 59
  planning for 64
  for shady walls 64
  summer pruning 124
  supporting 64-5
  training climbing roses 95-6, **96**
cloches 21, 22, 28, 30, 35, 56, 83, 125, 160
  floating 35
  polythene tunnel 35, **35**
  tent or barn 35
clubroot 82
Cobaea 59
coconut fibre or coir 11, 15
Colchicum *123*, *141*
cold frames 18, 40, 44, *49*, 81, 83, 92, 156, 183
  hotbed made inside 183
  making or buying 51, **51**
coleus 75, *81*
columbines 42
Colutea *171*
compost 15, 17, 18, 42, 43, 61, 65, 69, 82, *84*, 85, 91, 93, 94-5, 114, 1239, 152-3, 172
  containers/bins for 85, **85**
  heaps 85
conifers 63, 30
  hedges 114, 128, 157-8

re-shaping after snow and frost damage 30
taking cuttings 115, **115**
conservatories 30, 106
container plants/containers 14, 40, 44, 74, 90, 93-5, *94*, 122, 124, 152
alpines 18, *18*
controlling vine weevils 80
growing tender plants in pots 93-4
planting up patio containers 94-5
planting up pots for winter and spring 152-3
sowing for late colour 124
for winter plantings 152
Convolvulus 141
Cordylines 63
Coreopsis 42
cornflowers 111, *119*
corn salad 128
Cornus 45, 156, 179
Cortaderia *134, 174*
Corylus *24*
Cosmos 74, 137, *138*
Cotinus 21
Cotoneaster 156, 179, *184*
couch grass 100
courgettes 49, 82, 83, 115, *131*, 142, 160, 183
crab apples 155
Crambe 17
Crataegus 157
cress, land/American 116
Crocosmia *120*
Crocus *30*, 123, 140, 153
crown imperials 42, *63*, 140
cucumbers 33, 49, 82, 144, 183
Cupressocyparis 114
cuttings 44
basal 29, **29**
bedding plants 136
clematis **112**
conifer 115, **115**
dahlia 76
hardwood 156, **156**
making frame for 81, 125
root 16-17, **17**
roses 139, **139**, 156
semi-ripe 51, 125
soft 40, 51, **80**, 80-1, 125
tender bedding plants 41
Cyclamen *26*, 43, 80, *162*
Cytisus 95

D

daffodils 63, 78, 111, 140, 141, 153, 179
Dahlia 29, 75-6, 77, 137, 144
Daphne 53, 179
Datura 94, *162*
deadheading 75, 122, 125-6
deep beds, building 117, *117*
Delphinium 14, 42, 60, 74, 77, 110
Deutzia 77, 95
Diascia 95, *98*, 136
Dicentra 17, 42, 78, 144
Dictamnus 17
digging 161, *161*
Digitalis *102*
diseases 10, 82
clematis wilt 112, 155
clubroot 82
halo blight (tomatoes) 115
mildew 34, 82, 95
rose replant disease 168
tulip fire 140, 166
virus 82
see also pests
dividing
daffodils 111
flag irises 109, **109**
perennials 138
violets 60
dogwoods 45, *45*, 77, *155*, 179
Doronicum 71
drainage 14, 18, 21, 41
drying/dried flowers 108

E

earthworms 161
Echinacea 17
Echinops 42
Echium 141
elderberry 156
elders 21
ground 100
Elaeagnus 153, *185*
elephant's ears 179
endive 51, 128
Epimedium *52*
Erica *16, 37*, 179
Eryngium 17, *146*
Erysimum 111
Escallonia 156, 157
Eschscholzia 141
Eucalyptus 125
Euonymus *36*
Euphorbia *76*
Euryops 112
evergreens *10, 16, 24, 36, 37*, 48, *52, 53*, 64, 78, 94, 128, 138, 153, 173, 179, *184, 185*

F

Fagus *180*
Fallopia (formerly Polygonum) 64
Felicia 95
fennel 116
bronze 49
ferns 14
fertilisers 6, 15, 65, 69, 82, 137, 152, 155
chemical 10, 69
nitrogenous lawn 47
organic 10, 22, 49, 60, 69, 75, 91, 116, 138, 140
slow-release 47, 81, 93
rose 60, 69, 168
figs 156
firethorn 65
flame gun 100
flea beetles 142
flowering currant 65
forcing
chicory 97-8, 170, **170**
hyacinth indoors 141
rhubarb 34, *34*
spring bulbs 30
strawberries 22, 130, **130**
forget-me-nots 90, 153, 166
Forsythia 156
foxglove tree 21
foxgloves *92, 96, 102*, 122
fried egg plant 122
Fritillaria/fritillary *42, 43*, 63, *63*, 140
frost *12, 18*, 30, 83, 171, 173, *173, 180*, 182
fruit/fruit trees 14, 22, 28, 58, *69*, 74, 84, 90, 122, 129-31, 136, 144, 152, 155, 160, 166, 170-1, 182
caging soft 180
choosing trained tree fruit 68
controlling pests 98
cordons 68, **68**, 98, 130-1
espalier 68, **68**, 130, 131
fans 68, **68**, 130, 131
forcing rhubarb 34, *34*
growing blackberries 183
hardwood cuttings 156, **156**
netting 10
nicking and notching tree fruit 84, **84**
picking and storing tree fruits 144, *144*
planting bush fruit 34
planting fruit trees 170-1
protecting tree fruit 144
pruning 84, **130**, 130-1, 160, 171
raspberries 34, 98, **100**, 131
shaping up young trees **20**
strawberries 22, 129-30, **130**
training fruit trees **68**, **130**
training in bush fruit shoots 98
tying down fruiting shoots 171
see *also* apples; pears
fruit cage 160
Fuchsia 6, 29, 30, 40, **41**, 75, 95, 136, 137, 145
fungicide 17, 80, 80, 81, 136

G

Galtonia 141
garlic 14-15, 115, **159**, 159, 159
Garrya 64, 65, 156, *184*
Gaultheria (Pernettya) *24*
geraniums 76, 110, 178
Gerbera *81*
Geum 42
Gladioli 63
glass, sowing under 15-16
see *also* cloches; cold frames; greenhouses
gloxinia 30
Godetia *109, 141*
gooseberries 34, 98, *98*, 130, 156, **156**, 160, 171
grapes 156
grass, ornamental *134*
grass path *114*
greenfly 9, 56, 83
greenhouses 18, 23, 28-9, 30, 33, 41, 44, 66, 80, *81*, 82, 101, 106, *124*, 144-5
choosing 145, *145*
early blooms in 144
insulating 173
grit 18, 44, 61, 81, 92, 166
groundsel 100
guelder rose, dwarf *146*
Gypsophila 29, 138

H

halo blight 115
Hamamelis *24*
Hamilton, Tony 12, 38
hazel *24*, 41, *67*, 157
hazelnuts, pruning 22
heathers 45, 179
Hebe 45, 47, 63, 125
Hedera *24*, 165
hedges 14, 40, 58, 108, 122, 152, 156, 157-8, *158*, 164
choosing coniferous and deciduous 157-8
controlling leylandii 114
formal 66, 128
planning for 157
planting 158, **158**
starting dwarf 48
trimming 66, 128, **128**
heliotrope 94
Helleborus/hellebore *10, 26, 29, 37*, 91-2, 122, 123, 139, 144, 179
herbs 14, 21, 49, 58, 108, 116, *116*

Hesperis 122
Heuchera 42
hibiscus, Chinese 94
hollyhocks 77, 106
honeysuckle 64, 65, *118*, 182
hormone rooting powder 80, 136, 156
hornbeam 128
horticultural fleece 21, 22, 35, 50, 67
Hosta 72, 78, 140, 141, 144
houseleeks 18, 63
hoverfly 9
hyacinths, forcing, indoors 141
Hydrangea 30, 133
  climbing 64, 65
hypericum, dwarf 63
hypertufa 11
hyssop 116

I

Iberis 141
ice plant 138
Iceland poppy 90, 103
Imperata *146*
Ipomaea 59, *119*
Iris 30, *103*, 109, 179
  dividing **109**
Irish yew 30
ivy *24*, 64, 65, 100, *163*, 182

J

Jacob's ladder 122
Japanese anemones 16-17, 138, *163*
Japanese blood grass *146*
Jasminum/jasmine 65, 156, *185*
Juniperus/juniper *16*, 30, 63

K

katzura tree 155
Kerria 156
knapweed 111, *119*
kohl rabi 67, 116
  varieties 116, 182
Kolkwitzia 95

L

ladybirds 56
lady's mantle 91
Lathyrus 59
laurel 156
Lavatera 74, *132*
lavender 48, 63, *103*, 112, 155
lawns 40, 58, 74, 108, 122, *126*, 136, 152, 166, 168, *168*
  assessing mowers 65-6
  drainage 14, 21, 21
  early autumn care 142, *142*
  feeding 81
  keeping in top condition 114
  laying turf 168
  mowing 47, 114
  preparing to sow 126
  repairing damage to 47
  reviving growth 47
  sowing 126, 128
Lawson's cypress 30
leafmould 172, *172*
leeks 66, *146*, 182
  varieties 66, 170, *170*, 182
Lenten roses *37*, 92
lettuces 21-2, 49, 50, 51, 67, 83, 116, 128, 145, 160, 183
  varieties 22, 49, *98*, 116, 128
leucanthemums (shasta daisies) *109*
Leycesteria 30, 156
Leyland cypress 114, 157-8, 158
light box for seedlings 28, **28**
lilacs 95
Lilium/lilies *92*, *112*
  planting 167
  starting, in pots 180, **180**
  varieties 123, 180
lily of the valley, planting 42-3
limestone 11, 61
Limnanthes 122
Livingstone daisies 63
lobelia 14, 75, 95, 124
Lonicera 65, 66, *118*, *175*
loosestrife 29
lovage 49
lupins 9, 42, 60
Lysimachia 29
Lythrum 29

M

Macleaya 29
Magnolia *42*, *47*
Mahonia, *18*, 30, *185*
mallows 74, *106*
Malus 155
manure *69*, 82, 161
  growing your own (green) 69
  horse (for hotbed) 183
  pelleted chicken 10, 11, 50, 69, 82, 93, 129, 138
  see also compost
hotbed, making a 183, *183*
maples 21, *146*, 155
marestail 100
marguerites 41, 63, 75, *94*, 95, *98*, *111*, *123*, 136, 137
marigolds 6, 122
marjoram 29, 49, 116
marrows 83, 142
meadow rue 29
Meconopsis *78*, 122
melons 144, 183
michaelmas daisies *150*, *155*
mildew 34, 95
Milium 122
Mimulus 75
'mini-veg' 50, 182
mint 116
mock orange 95, *102*
modules, sowing in, 14-15, **15**, 42
Monarda *132*
morning glory 59, *119*
moss killers 47
moths
  codling 98
  plum fruit 98
  winter 160
'mounding' 91
mowers
  assessing 65-6
  mulching 114
  rotary 130
  see also lawns
mulch, mulching 61, *61*, 63, *69*, 101, 161
  lawns 114
  roses 65
Muscari 153
mustard greens (Chinese mustard) 129

N

Narcissi *38*
nasturtium 9, 59
Nemesia 74, 95
Nepeta 17, 42
Nerine 123-4, *141*
nesting boxes 9-10
nettles 100
Nicotiana 74
Nigella 141
nitrogen 69, 75

O

oleander 94
Olearia 156
oleaster *185*
onions 6, 38, 78, *83*, 97, *137*, *142*
  ornamental see Allium
  planting autumn onion sets 142
  preparing for lifting 142
  varieties 49, 142
  salad 49, 67
  spring 67, 128
organic gardening 6, 9, 10, 47, 100
Osteospermum 63, 136, *111*
Oswego tea *132*
Oxalis 100

P

Paeonia 77, *86*, 138
pampas grass *134*, *174*
pansies *59*, *75*, 90, 91, 153
Papaver 92, *103*
parsley 49, 97
parsnips 97, 159
  varieties 49, 182
Parthenocissus (Ampelopsis) 65, *163*
pasque flowers *71*
Paulownia 21
pears/pear trees 68, 130
  choosing 170
  guarding against winter moth 160
  nicking and notching 84
  picking and storing 144
  planting 170-1
  varieties 171
  weeping willow-leafed *56*
peas 49, 66-7, *83*
  varieties 49, 67
Pelargonium *41*, *75*, *81*, *94*, 95, 136, 137
  growing from seed 178
Pennisetum *134*
pennyroyal 49
Penstemon 63, 111
peppers 33, 144, 183
perennials
  basal cuttings 29, **29**
  border 14, 16, *16*, 28, 29, 40, 42, 58, 60, *63*, 74, *76*, 77, 90, *91*, 91-2, 108, 109-11, 122-3, 136, *137*, 138
  collecting seeds 139
  cutting back 110-11
  dividing old 138
  growing from seed 42
  over-wintering tender 137
  planting new 138
  root cuttings 16
  self-set seedlings 139
  supporting border plants 77, **77**
  top dozen varieties 42
periwinkle 52
pesticides 6, 56
pests 9, 82, **97**
  blackfly 83
  cabbage root fly 10, 97, 97
  carrot root fly 10, 97, 98
  codling moths 98
  controlling fruit 98
  flea beetles 142
  greenfly 9, 56, 83
  plum fruit moths 98
  vine weevils 80
  winter moth 160
  see also diseases

Petunia *6*, 14, 41, 74, 75, *94*, 95, *98*, 124
pheromene traps 98
Philadelphus 77, 95, *102*, 156
Phlox 17, 75, *118*
Phormium 134
phosphorus 69
pinks 14, 18, 42, 63, 75, *110*
  propagating 109-10, **110**
Platycodon 29
plums 84, 98
plunge beds 141, **141**, 166
polyanthus 43, 90-1
poor man's orchids 75
poppies *9*, *75*, *88*, 123
  Iceland 90, 103
  opium 122, 139
  oriental 16, 17, 92, *92*
  plume 29
  Welsh *78*, 122
potager *164*
potassium 69
potatoes
  chitting **22**
  early varieties 22
  guarding against frost 83
  lifting and storing 159
  planting early 50, **50**
  starting early 22
primroses, double *53*
Primulas 18, 80
privet 128, 156
propagation/propagating
  clematis 112, **112**
  pinks and carnations 109-10, **110**
  short-lived shrubs 112
  strawberries 130, **130**
  see *also* cuttings; seeds
propagators 14, 23, *23*
pruning 88
  apple and pear trees 68,
  blackcurrants 160
  clematis 30, 112
  deciduous trees to shape 180, 182
  flowering quinces 65
  fruit trees **130**, 130-1, 171
  hazelnuts 22
  plums and cherries 84
  raspberries 34
  roses 32, **32**, 65, 124, 126, 168
  to prevent wind damage 182
  shaping up young trees 20, **20**
  shrubs 21, 30, 45, **45**, *45*, 95
  summer, 98, **130**, 124-5, 130, 130-1
  wisteria 21, 124
Prunus *70*, 179
Pulmonaria 144
Pulsatilla 71
pumpkins 129, 142
Pyracantha 64, 65, 180, *180*
Pyrethrum 29
Pyrus *56*

Q

quickthorn (hawthorn) 128, 157
quinces 65, 156
  flowering *53*, 65

R

radishes 49, 50, 67, 82, 128, 183
  varieties 49, 128
Raoulia 63
raspberries 34, 88, 131
  growing as a pillar 98-100, **100**
red currants 34, 98, 130, 156, 171
rhubarb, forcing 34, *34*
Rhus 17
Ribes 65
rock roses 63
rockeries/rock gardens 11, 18, 60, 61
Rodgersia 140
Romneya 17
Rosa/roses *4*, 58, 74, 90, 91, 95-6, *103*, *112*, 136, 156, 157, *164*, 166, 182
  climbing 64, 95-6, **96**, 182
  cutting back 168, 182
  cuttings 139, **139**, 156
  deadheading 122, 125-6
  feeding and mulching 65
  growing in containers 44
  planting 168, 168
  pruning 28, 32, 32, 44, 65, 124, 126, **168**
  rambler 64, 65, 95, *106*, 124, 182
  from seed 139
  varieties, bush 96, 126, *126*, 138
  varieties, climbing 65, 95, *106*, 124, 126, 138
  varieties for containers 44
rose replant disease 168
rosemary 63
Rubus 45
Rudbeckia 42
Russian vine 64

S

sage, purple *150*
Salix 45
salsify 82, 159
Salvia 14, 74, 95, 137
Sambucus 21
Santolina 30, 66, 125, 155
saxifrage 18, 63
Schizanthus 75
Scilla *38*, *43*, 179
scorzonera 82, 159
scree garden/raised bed *60*, 61
sea holly 63, 146
seaweed 10
Sedum *16*, 18, 63, 100, 138, *146*, *153*
seed trays, 15, **15**, 42
seeds 12, 16
  collecting 139
  growing perennials from 42
seedlings 12, 28, 28-9
  looking out for 122
  protecting young vegetable 128-9
Sempervivum 18
shallots 32-3, 115
shrubs *12*, 14, 20, *24*, 285, 58, 74, 90, 95, 108, 122, 124-5, 152, 153-7, 182
  best time for planting 153-4
  growing from hardwood cuttings 156
  moving large 47, **47**, 156, **157**
  planting deciduous 155
  planting evergreens 156
  propagating short-lived 112
  pruning 21, 30, 45, **45**, *45*, 95, 124-5
  taking cuttings **80**, 80-1, 125, **156**, 156
sidalcea 29
silk tassle bush 65, *184*
silver birch 155
Skimmia *24*, 179
slug pellets 56, 131
slugs 9, 56, 131, 140, 161
smoke bush 21
snakeshead fritillary *43*
snowdrops *26*, *30*, 43, **43**, 179
Sorbus *163*
sorrel 116
sowing
  annuals outdoors 58, **59**
  biennials 90
  container plants for late colour 124
  crops in succession 49-50
  in modules and seed trays 14-15, **15**
  warmed soil for early 33
spinach 49, 67, 160, 183
  beet (perpetual) 116
Spiraea *76*, 156
spring greens 142
squashes, storing 142
Stachys *112*, 155
sumach 155
sweetcorn 49, 50
stonecrops 18, 100, *153*
strawberries 88, 160
  varieties 22, 129
  forcing 22, 130
  planting 129-30
  propagating 130, **130**
summer hyacinths 141
sunflowers *123*, *129*
swede 82
  varieties 82
sweetcorn 49, *142*
sweetpeas 9, 14, 16, 41, **41**, 51, 59
sweet rocket 122
sweet williams 90
Swiss chard 49, 116

T

Tamarix 30, 156
Taxus 157
Tellima 78
Thalictrum 29
'thatch' (dead grass) 47, 142, *142*
thrift 63
Thuja 157
thyme 49, 63
Tiarella 78
tobacco plants 74-5
tomatoes 23, 33, 49, 50, 82, 83, *101*, *142*, 144,160, 183
  blossom end rot and halo blight 115
  under glass 33, 82, *82*, 115
  outdoors 83, 115
  varieties 33
trees *12*, 14, 20, *24*, 28, 58, 74, 152, 153-6
  best time for planting 153-4
  general rules for planting 155
  planting bare-rooted **155**
  planting evergreens 156
  pruning 21, 68, 180, 182
  reshaping conifers after snow and frost damage 30
  shaping up young 20, **20**
  for small gardens 155
  staking 20, *20*, 155, **155**
  see also fruit trees
Tropaeolum 59
tufa rock 18
tulip fire (fungal disease) 140, 166
Tulipa/tulips *56*, 63, *75*, *76*, 78, 140, 153
  varieties *53*, 72, 78, *86*, 167
  digging up 78
  planting 166-7
turnips 49, 50, 67, 116, 159, 182, 183
  varieties 49, 116, 182

V

valerian *92*, 122
vegetables 14, 23, 28, 32-3, 38, 40, 49-50, 58, 66-7, 74, 82-3, *83*, 88, 90, 97-8, *98*, 108, 115-17, *117*, 122, 128-9, *131*, 136, *142*, 142, 152, 159-60, 166, 182
  building deep beds for 117, *117*
  early sowings under cloches 32
  fitting in 49
  growing tender 82-3
  guarding against frost and greenfly 83
  hardening off early, in cold frame *49*
  harvesting summer 115
  lifting and storing roots 159
  'mini veg' 50, 182
  pests 97, **97**
  planning for autumn 115-16
  planning for an early start 21-2
  planning late crops 67
  planning small-scale plot 49-50
  protecting late crops 160
  protecting young seedlings 128-9
  root crops for winter 82
  tender greenhouse crops 33
  see also under individual vegetables
Verbascum 17
Verbena 95
vermiculite, horticultural 15, 90, 91, 136
Viburnum *18, 37, 86, 146*, 153, 157
Vinca *52*
vine weevils 80, *81*
Viola *10, 59, 72*, 91, 110, 179
violets, sweet 60
virginia creeper 64, 65
Vitis *174*

W

wallflowers *75*, 90, 111, 153, 166
watering 44, 60, 63, 65, 106, 114, *124*, 155, 156, 158, 168
  container plants 94-5
  seedlings 29
  soker/'leaky pipe' hose 101, 130
  sprinkler 101
  techniques 100-1
'weed and feed' dressings 81
weed killers 47, 100
weeding 23, 47, 100, 101, 122, 142, 155
Weigela 95, 156
white currants 98, 156
willow-leafed jessamine 93-4
willows 45, *67*, 77, 156
wind damage, preventing 182
wisteria 21, 64, 124
witch hazels 24
woodlice 9

Y

yarrow 138
yew 66, 128, 157, *158*
Yucca 63

acknowledgments

The publishers would like to thank those photographers who gave permission for their photographs to be reproduced in this book.

All photographs are by **Stephen Hamilton**, with exceptions on the following pages:

John Glover: 16 left; 30; 36 below; 54-55; 61; 64; 68; 70 below right; 71 above; 106-107 Sleightholmedale Lodge, Yorkshire; 108-109 Glover; 117 The Croft, Cheshire; 120-121; 125 Savill Gardens, Windsor; 131 Preen Manor, Staffordshire; 132 above; 133 below; 147 above left; 147 below; 167; 174 below RHS Wisley; 175 above; 179.

Andrew Lawson: 18 Gothic House, Oxfordshire; 25 above left; 25 above right; 31; 37 above; 37 below left; 38-39; 43; 48; 56-57; 59 below right; 67 RHS Rosemoor Gardens, Devon; 70 below left; 76 Gothic House, Oxfordshire; 86 above; 99 Chilcombe House, Dorset; 102 below right; 103 above; 116; 127; 132 below left; 138 Gothic House, Oxfordshire; 141; 150-151 Eastgrove Cottage, Worcestershire; 153; 158 above; 162 below; 164-165 Barnsley House, Gloucestershire; 175 below left; 175 below right; 185 above left; 185 above right.

Marianne Majerus: 4-5

S+O Mathews: 180

Clive Nichols: 2-3 (designer: Rupert Golby) RHS Chelsea; 16-17 Wollerton Old Hall, Shropshire; 24 below; 37 below right; 44 (designer: C. Cordy); 45; 62 Beth Chatto's garden, Essex; 72-73 Chenies Manor, Buckinghamshire; 79 Barnsley House, Gloucestershire; 83 Ivy Cottage, Dorset; 96 Mrs Glaisher, Hildenborough, Kent; 104-105 Castle Howard, Yorkshire; 129 HMP Leyhill/Hampton Court Show; 133 above; 134-135 The Old Vicarage, Norfolk; 148-149 University Arboretum, Nuneham Courtenay, Oxfordshire; 174 above; 181 The Dingle, Wales; 184 right.

Hugh Palmer: 25 below Brook Cottage, Oxfordshire; 29 Erway Farm House, Shropshire; 92 Crathes Castle, Kincardineshire; 163 below Cherrybank Gardens, Perthshire.

Graham Strong/Clive Nichols Photography: 35